Economies of Death

T0362090

Economies of Death: Economic logics of killable life and grievable death examines the economic logic involved in determining whose lives and deaths come to matter and why. Drawing from eight distinct case studies focused on the killability and grievability of certain humans, animals, and environmental systems, this book advances an intersectional theory of economies of death.

A key feature of late-modern capitalism is its tendency to economically order certain human and nonhuman lives and environments, while appropriating and commodifying certain bodies and spaces in the process. Spanning the social sciences and humanities in its contributions and scope, each chapter shows how living beings and places are stripped down to the calculus of their end, with profound ethical and political implications for these entities and the world around them. From the genocide in Cambodia to the way some animals are considered 'pets' and others 'food'; from September 11, 2001 and Afghanistan to the politics of redemption for prisoners and ex-racehorses in Kentucky, these case studies draw from and develop an enriched understanding of bio- and necropolitics, posthumanism, killability, and grievability. In drawing together the objectification of humans, animals, and environments (and the power-laden hierarchies that maintain this objectification), this volume highlights how death across these subjects informs and responds to broader geo-economic processes.

This book aims to examine the reach of economies of death across such diverse subjects, challenging readers to consider the everyday calculus they make in determining whose lives mean more and why.

Patricia J. Lopez is a Postdoctoral Fellow in Geography at Dartmouth College in Hanover, New Hampshire, USA.

Kathryn A. Gillespie is a Lecturer in Geography, the Honors Program and the Comparative History of Ideas Program at the University of Washington, USA.

Routledge Frontiers of Political Economy
Titles 1–99 in this series can be found on the Routledge website: http://www. routledge.com/books/series/SE0345

Economies of Death

Economic logics of killable life and grievable death

Edited by
Patricia J. Lopez and
Kathryn A. Gillespie

Routledge
Taylor & Francis Group

LONDON AND NEW YORK

First published 2015 by Routledge

2 Park Square, Milton Park, Abingdon, Oxfordshire OX14 4RN
52 Vanderbilt Avenue, New York, NY 10017

Routledge is an imprint of the Taylor & Francis Group, an informa business

First issued in paperback 2020

British Library Cataloguing in Publication Data
A catalogue record for this book is available from the British Library

Library of Congress Cataloging in Publication Data
Economies of death : economic logics of killable life and grievable death /
edited by Patricia J. Lopez and Kathryn A. Gillespie.
1. Death–Economic aspects. 2. Grief–Economic aspects. 3. Human rights.
4. Animal rights. 5. Human-animal relationships. I. Lopez, Patricia J.
II. Gillespie, Kathryn (Kathryn A.)
HQ1073.E25 2015
306.9–dc23
2014042051

ISBN: 978-1-138-80576-7 (hbk)
ISBN: 978-0-367-59933-1 (pbk)

Typeset in Times New Roman
by Taylor and Francis Books

Contents

Contributors

Irus Braverman is Professor of Law at SUNY Buffalo Law School. Her main interests are in the interdisciplinary study of law, geography, anthropology, and animality. Braverman is the author of *Planted Flags: Trees, Land, and Law in Israel/Palestine* (Cambridge, 2009), *Zooland: The Institution of Captivity* (Stanford, 2012), and *Wild Life: The Institution of Nature* (Stanford 2015). She also co-edited *The Expanding Spaces of Law: A Timely Legal Geography* (Stanford, 2014).

Jennifer L. Fluri is Associate Professor in the Department of Geography at the University of Colorado-Boulder. Her research examines geopolitics, gender politics, and the geo-economics of international military, aid, and development interventions in South Asia. Her research appears in several peer reviewed academic journals. Her forthcoming book co-authored with Rachel Lehr, explores intimate geopolitics through several different entanglements between Americans and Afghans and the various currencies from gender to grief that have manifested from discursive framing of 9/11 and the U.S.-led war in Afghanistan. Fluri and Lehr's article in this volume is a modified version of a chapter in this book.

María Elena García is Director of the Comparative History of Ideas program and associate professor in the Jackson School of International Studies at the University of Washington. She received her Ph.D. in Anthropology at Brown University. Her first book, *Making Indigenous Citizens* (Stanford, 2005) examines Indigenous politics and multicultural activism in Peru. Her work on Indigeneity and interspecies politics in the Andes has appeared in multiple edited volumes and journals. Her second book project, *Dancing Guinea Pigs and Other Tales of Race in Peru*, explores the cultural politics of contemporary Peru, especially in relation to food, race, and violence.

Kathryn A. Gillespie is a Lecturer at the University of Washington in Geography, the Honors Program and the Comparative History of Ideas Program. Her work explores structures of power and privilege related to nonhuman animal lives, bodies, and deaths. She is working on a book, *The Cow with Ear Tag #1389* (under contract with University of Chicago Press), about the (un)grievable lives of cows in dairy production in the Pacific Northwestern United States. She co-edited *Critical Animal Geographies: Politics, Intersections and Hierarchies in a Multispecies World* (Routledge, 2015) and has articles published or forthcoming in *Gender, Place and Culture*, *The Journal for Critical Animal Studies* and *The Brock Review*.

Rachel Lehr earned her Ph.D. in linguistics from the University of Chicago writing a descriptive grammar of Pashai, a minority language spoken in eastern Afghanistan. For more than 20 years she has examined the languages and cultures of central and south Asia, while living and working in the region. The article in this volume is a modified version of a chapter in a forthcoming book she has co-authored with Jennifer Fluri exploring American–Afghan entanglements in the post-9/11 era. Dr. Lehr, a research associate in the Department of Geography at University of Colorado-Boulder is currently working with Fluri on a multi-year study of Afghan women's civil society organizations.

Patricia J. Lopez is a Postdoctoral Fellow at Dartmouth College in the Department of Geography. Her research focuses on the intersections of health, geopolitics, humanitarianism, militarism, and citizenship. She is particularly interested in uncovering the impacts of historical and contemporary militarized humanitarianism on health citizenship, with a focus on U.S. interventions in Haiti. Her current project explores the birth of the verticalized health intervention in development as it unfolded during the Cold War.

Tamar V.S. McKee, inspired by postcolonial and posthumanist perspectives, is fundamentally interested in what it means (and costs) to be human and humane in the Anthropocene. Her research interests have included the persistence, persecution, and politics of Tibetan cultural identity as evidenced through contemporary art and horse festivals, and, most recently, how the famed horse culture of Bluegrass Kentucky is challenged by the complex practice of Thoroughbred ex-racehorses rescue as seen through the entanglement of animal rights, human incarceration, and globally faltering economic times. With a Ph.D. in Anthropology from the University of British Columbia, McKee calls Squamish, British Columbia home.

Jack Taylor is Assistant Professor in the Department of English at the University of Hawai'i-Manoa. His primary research and teaching interests include African American literature and visual culture, African and Caribbean literature, and critical theory. He has recently published an interview entitled "Revolution at the Point of Production: An Interview with Mike Hamlin of DRUM and The League of Revolutionary Black Workers" in the journal *Spectrum* published by Indiana University Press. With Morgan Shipley, he recently published an article on *The Wire*. He is currently working on a book concerning the interconnection of African American literature, theory, and biopolitical philosophy.

James A. Tyner is Professor of Geography at Kent State University. His research interests center on war, violence, and genocide, with a specific focus on Cambodia. He has published 13 books and approximately 50 research articles and chapters. His most recent book is *Genocide and the Geographical Imagination: Life and Death in Germany, China, and Cambodia* (Rowman & Littlefield, 2012).

L.A. Watson is an interdisciplinary artist and writer working in the field of critical animal studies. Watson earned her B.A. in Gender and Women's Studies from the University of Kentucky and an MFA from Vermont College of Fine Arts. Her work has been exhibited both nationally and internationally. She recently co-curated the exhibition "Uncooped" at The National Museum of Animals & Society and designed and published the "Uncooped" book to accompany the exhibition. Watson is a member of the artist coalition ArtAnimalAffect and works in her home studio in Kentucky. More work can be viewed at: www.lawatsonart.com

Jen Wrye is a Sociology Instructor at North Island College on Vancouver Island in British Columbia, Canada. Her work focuses on food systems, animal–human relations, and the scholarship of teaching and learning. Her dissertation, *Nutritionism & the Making of Modern Pet Food*, is currently being revised for publication. Jen's new work investigates local food production and consumption.

Acknowledgments

We would like to thank Andy Humphries, Laura Johnson, and Lisa Thomson for their keen editorial assistance in producing this book. We are also grateful to three anonymous reviewers for their productive feedback at the proposal stage. A series of three sessions on Economies of Death at the 2014 Annual Meeting of the Association of American Geographers provided thought-provoking and fruitful inspiration as we formulated this book project. We thank the authors who have worked diligently to craft such interesting and provocative chapters for this volume. It has been a true pleasure to work with such brilliant and dedicated people.

We are grateful to University of Georgia Press for granting permission to print Jennifer Fluri's and Rachel Lehr's chapter in this text, which is part of the forthcoming book, *American-Afghan Entanglements: Development Geopolitics and the Currency of Gender*, by Jennifer Fluri and Rachel Lehr.

We would also like to thank Taylor & Francis, and Routledge specifically, for permission to reprint Irus Braverman's chapter, which is based on her original chapter in *Critical Animal Geographies: Politics, Intersections and Hierarchies in a Multispecies World*, edited by Kathryn Gillespie and Rosemary-Claire Collard (Routledge, 2015).

We are also indebted to those who have granted permission for the use of images reprinted in this book: Document Center of Cambodia, The IUCN Red List of Threatened Species © IUCN, Mike Parr, L.A. Watson, and Caretas photographic archive.

And of course, we are forever grateful to our families—both the bipedal and quadrupedal members—for their unending support and patience through this process.

1 Introducing economies of death

Kathryn A. Gillespie and Patricia J. Lopez

We first engaged in conversations that would lead to this project in the summer of 2009 as we clambered through prickly blackberry bushes at a local-to-Seattle park and filled our buckets with berries, our fingers stained purple and our arms scratched by thorns. As we picked the berries, we talked about death and dying, violence and killing, grief and mourning. And as we slowly stirred the bubbling jam and prepared the jars for canning later that morning, we continued our conversation.

At first glance, it would seem that our individual research projects have very little in common: one of us is actively involved in studying the effects of ongoing military intervention and aid on health citizenship in Haiti (Lopez) and one of us studies the violent impacts of commodity production on animal bodies, particularly those used for dairy production in the United States (Gillespie). Indeed, these projects focus on distinct situations and bodies with significant differences between them. And yet, our theoretical frameworks find many points of contact and overlap. We are both concerned with economic logics governing life and death and how certain lives and bodies are made killable and disposable. We have both experienced a profound sense of grief as we conducted our research and, as a result, noticed the ways that grief and grievability function politically to designate whose lives matter and whose do not.

Related questions began to emerge through our conversations: How do uneven hierarchies of power operate to privilege some bodies and subjugate others? In what ways is the global accumulation of capital implicated in the appropriation of these lives and bodies? And how are these economic logics of efficiency, production and consumption, and capital accumulation reliant on various forms of death (e.g., killing, social death, and others)? What is involved in the social and political process of 'making killable' and how is this related to the actual act of killing? What political work is done when we grieve the 'ungrievable'? How can these questions that we pose (as scholars, activists, and people living in the world) inform analysis and praxis that attends to the ethical dimensions of these processes? We ask these questions as a starting point for this project and begin to think through them in this chapter, with the authors throughout the book, and in our concluding thoughts that suggest some future directions for work on economies of death.

One important contribution of this text is its commitment to thinking human and nonhuman animal death, killability, and grievability alongside one another. In this vein, we employ what Jasbir Puar (2007, 120) calls "reading sideways," wherein we engage "seemingly unrelated and often disjunctively situated moments and their effects." This process helps us to understand a multiplicity of power dynamics and the ethical dimensions of varied and ambivalent social–political–economic relations in different contexts. Thus, like Jin Haritaworn, Adi Kuntsman, and Silvia Posocco (2014, 5), whose text on queer necropolitics "read[s] livability alongside killability, rescue alongside disposability, protection alongside abandonment and celebration alongside violent erasure," the project of our text is to read killability alongside grievability, political economy alongside ethical consideration, and the 'human' alongside the 'animal.'

We argue that examining the way humans and animals are made killable and grievable is a productive project for seeing connections that span beyond species boundaries. At the same time, we acknowledge, and are concerned with, the long history of 'dehumanizing' and 'animalizing' certain human groups, particularly people of color and the economically marginalized. As processes, 'dehumanization' and 'animalization' normalize violence against bodies, dispossess them of their political subjectivity and render them as "bare life" (Agamben 1998). Dehumanization and animalization are both reliant on devaluing certain lives and bodies based on particular socially constructed 'differences' (e.g., race, gender, sexuality, species, intelligence and cognition, etc.), and they materialize in slavery, genocide, land dispossession, incarceration, foreign policy, war making, hate crimes, sexual violence, and other historical and contemporary practices that are reliant on racist, sexist, and heterosexist ideologies.

We aim to maintain the usefulness of these concepts to describe processes that subjugate and strip away dignity from marginalized bodies, yet at the same time we are interested in troubling the language of 'dehumanization' and 'animalization.' Both of these concepts rely on rendering the subject as less-than-human (i.e., that the state of not being human is justification for violence) and, in doing so, reinforce the human–animal divide. Post-humanist scholars, of course, have troubled this socially constructed divide (reminding us that humans themselves are animals) and are dedicated to 'decentering the human' and moving toward post-anthropocentric ways of being in the world (e.g., Braidotti 2013; Haraway 2007; Wolfe 2009). Using the language of 'dehumanization' or 'animalization' to describe fundamentally exploitative processes reproduces the notion of human exceptionalism whereby humans, based on their species membership, are entitled to better treatment than nonhuman animals. Thus, 'animalization' as a discursive construct maintains the subordination of the actual animal as it leaves intact a system whereby it is acceptable to treat animals 'like animals.' 'Like animals' signals something—a lesser status, a status that justifies substandard or inhumane treatment. Indeed, even 'inhumane,' rooted in 'human' and 'humanity,' renders (some) humans as sacred subjects against which other species and entities are measured (and fall short).

This is not to say that human and nonhuman animals or their experiences are the same; rather, it is to say that 'animalization,' as a process that subjugates both humans *and* animals, is rooted in deeply uneven hierarchies of power. Ours is not a project of calculating whose lives (do or should) matter more; but rather, we attempt to resist hierarchization in our approach, rejecting anthropocentrism, white supremacy, heteronormativity, and other similar systems of dominance. Indeed, it is precisely these hegemonic systems of power that work to naturalize the 'making killable' of marginalized bodies in global economic regimes. The discourses that frame these deaths—these acts of killing, these moments of 'making killable,' these technologies of erasure—as 'collateral damage,' 'the price of capitalism,' or as simply 'culture' or 'tradition' work to obscure the very real violence involved.

Looking at the killing and 'making killable' of humans alongside animals enables us to see the co-production of violence that permeates everyday social relations. In particular, it allows us to see the ways in which these everyday practices of 'making killable' become necessary in service to capital accumulation. It is not merely the act of violence and killing that we are concerned with in this text, but also the act of making this violence mundane. Indeed, the work of making these acts of killing mundane is *central* to the process of 'making killable.' 'Economies of death,' as a theoretical framework, acknowledges that, of course, all living beings die: we all encounter death repeatedly throughout our lives as we lose those we love and we eventually all die ourselves. Thus, death is an inevitable process—a part of life, another phase of being (and not being) in the world. Death, in part, gives life meaning and transforms the body into something new—into decomposing flesh that feeds microorganisms and helps natural ecologies flourish, into ash dispersed in the wind, into something we fear, honor, and are disgusted by. We are not, then, opposed to death itself; rather, we are concerned with the way economic processes of commodification and capital accumulation make lives killable, and exploit bodies, lives and labor in ways that bring on premature death (Gilmore 2007; Tyner 2014).

Over several years, we engaged in conversations about these themes and first expanded this dialogue by organizing a set of sessions at the 2014 Annual Meeting of the Association of American Geographers in Tampa, Florida. These sessions on economies of death were scheduled in the final three session slots on the last day of the conference. Many people had already left Tampa while others had taken off to the beach to enjoy the Florida sunshine instead of spending another day in hotel conference rooms. In spite of this timing, the room was full for each session; some scholars even changed their flights so that they could stay for the whole series of sessions. The room filled with people and their luggage and the conversation we had across presentations and question/answer periods was dynamic, lively, and provocative. Clearly, there was significant interest in the subject from a range of scholars interested in violence and killing, death and dying, life and living, and the economic logics that make certain lives killable or grievable. In particular, it was productive thinking across species boundaries about these kinds of issues so that scholars who had focused primarily on human forms of violence and killing were suddenly considering violence against animals, and animal geographers who are typically siloed in their own sub-discipline were engaging in thinking with and about human case studies as well.

In addition to a range of critical feminist, Marxist, posthumanist, and anti-racist geographers, the sessions also attracted non-geographers, and we had presenters from such disciplines as Women's Studies and Art to frame a more interdisciplinary conversation. Thus, as we conceptualized the book, we were committed to curating a dialogue across disciplines in order to reach beyond geography and engage a more holistic vision of how economies of death operate in the world. In this spirit, *Economies of Death* includes eight substantive chapters that advance a theory of economies of death through distinct case studies, each focused on the impacts of economic logics of killability on humans, animals, and the environment. In its interdisciplinarity and intersectionality, this theory of economies of death can be taken up, applied, and grounded across multiple boundaries (of discipline, location, race, class, gender, species). As a result, the book should contribute to interdisciplinary and international conversations about these themes, with chapters written by scholars across the social sciences and humanities and global case studies spanning from Afghanistan and Cambodia to Peru and the United States. Underpinning the project of defining this theory is a close consideration of the political and ethical implications of these economic logics of killability and grievability. This theory of economies of death is built from localized and grounded case studies, which engage in a knowledge-making practice and the construction of a theoretical framework that can be taken up and understood within the global political-economic landscape.

The text is organized to make accessible the different strands of theory that inform the broader project of economies of death and explore grievability, killability, and thanato/necropolitics within grounded empirical case studies. The first three chapters focus on timely topics: September 11, 2001 and Afghanistan (Fluri and Lehr), the redemption of prisoners and ex-racehorses (McKee), and genocide in Cambodia (Tyner). Next, we move into two case studies that challenge the violence of categorizations that order the mundane: endangered species conservation (Braverman) and the differentiation between animals as 'pets' and animals as 'food' (Wrye). The final three chapters lay bare what happens when we consider the intersections of various forms of violence that cannot be artificially separated by hierarchies of whose lives we value and why: lynching and the 'animalization' of African Americans (Taylor), the memorialization of animals killed on roads as activism (Watson), and the political economy of interspecies violence and suffering in Peru (Garcia). Each chapter in the book takes seriously the economic logics of killable life and grievable death to define a distinct theoretical framework of 'economies of death.'

By way of introducing this project, we lay out the various strands of theory that inform our work and the theoretical intervention of 'economies of death.' We take as a springboard Foucault's biopolitics and review the ways in which this framework has informed our project here. Even as Foucault's framework is useful here, it is also characterized by a deeply rooted anthropocentrism; thus, we engage with posthumanist critiques and applications of biopolitics to understand how this theoretical framework might inform cross-species analyses of the politics of life and death. We are particularly attentive to the precarity (in the Butlerian sense) of certain lives in biopolitical figurings of life and death. This precarity dictates which lives are grievable and killable and which are not. Butler, however, advances a theory of grievability primarily focused on which *human* lives are grievable or not. Thus, we engage a theory of grievability across species lines to include nonhuman species in this differential calculation of life and grief. These theoretical frameworks—biopolitics (and thanato/ necropolitics), precarity and precariousness, and killability and grievability— inform how we understand economies of death in this text.

Biopolitics, as a concept and framework, has been used in increasing measure over the past 20 years. Once the purview of a handful of Foucauldian scholars, today it permeates across disciplinary divides, finding traction in political, ethical, legal, genomic, and security studies, and moving among human, animal, and environmental subjects. Biopolitics encompasses everything from the "politics of life itself" in the molecular management of the self (Rose 2007; Rajan 2006), to the politics of *homo sacer* within (and without) "spaces of exception" (Agamben 1998; Minca 2006). Indeed, scholars such as Timothy Campbell (2011) and Roberto Esposito (2008) have hinted at (and sought to address) an overuse of the idea of biopolitics that points to it losing specificity of meaning. However, that biopolitics has been exercised so thoroughly as a theoretical tool to discuss the ubiquitous manner in which power reaches into every cell and every facet of life and living, drawing new forms of subjectification into focus, speaks to the undeniably fundamental relationship between bodies and power that spans disciplines.[1] It is this relationship that the authors of this book seek to uncover, tracing just some of the ways in which biopolitics, and its twin, necropolitics, seep across species divides and are informed by, and give expression to, economic logics of grievability and killability. To that end, we think it is worth revisiting biopolitics, tracing it as it unfolded in Foucault's own thought, and then as it has exploded to take on a host of meanings that always point back to, and interrogate, networks of "relationship between the population, the territory, and wealth" (Foucault 2007, 142).

For Foucault, the era of biopower marks the disruption in political praxis from the absolute power of the sovereign to "make die" and "let live" toward a life-oriented power to "make live" and "let die" materializing as the shift from the absolute command of law toward the disciplining of individual bodies and whole populations in a "calculated management of life" (Foucault 1990, 139–140; Foucault 2003, 241). Fueled by the emergence of the idea of "population" as an economic and political problem in need of management and calculation, new forms of governance were crafted around subjects who were no longer simply a group of individuals whose inclusion and exclusion were arbitrarily appointed by the sovereign, but rather, a group of people who live and die, get sick, marry and have a whole range of productive and reproductive functions that must be disciplined, ordered, optimized, and otherwise normalized. Marked by two poles—anatomopolitical, which governs individual bodies, and biopolitical, which governs the social body—biopower "brought life and its mechanisms into the realm of explicit calculations and made knowledge-power an agent for the transformation of human life" (1990, 143). In his lecture series, *Society Must Be Defended*, given at the Collège de France in 1976, Foucault's idea of biopolitics begins its slow unmooring from its strict delineation in biopower, broadening to encompass beyond the statistical enumerations of birth, death, and illness toward, for instance, natalist policies that seek to understand birth rates and to intervene to manage them more directly, the shift in medicine toward public hygiene, the establishment of economically rational mechanisms to manage the precariousness of life, such as insurance, savings, and safety, and mediating and controlling the relations between people and the environment (Foucault 2003, 243–245). This transition toward a broader encompassing of biopolitics, married as it was to governmentality, was not to mark an explicit transition from a society dominated by discipline to one based on government, but rather, was expressed as a "triangle: sovereignty, discipline, governmental management, which has population as its main target and apparatuses of security as its essential mechanism" (2003, 143). It is here where political economy becomes isolated as both a science and a technique.

Without technologies of power—without the segregations and social hierarchies—capitalism would not have developed as it did. Indeed, Foucault asserts, "bio-power was without question an indispensable element in the development of capitalism; the latter would not have been possible without the controlled insertion of bodies into the machinery of production and the adjustment of the phenomena of population to economic processes" (1990, 140–141). It is through technologies of biopower that government both constitutes its own rationality through the definition and management of problems and creates the very technologies and institutions which enable it (Foucault 2007; 2008). To be clear, this is not to imply a coherent unity and even importance of the state, but a "governmentalization" of the state expressed as a multitude of forces that bear down on populations and is operationalized through economic knowledge (2007, 144–145). Indeed, the instrumentalization of reason reaches into the species level of humans and nonhuman animals, technologizing subjectivity of individuals and subsuming them into a calculable logic against which livability, grievability, and killability are mediated.

However, as Shukin (2009, 11) asserts, Foucault's assemblage of biopolitical technologies of power bump up against and reveal a kind of speciesism that continues to foreground the human experience as primary to late modernism's attachment to the ordering of life and death. Michael Dillon and Luis Lobo-Guerrero (2009, 2) go so far as to call "banal" the "distinction between discourses of the human and discourse of life," noting that the Greek philosophers made no such distinction. The anthropocentrism of Foucault's biopolitics elides the reproductive and labor capital of animals and, more insidiously, the mundane ways in which spaces of exception and the mass suffering and death that occurs within them (such as auction yards and slaughterhouses) not only go unremarked, but mark out the boundaries between species and lives that are 'pertinent' or not. However, this deeply marked boundary is far more fluid than any of us care to admit. It is a fluidity marked out in everyday language—in the construction of some humans as more (mere) animal and some animals as anthropomorphic.

Foucault argues that life is the object of government, with biopower's limit approached in death. "Power," he asserts, "literally ignores death" (2003, 248). However, we, and the chapter authors in this book, argue that death is, itself, a technology of power that is as much about the right 'make live' and 'to let die' as it is to 'make dead.' Indeed, Agamben argues (2000, 5) "[t]he *puissance absolue et perpetuelle,* which defines state power, is not founded—in the last instance—on a political will but rather on naked life, which is kept safe and protected only to the degree to which it submits itself to the sovereign's (or the law's) right of life and death." Or, put more plainly as Mbembe (2003) argues, "to kill or to allow to live constitute the limits of sovereignty, its fundamental attributes." What constitutes naked life, *zoē* (also translated from the Italian, *vita nuda,* or 'bare life'), or "the life common to all living beings (animals, men, or gods)" as opposed to political life, *bios,* "which indicated the form or way of living proper to an individual or a group" (Agamben 1998, 9), hinges on a contemporary biopolitical *nomos* which is not only instrumentalized in the "the determination of a juridical and a territorial ordering (of an *Ordnung* and an *Ortung*)—but above all a 'taking of the outside,' an exception (*Ausnahme*)" (Agamben 1998, 19; see also: Minca 2006).

And yet, as so many have argued, what constitutes the 'exception' today is an everywhere place, unlocalizable; and, who may constitute a "bare life," or outside of human jurisdiction, slides too easily with the shifting boundaries of exclusion and inclusion (Agamben 1998, 72; Belcher et al. 2008; Butler 2004). Indeed, the state of exception is, itself, a technique of government and *homo sacer* the life exposed to death—a condition to which we are all potentially exposed. We take with all seriousness Rosi Braidotti's warning against the "emphasis on death as the horizon for the discussions on the limits of our understanding of the human" (2006, 40). We agree that the obsession with death stops short of drawing on all life, and take care to point out that it is an obsession in so far as it is attached to the primacy of human life while failing to recognize the calculus against which all living and dying—human, animal, and environment—is a reflection of the ever expanding exploitative nature of capitalist production. Death is not the finitude against which life must be understood; but rather, we examine the ways in which death is mobilized as an imperative of late liberal politics and capitalism.

Biopolitical registers of life and death—of making live/letting die and letting live/making die—are fraught with dimensions of both precarity and precariousness. It is important to note that precarity and precariousness are distinct states of being, and these concepts, though related, should not be used interchangeably. Butler writes,

> Precariousness and precarity are intersecting concepts. Lives are by definition precarious: they can be expunged at will or by accident; their persistence is in no sense guaranteed. In some sense, this is a feature of all life, and there is no thinking of life that is not precarious—except, of course, in fantasy, and in military fantasies in particular. Political orders, including economic and social institutions, are designed to address those very needs without which the risk of mortality is heightened. Precarity designates that politically induced condition in which certain populations suffer from failing social and economic networks of support and become differentially exposed to injury, violence, and death.
>
> (Butler 2009, 25).

As such, we are concerned with both the precariousness of life and the precarity to which certain populations are differentially subjected to violence and death.

The precarity of populations is intimately tied up with the project of making certain lives and bodies killable. For instance, racialized social relations in the United States, characterized by uneven social and economic hierarchies of support and privilege, make black bodies (and black *male* bodies, in particular) killable and disproportionately exposed to bodily violence, incarceration, and premature death. To understand precarity in the nonhuman context, farmed animals, for example, live and die in a constant state of precarity, driven by the social and economic conditions of commodification, whereby they are brought into being specifically to be commodified and killed.

Economies of Death makes a political and ethical intervention that critiques the conditions under which precarious populations (and the individuals that comprise them) live, struggle, and are killed by violent political economic systems like capitalism. Although there has been an intensification of the violence wrought by capitalist production (in animal slaughter, the degradation of the environment and desecration of ecological landscapes, the death and incarceration of so-called excess labor force, etc.) since the 1970s, it is important to stress that these are conditions inherent to capitalism writ large. Indeed, many have argued that the neoliberal moment is one of hyper-intensification and hyper-efficiency in the more globalized circuits of capital (Foucault 2008; Brown 2005; Wright 2006). This hyper-intensification, in fact, lays bare the violence that is fundamentally characteristic of capitalist social and political economic relations more generally.

Haraway argues in *When Species Meet* (2007) that it is not so much the act of killing that is the problem, but the act of 'making killable.' She writes about the inescapability of avoiding killing in our lives: "Try as we might to distance ourselves, there is no way of living that is not also a way of someone, not just something, else dying differentially" (Haraway 2007, 80). In some ways, we agree with this claim—that there are many difficult-to-avoid acts of killing we engage in (killing insects as we walk along the sidewalk or drive on freeways, for instance). And yet, we are critical of the ways in which Haraway's argument justifies various acts of killing that are, in fact, more easily avoidable. For instance, in the case of farmed animals or animals used in scientific experimentation, Haraway sees a problem only in making them killable, not in the fact that they are killed. This approach justifies a kind of "humane capitalism"—in which capitalists and consumers believe that suffering should be limited as we sacrifice others in service to capital accumulation and our own lifestyle preferences. This sets up a false construct of living and dying wherein killing certain bodies is taken-for-granted and ethical considerations focus only on *how* animals live and are killed, not *whether* they should be killed at all.[2] Further, "Haraway would not make the same argument about cosmopolitical engagements of this sort if the 'other' were human" (Gruen 2014, 132); thus, there is an inherent speciesism to Haraway's claims about killing—namely, that animals, and especially certain species of animals, are more or less sacrifice-able under capitalist regimes of power. We disagree in certain fundamental ways with this approach and reject the hegemonic logic of the hierarchization of some species' lives and deaths over others.

In spite of the particular ways in which we disagree with Haraway's argument and what it justifies, we take up this notion of 'making killable' as a central theoretical strand in our advancement of economies of death. Central to this project are the economic logics that govern which bodies are made killable and which bodies are not. Marginalized human and animal bodies are continuously made killable in service to capital accumulation—their bodies used, worn out, discarded, and killed. Importantly, the process of making bodies killable is characterized by both the Foucauldian act of 'making die' (direct forms of killing) and 'letting die' (passive forms of letting bodies deteriorate and die through neglect or insufficient care).

The process of making certain bodies killable impacts which lives and deaths are grievable. Judith Butler writes, "Some lives are grievable, and others are not; the differential allocation of grievability that decides what kind of subject is and must be grieved, and which kind of subject must not, operates to produce and maintain certain exclusionary conceptions of who is normatively human: what counts as a livable life and a grievable death?" (2004, xiv–xv). We take this question as one of the book's central starting points: whose lives count as livable and whose deaths are grievable? In the human realm, this differential calculus is borne out, as Butler (2004; 2009) argues, in war, for instance: certain human lives are framed as 'collateral damage,' as acceptable and, importantly, *un-grievable* losses in service to economic logics that drive the war machine. We also see the way certain human lives are made not grievable through racialized violence in the spectacle of lynching (see Taylor, this volume) and the erasures of human life and death in the wake of Shining Path violence in Peru (see García, this volume). At the same time, animal lives are also situated in this uneven hierarchy of grievability in innumerable ways: animals' lives are often positioned as inherently less grievable than humans' just by virtue of their species membership; certain animal species are privileged over others as we see, for instance, in the ability of people to keep some animals ('pets') as cherished members of their families and kill others with little thought for food (see Wrye, this volume); and in our conservation prioritization of some species over others (see Braverman, this volume, for a differential valuing of endangered species based on their charismatic quality).

Butler's work is focused on the way *human* lives are made grievable or not. Thus, we extend her theory of grievability to put forth a more posthuman consideration of "what constitutes a grievable or killable life." James Stanescu (2012) writes about the act of mourning animals as a political statement about their position in the world. Stanescu begins his analysis in the 'meat' section of the grocery store, where he is struck by a profound sense of grief over the cut-up and packaged corpses there in front of him. In the next moment, he is further moved by the fact that this grief is deeply unintelligible to the rest of the world (those who don't see the violence and grief in a package of 'meat'). Following Stanescu's call for extending Butler's work to the nonhuman realm, we are committed to the act of making human *and* nonhuman lives and deaths grievable as a political and ethical statement driving an enlarged ethic of care. In this act of making grievable, we aim to move toward a recognition of all lives being constituted as *bios*, or having political life (a la Agamben). Indeed, "animals are already subjects of, and subject to, political practices" (Hobson 2007, 251), and grieving animals helps us to acknowledge their political life.

Grief—the act of grieving—enables us to understand and empathize with the vulnerability of others and, rather than resulting in inaction, can prompt critical opposition to maintaining the vulnerability of certain populations (Butler 2004, 30). Grief, then, is not merely a solopsistic act of wallowing in our own sorrows; rather, it is both a political act against, and a way of making political, the suffering and oppression of others. Grief acknowledges that the life, suffering, and death of a body matters. Grief, in the best cases, can resist the differential valuation of lives and acknowledge that distance, perceived 'differences,' and political and economic interests should not govern who can and should be grieved. Mourning then "has all sorts of powers, potentialities and potencies. Mourning is never just about grief, but it is about celebrations, memories and stories. Mourning doesn't just bring with it moments of isolation, it also sets up connections and reaches out for relation" (Stanescu 2012, 580). With this relationality and the potential for connection in mind, *Economies of Death* takes as its starting point the practice of grieving marginalized human and nonhuman lives, deaths and acts of killing. As editors—together with our authors—we write from a place of profound grief as an act of recognition that all lives matter, all deaths are grievable, and the act of killing in service to capital accumulation is a deeply politically and ethically problematic structure of social and political economic relations.

A note on the use of images in the book

Throughout the book, some authors have used images that readers may find difficult to view. Indeed, in a book about economies of death, it might be expected. We, collectively, the editors and the authors who have chosen to use the images, have discussed each decision, chewing on the weight of what the images will add as opposed to how they may simply work to reinscribe the objectification of those whose death has been archived and to replicate the very spectacle of violence itself (Giroux 2007; Polchin 2007). No author or editor uses images of death lightly or easily, but their inclusion, for us, is deeply tied to the (re)construction of collective memory—a recognition and visual representation of just four moments in which economic logics of killability were not only laid bare in the actual physical death of others, but were recorded—some for the sheer spectacle of the spectacle (as in the lynching photographs in Taylor's chapter), others to record the atrocities *against forgetting* (as in the images in Tyner's and García's chapters), and some that render ghostly memorials (Watson's chapter). Three of the chapters (Fluri and Lehr's, Taylor's, and García's) specifically address public exhibitions of images—one of lively pictures of dead people and two of the acts of violence, and all as modes of remembrance and historical witnessing (although only two of these chapters include images). This act of historical witnessing, however uncomfortable it may be, can, of its own accord, and when done with consciousness, be an ethical act in and of itself—an invitation to remember and to reflect more deeply upon the history that we are not always comfortable remembering (Apel 2004; Lydon 2010; Sontag 2013). It is in this vein that we have made the decision to include the images that we have. It is our hope that we have done so with respect and afford those whose images are published herein the dignity that we believe all beings—human and nonhuman—deserve.

References

Agamben, Giorgio. 1998. *Homo Sacer: Sovereign Power and Bare Life.* Stanford: Stanford University Press.
——2000. *Means Without Ends: Notes On Politics.* Series: Theory out of bounds: 20. Minneapolis: University of Minnesota Press.

Apel, Dora. 2004. *Imagery of Lynching: Black Men, White Women, and the Mob.* New Brunswick, NJ: Rutgers University Press.

Belcher, Oliver, Lauren Martin, Anna Secor, Stephanie Simon, and Tommy Wilson. 2008. Everywhere and Nowhere: The Exception and the Topological Challenge to Geography. *Antipode.* 40 (4): 499–503.

Braidotti, Rosi. 2006. *Transpositions: On Nomadic Ethics.* Malden, MA: Polity Press.

——2013. *The Posthuman.* Malden, MA: Polity Press.

Brown, Wendy. 2005. *Edgework Critical Essays on Knowledge and Politics.* Princeton, N.J.: Princeton University Press.

Butler, Judith. 2004. *Precarious Life: The Powers of Mourning and Violence.* London: Verso.

——2009. *Frames of War: When Is Life Grievable?* New York: Verso.

Campbell, Timothy C. 2011. *Improper Life Technology and Biopolitics from Heidegger to Agamben.* Minneapolis: University of Minnesota Press.

Dillon, M. and L. Lobo-Guerrero. 2008. Biopolitics of Security in the 21st Century: An Introduction. *Review of International Studies.* 34 (2): 265–292.

Esposito, Roberto. 2008. *Bíos: Biopolitics and Philosophy.* Minneapolis: University of Minnesota Press.

Foucault, Michel. 1990. *The History of Sexuality: An Introduction. Vol. I.* New York: Vintage Books.

——1995. *Discipline and Punish: The Birth of the Prison.* New York: Vintage Books.

——2003. Society Must Be Defended: Lectures at the Collège de France, 1975–76. Mauro Bertani, Alessandro Fontana and François Ewald (eds.) and David Macey (Trans.). New York: Picador.

——2007. Security, Territory, Population: Lectures at the Collège de France, 1977–78. Michel Senellart, François Ewald, and Alessandro Fontana (eds.) and Graham Burchell (Trans.). Basingstoke: Palgrave Macmillan.

——2008. The Birth of Biopolitics: Lectures at the Collège de France, 1978–79. Michel Senellart (ed.) and Graham Burchell (Trans.). Basingstoke: Palgrave Macmillan.

Gilmore, Ruth Wilson. 2007. *Golden Gulag: Prisons, Surplus, Crisis, and Opposition in Globalizing California.* Berkeley: University of California Press.

Giroux, Henry A. 2007. Beyond the Spectacle of Terrorism: Rethinking Politics in the Society of the Image. *Situations: Project of the Radical Imagination.* 2 (1): 17–52. Available online http://ojs.gc.cuny.edu/index.php/situations/issue/view (accessed October 10, 2014).

Gruen, Lori. 2014. Facing Death and Practicing Grief. *Ecofeminism: Feminist Intersections with Other Animals and the Earth*, Carol Adams and Lori Gruen (eds.). New York: Bloomsbury, pp. 127–141.

Haraway, Donna. 2007. *When Species Meet.* Minneapolis: University of Minnesota Press.

Haritaworn, Jinthana, Adi Kuntsman, and Silvia Posocco. 2014. *Queer Necropolitics.* Hoboken: Taylor & Francis

Hobson, Kersty. 2007. Political Animals: On Animals as Subjects in an Enlarged Political Geography. *Political Geography*, 26 (3): 250–267.

Lemke, Thomas. 2011. *Biopolitics: An Advanced Introduction.* Translated by Eric Frederick Trump. New York: New York University Press.

Lydon, Jane. 2010. 'Behold the Tears': Photography as Colonial Witness. *History of Photography.* 34 (3): 234–250.

Mbembe, Achille. 2003. Necropolitics. *Public Culture*. 15 (1): 11–40.

Minca, Claudio. 2006. Giorgio Agambenand the New Biopolitical Nomos. *Geografiska Annaler. Series B, Human Geography*. 88 (4): 387–403.

Polchin, James. 2007. Not Looking at Lynching Photographs. Frances Guerin and Roger Hallis (eds.). *The Image and the Witness: Trauma, Memory, and Visual Culture*. New York: Wallflower Press.

Puar, Jasbir K. 2007. *Terrorist Assemblages: Homonationalism in Queer Times*. Durham: Duke University Press.

Rabinow, Paul and Nikolas Rose. 2006. Biopower Today. *BioSocieties*. 1 (2): 195–217.

Rajan, Kaushik Sunder. 2006. *Biocapital: The Constitution of Postgenomic Life*. Durham: Duke University Press.

Rose, Nikolas. 2007. *The Politics of Life Itself: Biomedicine, Power, and Subjectivity in the Twenty-First Century*. Princeton: Princeton University Press.

Shukin, Nicole. 2009. *Animal Capital: Rendering Life in Biopolitical Times*. Posthumanities Series, 6. Minneapolis: University of Minnesota Press.

Sontag, Susan. 2013. *Regarding the Pain of Others*. New York: Macmillan.

Stanescu, James. 2012. Species Trouble: Judith Butler, Mourning, and the Precarious Lives of Animals. *Hypatia*, 27 (2): 567–582.

Tyner, James A. 2014. Population Geography II: Mortality, Premature Death, and the Ordering of Life. *Progress in Human Geography*. Online DOI: 10.1177/0309132514527037.

Wolfe, Cary. 2009. *What is Posthumanism*. Minneapolis: University of Minnesota Press.

Wright, Melissa W. 2006. *Disposable Women and Other Myths of Global Capitalism*. New York: Routledge.

Notes

1 For a rather thorough overview of the history and different theoretical debates around biopolitics, see Thomas Lemke's (2011) *Biopolitics: An Advanced Introduction*.

2 We do see that there are certain situations where the act of killing is one not characterized by economic gain or self-interest, and where it is in the best interest of the one being killed: in the case of physician-assisted suicide, or euthanasia in the case of an ailing and dying animal. In situations like these, where the suffering of a body will only be relieved by death, we see killing as an act of kindness.

2 The currency of grief

9/11 deaths, Afghan lives, and intimate intervention

Jennifer L. Fluri and Rachel Lehr

Grief is most often defined as an emotive response to tragedy and loss. This emotion can be a tactile feeling or animated to reflect a deep personal experience of loss or trauma. What happens when personal grief becomes public, collective, and even geopolitical? Some suggest that national tragedies such as the events of 9/11 in the U.S. were expressed through public spectacles of grief. The articulation of public sorrow by way of presidential speeches, political discourses, and media narratives accumulated into a grand narrative that manipulated and shaped national-collective suffering in order to legitimate political/military action (Burk 2003; Dahlman and Brunn 2003; Engle 2007; Fried 2006; Saal 2011; Simko 2012). Indeed, as Kevin Rozario (2007) argues, natural and human-caused disasters have had a significant historical framing within the U.S. that often impacted collective national-identities since the arrival of the Puritans. After September 11, 2001 national identities were solidified. At the same time, the U.S. government seized the opportunity to create new security regimes and to invade/occupy Afghanistan and Iraq.

This chapter examines the geopolitics of grief in order to illustrate the intersections of intimate, national, and global appropriations of 9/11 grief and Afghan suffering respectively.[1] We include a review of the literature about 9/11 grief and the various ways in which it was mediated and shaped to meet a particular representation of the U.S. nation and nationalistic ideologies of morality, justice, and revenge. We examine Agamben's (1998, 1999) concept of bare life and how the gendering of this representational ontology has become a form of development currency. By combining Agamben's (1998, 1999) theories on bare life, sovereignty, and potentiality with Judith Butler's extensive analysis of 'precarious life' we explicate the ways in which these political theories, when mapped onto different bodies, yield various forms of currency. We examine the ways in which the grief of surviving family members of 9/11 victims became a form of political currency. We critically analyze the grievability of Afghan women and children's living-suffering and American victims of 9/11 respectively. We argue that certain taxonomies of grievability and potentiality have become particular forms of political and economic currencies. Our analyses include empirical examinations of two organizations founded by surviving family members of 9/11 victims. Beyond the 11th was founded by two women whose husbands died on the planes flown into the World Trade Center, and The Peter M. Goodrich Memorial Foundation was founded by the parents of Peter, who was a passenger on Flight 175.

Assistance and development as extensions of geopolitics become tools for demarcating the 'ethically superior' from those associated with the dispossession of human rights (Abu-Lughod 2013). Humanitarian aid operates to theoretically reinforce rights-based claims while remaining constrained by the limited ability of organizations to actually orchestrate justice (Laurie and Petchesky 2008). Human rights concepts are often represented as undeniable and universal. However, careful study of human rights histories and discourses by several scholars reveals that these so-called 'universal' claims are attentive to 'western-European enlightenment', which favors individualism and autonomy—fitting neatly within capitalist economic structures (De Waal 1998; Forsythe 2005; Hancock 1989; Hunt 2008). These concepts often stand in contrast to the organization and functionality of family-based networks and structures of community that predominate in Afghanistan (Johnson and Leslie 2004). The ontologies of bare life as discussed by Agamben and the gendered potentialities of aid/development to 'rescue' bare life are central to our critiques throughout this chapter (Fluri 2012). It is at the intersection of ontological positioning, geopolitical discourse, and international 'assistance' that currency emerges. The development and assistance-driven translations of gender, suffering, and grief into currency illustrate a particular manifestation of death economies. This death economy culminates in gendered geopolitics that manipulates emotions associated with trauma and suffering into a complicated mix of financial and political currencies.

For the individuals who lost loved ones on 9/11 their mourning is deeply personal and simultaneously shared as a collective experience of suffering by citizens of an 'injured nation'. This grief was subsequently woven into various discourses that sought to validate the U.S. military response culminating in the October 7, 2001 invasion of Afghanistan (Engle 2007; Gunn 2004). In contrast, as Karen Engle argues, Afghan deaths were not framed as worthy of grief nor part of the political representations of 9/11 and its aftermath, i.e. the Global War on Terror. At the same time, however, we argue that Afghan-life portrayed through the frame of gendered suffering under the Taliban regime elicited a particular form of representational grief. This grief was not attached to Afghan civilian deaths, but rather to the objectified oppressed-Afghan-life, predominantly symbolized by the burqa-clad woman.

On November 17, 2001, Laura Bush addressed the traumatized people of the United States as a self-appointed spokesperson for Afghan women. Highlighting American sorrow and sympathy for Afghan women and children, she declared:

> The plight of women and children in Afghanistan is a matter of deliberate human cruelty, carried out by those who seek to intimidate and control. Civilized people throughout the world are speaking out in horror—*not*

only because our hearts break for the women and children in Afghanistan, but also because in Afghanistan we see the world the terrorists would like to impose on the rest of us.[2]

This speech was intended to evoke an emotional response of sympathy and sorrow toward the 'heart breaking' plight of Afghan women and children. As discussed by several feminist scholars, this speech was a focal point for framing the 'saving women' trope that helped to situate and further justify U.S. military actions in Afghanistan (Abu-Lughod 2002, 2013; Hunt 2002; Hirschkind and Mahmood 2002; Young 2003). This rallying cry also came at a time when the U.S.-led war in Afghanistan was marked by thousands of Afghan civilian deaths and the return of Afghanistan's civil-war era warlords. The invocation of these tropes helped to de-historicize U.S. policies that abetted if not preempted the events of 9/11 (Maley 2006; Mamdani 2005).[3] Simultaneously this helped to reinforce the 'need' for U.S.-led intervention (Rashid 2000, 2008; Mamdani 2005). As Mahmood Mamdani (2005) argues, the U.S. was actively involved in perpetuating the conflict and helping to finance a pan-Islamic Jihad against 'godless communism' during the Cold War. What International Relations scholars often refer to as 'blow-back'—the growth of violent political Islam against the U.S.—grew from these foreign policy initiatives in the 1980s.

In order to examine the ways in which grief is interlinked with politics we draw upon Judith Butler's theories on grief, conflict, and non-violence post-9/11 (Butler 2006, 2009). We use this theoretical framework to describe how grief is put to work in order to become a politically viable tool for shaping and sustaining the grand narratives associated with U.S. interventions in Afghanistan. We argue that the political use of grief operates as a form of currency. We examine the intimate engagements between Americans and Afghans through '(un)common' experiences of grief.

Butler (2006, 2009) explores the ways in which grief is identified and incorporated into the political framing of 9/11 and its aftermaths (in both Afghanistan and Iraq). Framing, she argues, represents not only the intention but also the non-intentionality of operational power at work toward demarcating what, and how a thing (such as grief), is represented as 'reality'.[4] Thus, media and the ability of those in power (i.e., Mr. and Mrs. Bush) to have a privileged access to media, have a significant and at times overarching role in shaping 'reality' to meet their particular political ideologies (Bligh et al. 2004a). The tragedy of 9/11 exemplifies a form of 'mediated trauma'[5] that incorporates nationalistic symbols and ideologies (Kaplan 2005).

Butler's (2006, 2009) theoretical discussions about mediated representations of U.S. grief and political responses to 9/11 focus on grief and precarious life. Butler defines precarious life as one that is 1) dependent on others, 2) part of social life, and 3) including obligations towards others. Butler's theoretical discussion of precariousness and grief connects these concepts to the ways in which they were framed, visualized, and represented as part of post-9/11 U.S.

responses. Part of this framing included legitimizing international aid and development claims over geographic spaces and people in Afghanistan under a larger umbrella defined as 'alleviating Afghan suffering'. Aid and development programs were further tasked with cultivating Afghan potentiality toward a 'modern' country in an image more recognizable to the U.S. and its allies. The political economy of development is designed to benefit the economic and political interests of donor rather than recipient countries (Harvey 2005). Concurrently the discursive representations of post-9/11 aid and development in Afghanistan highlighted the plight of Afghan women in order to reinforce myths of political saving and economic rescue.

Agamben's theoretical analysis of potentiality provides us with an instructive method for investigating this concept within a general framing of international aid and development (Agamben 1999). Agamben discusses Aristotle's definition of potentiality in two ways (1) as a child whose potentiality requires him/her to "suffer an alteration (to become other) through learning" in order to gain knowledge, and (2) as an adult who possesses knowledge while remaining in a state of potentiality until he/she brings his/her knowledge into actuality (Agamben 1999, 179). Individuals living in spaces targeted for international development are discursively imagined by development organizations and workers in the child/learner state of potentiality. This development framework places Afghans in a state of potentiality that requires a transformation in order for their potentiality to be actualized. International development workers' potentiality is subsequently actualized through their provision of knowledge and 'expertise' (Kothari 2005).

Development programs attempt to insert international interventions as both necessary and essential for actualizing the potentiality of Afghans and development workers respectively. Not surprisingly, in light of these theoretical definitions of potentiality, international workers commonly described adult-Afghans as children.[6] This appellation reflects larger aid and development discourses that are framed by paternalistic assistance structures (Sheppard et al. 2009). An often-repeated mantra among international development workers is the need to build 'Afghan capacity'. Capacity is defined within a particular development framework in order to meet specific criteria set by organizations. Therefore most development workers have been unable or unwilling to see the existing capacities and capabilities of Afghans (Fluri 2009). Development promises the alleviation of suffering through the actualization of potentiality. By suggesting that Afghans lack capacity and by categorizing them in the learner 'child-like' status, the development worker discursively defines his/her own position as 'expert'.

These problematic framings situate Afghan life as both precarious and in a state of learner-potentiality. The link between potentiality and suffering brings us back to Butler's concern about the precariousness of life and its intersected connection to grief. Butler defines "grievability [as] a presupposition for a life that matters" (Butler 2009, 14). She links the value of life with whether or not a life, when it is extinguished, is mourned. Therefore, suggesting that when a death is not grievable, that former life has not been counted, and consequently has been rendered expendable. The ability to extinguish life must also be considered as part of this framing of grievability and value.

Agamben's examinations of sovereignty suggest a binary framing between political life—called 'bios' a full complete and meaningful life, in contrast with natural life—identified as *zoē* a life in its most basic form of physical aliveness.[7] Agamben, in his discussions of state-sovereignty, suggests that the ability to kill or be killed is foundational to political life; "the first foundation of political life is a life that may be killed, which is politicized through its very capacity to be killed" (Agamben 1998, 89). Agamben defines the 'zone of indistinction' as the separation of 'political' (*bios*) from 'natural' life (*zoē*). When life is indistinct, in Agamben's terms, and not grievable, in Butler's terms—it rests in a precarious place of expendability—*a political life, but one without value*. Sovereignty for Agamben is the power to take life—to determine which lives are 'worth living', expendable, or collateral—and to 'untie' a person from political life. He argues that the 'untying' of life implies and produces *bare life* "which dwells in the no man's land"—the zone (or space) of indistinction (Agamben 1998, 56). This form of political theorizing links sovereignty with the ability to legitimately express power through violent means (Elden 2013).

Derek Gregory (2004) takes up Agamben's theories on sovereignty as part of his analysis of U.S. military intervention in Afghanistan post 9/11. Through his analysis he defines the spaces of Afghanistan writ large, including Taliban, Al-Qaeda, refugees, and civilians within Agamben's *zone of indistinction*—where people can be killed with impunity. These political theories resonate at a macro-scale (Graham 2004; Elden 2013). When civilian lives in conflict zones such as Afghanistan are reduced to *bare life 'zoē'* by powerful sovereign states (i.e. the U.S.) with the 'legitimate' ability to kill, it suggests that—in Butler's terms—there is no recognition of these deaths as grievable and no accounting of those lives having meaning enough to be counted or accounted for. Therefore deaths may be recognized but not receive any recognition as being lives that are worthy of U.S. grief. Critical scholars continue to question the legitimacy of the state's ability to decide which deaths count as grievable and which are relegated as collateral (Hyndman 2007; Hyndman and De Alwis 2004; Roy 2002).

We challenge these macro analyses of state-sponsored violence in order to critically evaluate the spatial confinement of bare life solely within a zone of indistinction. As Ong (2006) argues "bare life does not dwell in a zone of indistinction, but it becomes, through the *interventions* of local communities, NGOs and even corporations, shifted and reorganized as various categories of *morally deserving humanity*" (24, *emphasis ours*). Dunn and Cons (2014) critique the concept of bare life—by identifying refugee camps not as indistinct zones, but rather as 'sensitive spaces', which demonstrate that concepts such as sovereign control, citizenship, territorial integrity and identity are "untenable and unstable" in such spaces, and subsequently undermine conventional "ideas of security and belonging" (96). They refocus critical attention toward 'aleatory sovereignty' as a 'rule by chance' to offer a more nuanced understanding of sensitive spaces, authority, power, and control. Thus, experiences of life in a conflict zone are far more complex, rich, full, and layered than macro-scale geopolitics and analyses at this scale suggest (Dunn and Cons 2014).

We argue that while Afghan civilian bodies do not resonate as grievable in the U.S., and are defined as collateral damage by the military, they simultaneously operate as political currency.[8] U.S.-led international forces, the Afghan government, and insurgents all point to civilian deaths when caused by their respective enemies in an effort to delegitimize the violence of the 'other'. Civilian deaths, particularly those of 'women and children' are therefore a currency, discursively exchanged to invalidate certain acts of violence. Afghan deaths are not grievable by U.S. citizens however they do retain geopolitical currency. U.S. citizens are not expected to grieve for the loss of Afghan lives, but to view 'innocent' deaths caused by insurgents as outrageous acts of violence.

Afghan deaths remain anonymous and unrecognized within U.S. public forms of grief and remembrance. Exceptions to the anonymity of Afghan civilian deaths are used to provide a modicum of qualification by invoking the gender and age of victims. Identifying women and children among the civilian dead (particularly when the 'enemy' causes these deaths) presents a seemingly apolitical 'innocence'. This 'innocence' recalibrates anonymity in order to signal a measure of grief. This grief is not for the actual loss of these particular lives, but rather serves to contest the perpetrators of violence. We argue that this modicum of grief operates as political currency—in order to frame the enemy as 'other' and their violence as illegitimate (Enloe 2000a, 2000b). Insurgents are further associated with causing Afghan women's and children's living-suffering. This living-suffering is represented as grievable, and development is identified as the source of its alleviation.

Mbembe (2003) argues that contemporary forms of colonial occupation occur through a "concatenation of multiple powers: disciplinary, biopolitical, and necropolitical" (29). His theorization of contemporary necropolitics critiques the maximum destruction brought forth by modern warfare and precarious forms of social existence. He argues that necropower operates as a platform for territorial and corporeal control, which blurs the lines "between resistance and suicide, sacrifice and redemption, martyrdom and freedom" (Mbembe 2003, 39). This blurring is indeed a condition of modern political conflict. Conflict development exemplifies an intersectional link between the living bio-politics of social engineering and necropolitics—i.e., controlling death. Militarized development blurs the expected demarcations between humanitarian assistance, development, and military action. In the Afghanistan context, U.S. militarism is often represented as humanitarian through the intersectional actions of military occupation and development assistance. The provision of death-producing violence and life-sustaining aid positions the U.S. (and coalition forces) as a powerful arbiter for the control of life and death in this space.

Development potentiality, when situated within Butler's grievability analysis, employs multiple scales and sites of grief, which are put to work as part of U.S.-led geopolitical framing. In U.S. public discourse, grievable deaths are those lives lost on 9/11 and American lives lost in the line of duty (both military and civilian). Engle (2007) argues that Afghan lives lost as a result of the U.S. response to 9/11 do not receive significant reporting at the individual scale because those deaths are not recognized as 'mournable losses'. Afghan deaths as a result of Taliban, Al-Qaeda and other insurgent violence are mobilized as political currency; while civilians killed by the U.S., as part of 9/11 retaliation, remain anonymous and are not included within 9/11 frames of grief.

Although Afghan deaths (particularly those committed by U.S.-led international forces) are not necessarily identified in the U.S. media lexicon as grievable, Afghan *aliveness*—and in a state of suffering or oppression—particularly those of women and children, remains *grievable*. The framing of *Afghan-aliveness as grievable* situates 'them/Afghans' in a state of potentiality. This epistemologically frames development as a transformative process from Afghan precariousness and livable-grief toward a life 'worth living'. Similarly, gendering the grievable-object of life as apolitical women and children morally situates them as the representative space upon which to enact assistance and development.

Butler (2009) argues "there can be no sustained life without ... sustaining conditions, and those conditions are both our political responsibility and the matter of our most vexed ethical decisions" (23). Gregory, as part of his critique of the U.S. suggests "without sustained reconstruction of the Afghan economy, and without a concerted effort to establish the institutions of a genuinely civil society, the same matrix that supported the growth of al-Qaeda will reassert itself" (Gregory 2004, 73). Development's promise and disciplinary framework offers a pre-emptive strike against future terrorism, not only through reconstruction but also by creating the conditions for future allies rather than adversaries (Duffield 2001, 2007; Essex 2013). Poverty, illiteracy, and under-development are also framed as underlying causes of terroristic violence. Mark Duffield's research is of particular note because he details the overt linkage between international development and "structural conflict prevention" that defines the work of the United States Agency for International Development (USAID) (Duffield 2001, 120). When we take a closer look at the more intimate interactions between Americans and Afghans by way of aid and development, a nuanced and manipulative representation of precariousness, grief, and suffering emerges.

We do not suggest that reconstruction and relief efforts in Afghanistan are unnecessary or unimportant, rather it is the false link between aid/development and stalling or stopping (terrorist or military) violence that we critique. This connection is not clearly demarcated and, in many respects, development efforts in Afghanistan have increased or perpetuated violence and poverty rather than sustaining peace (Fishstein and Wilder 2012, Wilder and Gordon 2009). There remain multiple and intersecting matrices between the institutions that promote peace building through aid and development and those that produce and profit from state and private military violence.

Part of this quandary can be found in much of liberal political beliefs and theories on morality and the universality of human rights (Goodhand 2006). These claims often miss out on the specificities that help to illustrate how grief and suffering become currencies—that can be exchanged—to produce new forms of wealth, power inequities, and violence. As Joseph Slaughter (2007) argues:

> We knew that the Taliban were a violent and oppressive regime, especially toward women, but we did not acknowledge that fact until we needed a humanitarian rationale for prosecuting the so-called War on Terror in Afghanistan. More perversely, we Americans somehow manage collectively not to know that we are torturing (or outsourcing the torture of) 'enemy combatants'—a pseudo-legal designation that places the individual outside the realm of legal personality and rights—at Guantanamo Bay and elsewhere.
>
> (12)

The efforts to alleviate humanitarian suffering and the grievable-object-of Afghan aliveness exemplify the crux of neo-colonialism and humanitarian Imperialism (Bricmont 2006). The political work of emotion/affect, particularly in our case studies, illustrates how 9/11 grief provides personal, individual, and nearly irrefutable claims that the efforts of 9/11 survivors within an aid and development framework are 'good' in an effort to stamp out 'evil'. Development as neo-colonialism operationalizes assistance as a conduit for political influence and territorial control (Escobar 1995; Duffield 2001). Emotive and intimate connections between Americans and Afghans provide an alternative lens through which to view U.S. interventions. The emotive representations of *American-Afghan entanglements*—intimately connected through 'shared' grief—are exchanged by way of development assistance. In this way the currency of 9/11 grief translates into donor funds to assist Afghans. Simultaneously it translates into American's emotive connections to Afghans through a sense of shared grief.

We realize that this particular critical lens, that of the grief of 9/11 surviving families, is both difficult and wholly unpopular. We argue that we must critically examine this assumed 'good' (i.e. assistance) toward a more complex power geometry for understanding what Ong identifies as the numerous categories of *morally conditional humanities* (Ong 2006; Massey 1993). Ong argues "the counter politics of survival are crystallized through the interrelationship of biopolitics, labor markets, and systems of virtue. Such ethical problematizations may circumvent human rights or citizenship, coming to rest on resolutions that reflect contingent and ambiguous ethical horizons of the human" (Ong 2006, 25). Thus, liberal and progressive ideologies of humanitarianism and feminism can be (and have been) manipulated as weapons to produce the same violence and dispossessions that rights-based claims seek to challenge.

Grief as currency—setting the stage for 9/11 and beyond

The scaling of personal grief to national grief elicits political recognition, which translates into currency. Olds, Sidaway and Sparke provide a sharp and poignant discussion about the way in which the individuation of grief associated with 9/11 was also a racially contingent representation, focusing on a 'white selfhood' that included "a geopolitical cover-up of the terror and death suffered by nonwhite people" (2005, 478). They argue that this racialized representation, in addition to the loss of life, includes "the loss of a critical lesson in how to respond to terror and mass death with justice and humanity" (Olds et al. 2005, 478–479). Considering these arguments we investigate the intimately personal responses to 9/11 grief through two case studies. These case studies represent white-American economically privileged aid and development interventions as examples of justice and humanity.

The visual portraits of 9/11 tragedies through still and video photography and its repetition were central to the framing of U.S. nationalized grief. Spatially visual language such as the 'wounded skyline' to describe New York City on the afternoon of 9/11, and the repetition of images of destruction were followed by both spontaneous and carefully constructed memorials. Street memorials provided a visual disruption to pedestrian traffic that demanded reflection. These memorials, combined with images of missing persons, were decidedly intimate—personal—and not immediately tied to a communal sense of national identity or patriotism (Kaplan 2005). These nationalistic themes were incorporated within the more institutionalized memorials and framed remembrances of the 9/11 dead. The political haranguing about how to permanently memorialize the dead included concerns that the World Trade Center site would be turned into a voyeuristic attraction and the surrounding area into a mall, much of which has come to fruition in recent years (Haskins and DeRose 2003).

Film, theater, and literature provided an avenue for shaping emotive summaries of 9/11 and how 'we' as Americans were to remember these events (Greenberg 2003; Saal 2011). The often-cited *New York Times* "Portraits of Grief" section of its newspaper exemplifies the individuation of sorrow in order to shape a collective intimacy of shared pain. This distracted the populace from critically examining the "all-too-real consequences of U.S. government official policy of retaliation" (Engle 2007, 75). The profiles, and their accompanying photos, served to give meaning and to explain 9/11, which at that time was viewed as 'unexplainable' (Lule 2002). Lule (2002) further argues that these profiles affirmed dominant cultural values and beliefs in the U.S. at a time when people were questioning and challenging these beliefs in an effort to understand 'why' the U.S. was attacked on 9/11. As one of the first institutionalized attempts to commemorate the deaths on 9/11, it offered a public expression of American 'values' and featured an accounting of these lives as grievable (Hume 2003). These 9/11 obituaries ran in the *New York Times* from September 15 thru December 31, 2001, and were later published in a book containing a total of 1,910 Portraits of Grief (Miller 2003).

The Smithsonian, as a U.S. government institution, provided another institutionalized framing and remembrance of 9/11. The Smithsonian exhibit emphasized national unification around leaders and developed a sense of common symbols and icons to help discredit dissenting or alternative representations of 9/11. This exhibit, infused with nationalistic rhetoric, stood in stark contrast to spontaneous street and on-line memorials (Haskin and DeRose 2003). Amy Fried (2006) argues that the Smithsonian's use of personal narratives in its 9/11 exhibit precluded a meaningful critique or multiple analyses of these events.[9] In the early days after 9/11, although a 'disciplining' and 'homogenizing' of U.S. memorials and responses was actively being formed—"on the streets something fluid, personal and varied was taking place" (Kaplan 2005, 15). The street memorials generated by grieving loved ones and fellow citizens focused on the lives and deaths of people rather than a collective and jingoistic representation of the injured nation.

Memory and remembrance are important aspects of both personal and political grief. The political demands of the nation incorporated techniques of melodrama and storytelling to (1) "define America as a heroic redeemer," (2) depict Americans as a "unified moral nation," and (3) authenticate American virtue "by the resolution to undertake retributive action in response to victimization" (Anker 2005, 55). Some US-based imperial-feminist responses, such as that of the Feminist Majority Foundation, supported the incorporation of Afghan women's rights with U.S. military actions (Russo 2006). Meanwhile, many other U.S. and international feminist responses included multiple voices of caution, dissent, and concern about U.S. military reactions (Hawthorne and Winter 2003). Lorraine Dowler's (2002) critique of the removal or invisibility of women within the narrative of 9/11 heroes masculinized the space of ground zero, which included the visual embodiment of the former towers as a male police officer and fire fighter. This recasting in heroic-masculine terminology embraced new mythologies that positioned male first responders as 'supermen'—and women in the U.S. and Afghanistan in need of protection or saving respectively (see Kensinger 2009, 50). The masculinization of ground zero, coupled with the protection of the now-feminized homeland, was expanded by the imperative to 'save' Afghan women.

Conversely, scholars have highlighted responses to 9/11, which were neither political nor motivated by personal economic gain. Dahlman and Brunn (2003) argue that "the contribution of money, time, material aid and even blood mark significant forms of redistribution in society that do not conform to state or market institutions" (277). In this way, Dahlman and Brunn highlight the ways in which everyday responses to 9/11 did not neatly fit within geopolitical expectations or economic opportunities. While remembrances are not without contestation and challenge, the predominant messages and grand narratives shaped by nationally institutionalized remembrances of 9/11 positioned the U.S. as the wounded hero with the legitimate and even 'moral' obligation to seek retributive justice (Däwes 2007). 9/11 grief was not in and of itself a form of currency. When reinforcing the grand narrative trope of 'saving' Afghan women, 9/11 grief became a currency exchanged for effective fundraising.

9/11 grief currency

Inderpal Grewal's examination of consumer culture and politics helps to situate our reading of 9/11 grief as currency. Grewal illustrates the ways in which "consumer culture has a hand in producing political subjects and identities" (2003, 559). She argues that consumer culture has taken a central place in promoting the concepts and actualization of political liberalism and economic neoliberalism by producing possibilities of consumption and democracy, "American style" (Grewal 2003, 559). Grief currency becomes incorporated into memorials by linking the political re-telling of past events as opportunities for consumptive capitalism (Fried 2006). Organizations responding to 9/11 garnered a certain level of currency through their association with citizen-subjects, attending to the social and emotional recovery of New Yorkers, and the nation as a whole (Fullilove et al. 2004). Remembrances were marketed through the sale of souvenirs and commemorative gear. Walmart sold 4.96 million American flags within the first seven months after 9/11 compared with 1.18 million the previous year; the U.S. issued 9/11 commemorative postage stamp that yielded $30 million in revenue; both Quran and Bible sales increased by 800% and 30% respectively (Brunn 2004). 9/11 grief currency can be calculated in terms of actual funds, consumptive practices, and the valuation of 9/11 deaths through compensation programs for surviving families. The families of those who died on 9/11 received much larger compensation packages than those who were injured or became ill as a result of rescue and recovery efforts (Gilbert and Ponder 2014).

While Afghan civilian deaths may fall under the U.S. political rhetoric as expendable, collateral and therefore not grievable, at the same time, they do retain currency. We argue that Afghan-aliveness—portrayed through the gendered lens of Taliban and Al-Qaeda imposed suffering—expects a modicum of grievability within U.S. framings. This grief, when linked with development potentiality, also operates as a currency. Table 2.1 provides a visual matrix for illustrating how the taxonomies of grievability, potentiality, and currency are discursively framed through various representative lenses of U.S. gendered geopolitics in Afghanistan. The currency of 9/11 grief combined with Afghan 'need' further situates assistance as by definition 'good' and beyond reproach. We argue that it is imperative for us to be both cautious and critical of anything identified as undeniably 'good'. This can and often does manifest into

Table 2.1 Geopolitical Gendered Framing

	Grievable	**Not Grievable**	**Potentiality**	**Currency**
United States	Deaths—victims of 9/11	Deaths—non-U.S. citizen victims of 9/11	*Learned-Potentiality* International Development workers	Grief of mothers and wives of 9/11 victims
Afghanistan	Aliveness-suffering of woman and children under the Taliban/Al-Qaeda	Afghan Deaths	*Learner-Potentiality* Afghans	Afghan women and children

unequal power relations that manipulatively define assistance and development writ large as apolitical, benevolent, and altruistic. As part of our discussion of 9/11 grief and its currency, we focus on two case studies to illustrate the process of grieving, and healing from grief, through an intimate interconnection with Afghanistan.

We examine the public representation of two organizations, Beyond the 11th and the Peter M. Goodrich Memorial Foundation, each founded in response to the loss of loved ones on 9/11. Our analysis centers on the websites and documentary films made about these extraordinary people. Beyond the 11th was founded by Susan Retik and Patti Quigley after they lost their husbands who were passengers on the planes that hit the World Trade Center towers. This organization raises funds for projects to assist widows in Afghanistan (which was distributed in Afghanistan through the organization CARE International). Don and Sally Goodrich, the parents of Peter who died on Flight 175, founded the Peter M. Goodrich Memorial Foundation. This foundation has built schools in Afghanistan and provided young Afghans with the opportunity to study in the United States at the secondary and collegiate level.

We offer these examples not to critique the personal reactions of these individuals. As parents and partners, we may have made a similar attempt to form a healing-connection across social, economic, and political differences. We do not fault these individuals for attempting to formulate a non-violent and more humane response to their personal grief. Rather, we focus on the public and nationalized framing of their private grief. By examining the public framing of these organizations, we elucidate the ways in which the extraordinary actions of individuals become integrated into the grand narratives that structure gender, aid, and development efforts in Afghanistan.

The documentary film about the Peter M. Goodrich Memorial Foundation is titled, *Axis of Good: A Story from 9/11*, and the documentary about the widows that founded Beyond the 11th, is titled *Beyond Belief*.[10] The titles of both of these films offer poignant and emotive linguistic techniques to illustrate responses to grief as unique and exceptional acts of kindness in a time of crisis. The *Axis of Good* title suggests a counter-framing to former President Bush's 'Axis of Evil' representation of the enemy. It also situates the acts and actions contained in this film as by definition 'good', sitting within the larger economic and geopolitical framing of humanitarian aid. *Beyond Belief* similarly focuses on the exceptionality of these responses to grief— one that does not seek revenge through violence, but rather extends assistance through '(un)common' experiences of, and responses to, grief. In both cases these organizations operate from positions of relative economic privilege vis-à-vis the Afghans they engage with, and a modicum of power and authority associated with their status as Americans. Aid and development, as a system, are not critiqued in these films but assumed to be a duty and expected method to alleviate Afghan suffering.

The women featured in these respective documentaries are represented with a particular framing of intimacy through motherhood and home. Domestic spaces operate as a visual tool for drawing the viewer into private spaces and intimately connecting them to the lives of these individuals and their grief. *Beyond Belief* provides several scenes of Retik and Quigley engaging in daily activities associated with motherhood, i.e. waking up their children, taking them to school, preparing and eating meals. Similarly, the domestic sphere is a central technique for framing the audience's intimacy with the Goodrich family in the film entitled, *Axis of Good: A Story from 9/11*. The interviews and discussions with the respective families are also often portrayed in domestic spaces and several shots in both films show connections between family members in kitchens, dining rooms, and bedrooms, which help to frame the viewers' perception of these families through an intimate lens.

Sally Goodrich, as a mother who lost a son, is further represented as sacrificing time and attention toward her surviving children and grand-children in order to act as benefactor of schools in Afghanistan. The representational use of gender resonates through the existing shibboleth of motherhood as virtuous, altruistic, and moral and an illustration of care and kindness. A moral representation of motherhood and humanitarianism pro-vides a form of authority for situating these actions as beyond reproach. These respective women and organizations combine each woman's personal sense of loss and relative privilege as the basis for making connections with individuals in Afghanistan. Retik and Quigley accomplish this by supporting widows in Afghanistan, and Goodrich through education programs.

These documentary stories fit within a larger framework that de-politicizes and de-historicizes U.S. geopolitical interventions in the region. The focus on the benevolent work of these individuals in Afghanistan lessens the political tone and precludes any critique of U.S. foreign policy. The American women's compassionate work with Afghans associates their American-identities with morality similar to the institutionalized memorials and remembrances of 9/11 (Maney et al. 2005; Anker 2005; Wright 2012). In addition to the shared response to 9/11 grief for both charitable organizations, three common themes are presented in each documentary: (1) an emphasis on non-violence, love, and kindness, (2) the importance of making a personal connection through travel to Afghanistan to see the actual projects sponsored by their respective charities, and (3) 'meaning making' as a method for processing and healing from profound loss.

The emphasis on non-violence, love and kindness is illustrated through the way in which Quigley and Retik are discussed by the director of CARE International in Kabul, Afghanistan, Paul Barker when he states: "Given the choice between violence and love they choose love." Similarly Don Goodrich, states, "For every act of violence there needs to be an act of kindness or we devolve into violence." These films illustrate the importance placed on making a personal connection with Afghans. Sally Goodrich connects her own healing with a sense of shared grief and developing a common connection across difference. She states: "It wasn't until I encountered people [i.e., Afghans] who had suffered a great deal more, that I realized suffering is a bridge between people unlikely to communicate." Similarly, Retik, in preparation for her first trip to Afghanistan, identifies her ultimate goal as making "a true connection with at least one of the women" that she will meet.

Both Susan Retik and Sally Goodrich identify their charitable work as an essential part of their own personal healing. For example, Retik, in response to the descriptions of her as "so generous," states "well it really, really, really is as much for me as the people we are trying to help. I need this to keep busy and focused and feeling productive … ." Similarly, Sally Goodrich connects the work she and her husband are doing for Afghans as part of "always trying to figure out how to reconstruct our lives." She also sees the work she is doing in Afghanistan as "living out the best part of my kid." Quigley, in describing the post-traumatic stress associated with profound grief, states that her healing process is a form of post-traumatic growth. "You also have post-traumatic growth and that's when you are able to positively make it through a tragedy. There's some kind of good or growth forward." These quotes frame American privilege in contrast to grievable-Afghan-living-suffering. Conversely, Afghans are regularly identified as "having nothing." 'Nothing' is based on their perception of Afghans' economic and resource scarcity. Therefore, the extensive networks among Afghans, their agency, resilience, and capabilities are not discussed nor highlighted in either film, while their suffering and need are emphasized. Thus, the grief-currency of their living-suffering translates into funds to fill the 'void' associated with the perception of material 'nothing'.

Beyond Belief begins with the infamous image of a burqa-clad woman, Zarmeena, being shot to death by the Taliban in a Kabul football stadium. The documentary identifies this video as being shot by a hidden camera, but does not credit nor mention the Revolutionary Association of the Women of Afghanistan (RAWA) as the organization who filmed this execution. In addition to erasing the agency and actions of these female-Afghan activists, there is a public erasure of the corporeal injuries experienced by men under the Taliban regime. Showing only a portion of this footage—that of a woman being killed—renders absent and invisible the extensive images and video of the vast number of Afghan men who were publically executed or mutilated by the Taliban, also recorded by RAWA. The agency and ability of Afghan women to challenge their own repression is excluded from these representations, and Afghan women's agency prior to 9/11 is rendered entirely invisible. Afghan women's 'empowerment' and agency, an often-quoted goal of development assistance, is also rarely recognized. Within the post 9/11 'saving' and development framework, Afghan female-suffering commands far higher currency than their agency.

The focus on Afghan suffering incorporated into both films attempts to elicit viewer empathy. 9/11 grief is continually represented through an intimate lens. The currency of American grief is exchanged to generate funds that will alleviate Afghan suffering. Afghan women are interviewed and included, particularly in *Beyond Belief*, with emotional scenes between the 9/11 widows and their Afghan counterparts. Individual interviews with Afghan women focus on their living-suffering as widows and mothers and in situations of economic desperation and insecurity. In one scene U.S. sponsored violence is mentioned and quickly transferred to the Taliban and mitigated through a discussion of shared grief between the American and Afghan widows.

The scene begins with a number of widows in a room speaking (through a translator) to Retik and Quigley.

Modira Sahidi: I have a 25 year old daughter. When an American bomb hit our house her father died and she got injured. She was blinded. Her head and skull were fractured. The treatment she received didn't work, but I couldn't afford any more. My house is close, I wish you could come and visit her.

Retik: Now that we've met you *(pause)*. Before we met you we wanted to help you. Now that we met you we really want to help you. We will tell your stories when we go home and we will let people know. And we will continue to help support you and continue to work hard.

The next scene is at Modira Sahidi's house.

Modira Sahidi: She was sitting with her father when the rocket came through the window. The ceiling fell and we all screamed, What happened? We were afraid to move because another rocket might come. No one came, no neighbors, no one.

Retik: What do you think about the United States because your husband was killed as a result of bombing. Do you … *(explaining to the translator)* before she answers tell her I won't be offended whatever she says. To be honest …

Zainab Wahidi, local representative of CARE Afghanistan translates:
> Your husband died in an American bombing, what do you think about America?

Modira Sahidi: No, It was from God, God's will.

Zainab Wahidi, translates:
> What do you think about America? Tell us how you imagine it. Even if you think something bad don't be afraid to say it.

Modira Sahidi: Why should we say something bad about them? The Taliban are the bad people. Because of them, this is what happened.

Retik: It is the same living in the United States. Some people think blame Afghanistan, or some of the people of Afghanistan, for the attacks on the United States. And this is why we're trying to reach out because it's a terrible situation that one hurts another, that gets the repercussion, I don't know if you can translate all of that but …

Modira Sahidi: I think we have the same experience. In America's war—there and here—we became widows, and they became like us.

   The scene ends.

Interestingly, there is an identification of the U.S. role in the death of Afghan civilians; however, Modira Sahidi focuses on the Taliban, as the reason for U.S. bombing. The scene ends with a sense of shared experience, while identifying the conflict in both the U.S. and Afghanistan as "America's war." Retik signals a sense of common experience as operating outside the boundaries and cyclical aspects of political conflict—further depoliticizing international assistance. Sahidi's overall framing of her husband's death, provides an 'authentic' lens through which to reinforce U.S. violence as ultimately good for Afghanistan despite the deaths it causes. This scene along with the entire documentary provides no historical or political context for U.S.-led military or development interventions.

   In many respects these examples illustrate profound and notable attempts to create intimately emotive linkages based on a belief in shared grief. The framing of Afghan and American civilians as common victims of the 'same terrorists' responsible for 9/11 helps to shape an (un)common sense of victimhood, which operates as a subtle erasure of U.S. foreign policy and historical maneuvers in the region. The attempts by each organization to operate outside of politics and the bordered expectations of sovereign power and territorial control can be viewed as operating above politics despite U.S.-led military operations. Conversely, when compared with other institutionalized remembrances of 9/11 grief, these 'heroic' efforts fit within a de-historicized and de-politicized framing of the U.S. Thus, further reinforcing the just morality of these benevolent engagements in Afghanistan through various 'saving' and 'liberating' discourses. We argue that these public representations, through documentary and Internet websites, are by definition geopolitical despite the efforts of these individuals to situate themselves and their acts as above or outside of politics (Duffield et al. 2001; Drury et al. 2005; Donini 2007).

The use of documentary film attempts to articulate an alternative response to 9/11, which we argue further exemplifies 9/11 deaths as grievable. The greivability of the men lost on 9/11 translates into the grief-currency of the respective families with a focus on mothers and wives—and their subsequent ability to generate funds. The *Axis of Good* film begins at a church service where the Reverend explains that efforts are being made to build a school in Afghanistan in memory of Peter Goodrich, and asks the parishioners to donate money toward the project. Sally Goodrich clearly states that while they do not actively fundraise, people give them money in response to their story. "It is not that I don't need money, we do. It's that we don't actively fundraise, I believe that if we are doing something good, and people like it, they gravitate toward it—they will support it." Susan Retik more specifically links her grief and the sympathy of others with the ability of Beyond the 11th to successfully fundraise. For example in one scene of the film, Patricia Quigley states that she wants to "get away from being the 9/11 widow" and Retik responds "That's where the sympathy and that's where the money [comes from]. People [say] 'oh look at what they're doing'—it's what we have to use." This statement further exemplifies the connection between 9/11 grief and its currency to generate funds for this project.

These individuals do indeed offer an alternative response to grief and loss that intends to provide charity and service to make human-to-human connections across distant geographies through economic assistance. The intentions of these respective organizations are commendable. The power of these stories provide an irresistible lens through which to view American benevolence. These stories are also ripe for co-optation by the media and U.S. government in order to frame them within the grand 'saving Afghanistan' narrative. For example, Sally Goodrich was named ABC's person of the week (April 26, 2005) and Susan Retik received the Citizens Medal from President Obama in 2010.[11]

Conclusion

Americans and Afghans have been framed through a gender-specific and geopolitically inspired lens as suggested by the grievability-potentiality-currency matrix (see Table 2.1). This framing positions Afghans as victims, embodied as women and children, apolitical innocents in need of retributive justice from international entities. Afghan women and children as objectified images of human suffering offer a poignant example that resonates symbolically and fits neatly within larger geopolitical saving narratives. The female and child 'in need of saving' trope also resonates with the ways in which American women and children are portrayed as providing love, kindness, and assistance in Afghanistan. Therefore, we do not see the gendered framing of the family members of 9/11 victims as a challenge to the hyper-masculinized representation of U.S. State and military response, rather as the expected 'feminine' complement to male-military aggression and revenge (Goldstein 2003).

The objectified grievability of Afghan women's and children's living-suffering under the Taliban fits within broader discourses of development—learned and learner potentiality—and intersects with 9/11 grievability to produce interrelated currencies. The 9/11 grief-currency helps to raise funds for the seemingly apolitical, innocent, and docile suffering of Afghan women and children. This also operates as political currency framed through the 'saving women' trope and aid/development potentiality. Gendered currency operates in tandem with 9/11 grief-currency. When this form of currency takes political shape it works to erase the violence brought forth by both historical and contemporary U.S.-led interventions. The framing of grief and benevolence as displayed through these emotive lenses shrouds rather than illuminates and becomes subsumed within existing grand narratives rather than effectively challenging them.

We argue that individual and small-scale attempts by Retik, Quigley, and Goodrich illustrate a more pluralistic connection between 'morally deserving' humans. The public representations and frames through which these stories are told remain squeezed within existing tropes and grand narratives in order for them to be accessible to the general public and obtain the ability to elicit emotions. The careful crafting of how 'we' Americans were expected to emotively respond to 9/11 through various political discourses (as discussed in this chapter) set the scene of masculine-military revenge, and feminine-domestic-comfort from which these documentary narratives are framed. The currency of grief, gendered victimhood, and suffering must be considered as part of analyses of death economies and intimate geopolitics. We must remain critically vigilant of the value and valuation of life and death by uneven development paradigms fueled by gendered-nationalist rhetoric that fosters life, death, and grief currencies.

References

Abu-Lughod, Lila. 2013. *Do Muslim Women Need Saving?* Cambridge: Harvard University Press.

——2002. "Do Muslim women really need saving? Anthropological reflections on cultural relativism and its others." *American Anthropologist.* 104 (3): 783–790.

Agamben, Giorgio. 1999. *Potentialities: Collected Essays in Philosophy.* Stanford: Stanford University Press.

——1998. *Homo Sacer.* Daniel Heller-Roazen (Trans.). Stanford, CA: Stanford University Press.

Anker, Elisabeth. 2005. "Villains, victims and heroes: Melodrama, media, and September 11." *Journal of Communication.* 55 (1): 22–37.

Bligh, Michelle C., Jeffrey C. Kohles, and James R. Meindl. 2004a. "Charisma under crisis: Presidential leadership, rhetoric, and media responses before and after the September 11th terrorist attacks." *The Leadership Quarterly.* 15 (2): 211–239.

——2004b. "Charting the language of leadership: a methodological investigation of President Bush and the crisis of 9/11." *The Journal of Applied Psychology.* 89 (3): 562–74.

Bricmont, J. 2006. *Humanitarian Imperialism: Using Human Rights to Sell War.* New York: Monthly Review Press.

Brunn, Stanley D. 2004. *11 September and its Aftermath: The Geopolitics of Terror.* London: Frank Cass.

Burk, Adrienne L. 2003. "Private griefs, public places." *Political Geography.* 22 (3): 317–333.

Butler, Judith. 2009. *Frames of War: When is Life Grievable?* London: Verso.

——2006. *Precarious Life: The Powers of Mourning and Violence* London: Verso.

Dahlman, Carl and Stanley Brunn. 2003. "Reading geopolitics beyond the state: organisational discourse in response to 11 September." *Geopolitics.* 8 (3): 253–280.

Däwes, Birgit. 2007. "On Contested Ground (Zero): Literature and the Transnational Challenge of Remembering 9/11." *Amerikastudien/American Studies.* 52 (4): 517–543.

De Waal, A. 1998. *Famine Crimes: Politics & the Disaster Relief Industry in Africa.* Bloomington: Indiana University Press.

Donini, Antonio. 2007. "Local perceptions of assistance to Afghanistan." *International Peacekeeping.* 14 (1): 158–172.

Dowler, Lorraine. 2002. "Women on the frontlines: Rethinking war narratives post 9/11." *GeoJournal.* 58 (2–3): 2–3.

Drury, A. Cooper, Richard Stuart Olson, and Douglas A. Van Belle. 2005. "The politics of humanitarian aid: US foreign disaster assistance, 1964–1995." *Journal of Politics.* 67 (2): 454–473.

Duffield, Mark. 2007. *Development, Security and Unending War: Governing the World of Peoples.* Cambridge: Polity.

——2002. "Social reconstruction and the radicalization of development: Aid as a relation of global liberal governance." *Development and Change* 33 (5): 1049–1071.

——2001. *Global Governance and the New Wars: The Merging of Development and Security.* Vol. 87 London: Zed books.

Duffield, Mark, Joanna Macrae, and Devon Curtis. 2001. "Editorial: Politics and humanitarian aid." *Disasters.* 25 (4): 269–274.

Dunn, Elizabeth Cullen and Jason Cons. 2014. "Aleatory sovereignty and the rule of sensitive spaces." *Antipode.* 46 (1): 92–109.

Elden, Stuart. 2013. "Secure the volume: Vertical geopolitics and the depth of power." *Political Geography.* 34 (6): 35–51.

Engle, Karen J. 2007. "Putting mourning to work making sense of 9/11." *Theory, Culture & Society.* 24 (1): 61–88.

Enloe, Cynthia. 2004. *Curious Feminist: Searching for Women in a New Age of Empire.* Berkeley: University of California Press.

——2000a. *Bananas, Beaches and Bases: Making Feminist Sense of International Politics.* Berkeley: University of California Press, second edition.

——2000b. *Maneuvers: The International Politics of Militarizing Women's Lives.* Berkeley: University of California Press.

Escobar, Arturo. 1995. *Encountering Development: The Making and Unmaking of the Third World.* Princeton: Princeton University Press.

Essex, Jamey. 2013. *Development, Security, and Aid: Geopolitics and Geoeconomics at the US Agency for International Development.* Vol. 16. Athens: University of Georgia Press.

Fishstein, Paul and Andrew Wilder. 2012. "Winning hearts and minds? Examining the relationship between aid and security in Afghanistan." Medford, MA: Feinstein International Center, Tufts University.

Fluri, Jennifer. 2012. "Capitalizing on Bare Life: Sovereignty, Exception, and Gender Politics." *Antipode.* 44(1): 31-50.

——2009. "'Foreign Passports Only': Geographies of (post)conflict work in Kabul, Afghanistan." *Annals of the Association of American Geographers.* 99 (5): 986–994.

Forsythe, David P. 2005. *The Humanitarians: The International Committee of the Red Cross.* Cambridge, UK: Cambridge University Press.

Fried, Amy. 2006. "The Personalization of Collective Memory: The Smithsonian's September 11 Exhibit." *Political Communication.* 23 (4): 387–405.

Fullilove, M.T., L. Hernandez-Cordero, J. S. Madoff, and R.E. Fullilove. 2004. "Promoting collective recovery through organizational mobilization: The post-9/11 disaster relief work of NYC RECOVERS." *Journal of Biosocial Science.* 36 (4): 479–490.

Gilbert, Emily and Corey Ponder. 2014. "Between tragedy and farce: 9/11 compensation and the value of life and death." *Antipode.* 46 (2): 404–425.

Goldstein, Joshua S. 2003. *War and Gender: How Gender Shapes the War System and Vice Versa.* Cambridge: Cambridge University Press.

Goodhand, Jonathan. 2006. *Aiding Peace? The Role of NGOs in Armed Conflict.* Boulder, CO: Lynne Rienner Publishers.

Graham, Stephen. 2004. "Vertical geopolitics: Baghdad and after." *Antipode.* 36 (1): 12–23.

Greenberg, Judith. 2003. *Trauma at Home: After 9/11.* Lincoln: University of Nebraska Press.

Gregory, Derek. 2004. *The Colonial Present: Afghanistan, Palestine, Iraq.* Malden, MA: Blackwell Publishing.

Grewal, Inderpal. 2003. "Transnational America: Race, gender and citizenship after 9/11." *Social Identities.* 9 (4): 535–561.

Gunn, Joshua. 2004. "The rhetoric of exorcism: George W. Bush and the return of political demonology." *Western Journal of Communication (Includes Communication Reports).* 68 (1): 1–23.

Hancock, Graham. 1989. *Lords of Poverty: The Power, Prestige, and Corruption of the International Aid Business.* New York: Atlantic Monthly Press.

Harvey, David. 2005. *A Brief History of Neoliberalism.* Oxford: Oxford University Press.

Haskins, Ekaterina V. and Justin P. DeRose. 2003. "Memory, visibility, and public space reflections on commemoration (s) of 9/11." *Space and Culture.* 6 (4): 377–393.

Hawthorne, Susan and Bronwyn Winter. 2003. *September 11, 2001: Feminist Perspectives.* Vancouver: Raincoast Books.

Hernández-Cordero, J. Lourdes, and Mindy Thompson Fullilove. 2008. "Constructing peace: Helping youth cope in the aftermath of 9/11." *American Journal of Preventive Medicine.* 34 (3): S31–S35.

Hirschkind, Charles and Saba Mahmood. 2002. "Feminism, the Taliban, and politics of counter-insurgency." *Anthropological Quarterly.* 75 (2): 339–354.

Hume, Janice. 2003. "'Portraits of Grief,' reflectors of values: *The New York Times* remembers victims of September 11." *Journalism & Mass Communication Quarterly.* 80 (1): 166–182.

Hunt, Krista. 2002. "The strategic co-optation of women's rights." *International Feminist Journal of Politics.* 4 (1): 116–121.

Hunt, L. 2008. *Inventing Human Rights: A History.* New York: W.W. Norton & Company.

Hyndman, Jennifer. 2007. "Feminist geopolitics revisited: Body counts in Iraq." *The Professional Geographer.* 59 (1): 35–46.

Hyndman, Jennifer and Malathi De Alwis. 2004. "Bodies, shrines, and roads: Violence, (im) mobility and displacement in Sri Lanka." *Gender, Place & Culture.* 11 (4): 535–557.

Jetter, Alexis, Annelise Orleck, and Diana Taylor. 1997. *The Politics of Motherhood: Activist Voices from Left to Right.* Hanover:University Press of New England.

Johnson, Chris and Jolyon Leslie. 2004. *Afghanistan: The Mirage of Peace.* London: Zed Books.

Kaplan, E. Ann. 2005. *Trauma Culture: The Politics of Terror and Loss in Media and Literature.* New Brunswick: Rutgers University Press.

Kensinger, Loretta. 2009. "Radical lessons: Thoughts on Emma Goldman, chaos, grief, and political violence post-9/11/01." *Feminist Teacher.* 20 (1): 50–70.

Kothari, Uma. 2005. "Authority and expertise: The professionalisation of international development and the ordering of dissent." *Antipode.* 37 (3): 425–446.

Laurie, M. and R.P. Petchesky. 2008. "Gender, health, and human rights in sites of political exclusion." *Global Public Health.* 3: 25–41.

Lule, Jack. 2002. "Myth and terror on the editorial page: *The New York Times* responds to September 11, 2001." *Journalism & Mass Communication Quarterly.* 79 (2): 275–293.

Maley, William. 2006. *Rescuing Afghanistan.* London: Hurst & Company.

Mamdani, Mahmood. 2005. *Good Muslim, Bad Muslim: America, the Cold War, and the Roots of Terror.* New York: Three Leaves Press; Doubleday.

Maney, Gregory M., Lynne M. Woehrle, and Patrick G. Coy. 2005. "Harnessing and challenging hegemony: The US Peace Movement after 9/11." *Sociological Perspectives.* 48 (3): 357–381.

Massey, Doreen. 1993. "Power-geometry and a progressive sense of place." *Mapping the Futures: Local Cultures, Global Change.* J. Bird, B. Curtis, T. Putnam, G. Robertson and L. Tickner (eds.). London: Routledge, pp. 59–69.

Mbembe, Achille. 2003. "Necropolitics." Libby Meintjes (Trans.). *Public Culture.* 15 (1): 11–40.

Miller, Nancy K. 2003. "'Portraits of Grief': Telling details and the testimony of trauma." *Differences: A Journal of Feminist Cultural Studies.* 14 (3): 112–135.

Olds, Kris with James Sidaway and Matthew Sparke. 2005. "Guest Editorial: White Death." *Environment and Planning D: Society and Space.* 23, 475–479.

Ong, Aihwa. 2006. *Neoliberalism as Exception: Mutations in Citizenship and Sovereignty.* Durham: Duke University Press.

Petraeus, D.H. and J.F. Amos. 2006. *Counterinsurgency.* Field Manual, Marine Corps Warfighting Publication. Washington D.C., USA: Headquarters Department of the Army.

Rashid, Ahmed. 2008. *Descent into Chaos: The US and the Disaster in Pakistan, Afghanistan, and Central Asia.* New York: Viking.

——2000. *Taliban: Militant Islam, Oil, and Fundamentalism in Central Asia.* New Haven: Yale University Press.

Roy, Arundhati. 2002. *The Algebra of Infinite Justice.* New Delhi: Penguin Books India.

Rozario, Kevin. 2007. *The Culture of Calamity: Disaster and the Making of Modern America*. Chicago: University of Chicago Press.

Russo, Ann. 2006. "The feminist majority foundation's campaign to stop gender apartheid: The intersections of feminism and imperialism in the United States." *International Feminist Journal of Politics*. 8 (4): 557–580.

Saal, Ilka. 2011. "'It's about Us!'. Violence and narrative memory in post 9/11 American theatre." *Arcadia-International Journal for Literary Studies*. 45 (2): 353–373.

Sheppard, Eric, Philip W. Porter, David R. Faust, and Richa Nagar. 2009. *A World of Difference: Encountering and Contesting Development*. New York: Guilford Press.

Simko, Christina. 2012. "Rhetorics of suffering September 11 commemorations as theodicy." *American Sociological Review*. 77 (6): 880–902.

Slaughter, Joseph. 2007. "Human Rights, Inc." *The World Novel, Narrative Form, and International Law*. New York: Fordham UP.

Wilder, Andrew and Stuart Gordon. 2009. "Money can't buy America love." *Foreign Policy,* Washington, DC 1. Available online: http://www.foreignpolicy.com/articles/2009/12/01/money_cant_buy_america_lov (accessed December 1, 2014).

Wright, Melissa W. 2012. "Witnessing, femicide, and a politics of the familiar." *The Global and the Intimate: Feminism in our Time*. Geraldine Pratt and V. Rosner (eds.). New York: Columbia University Press, 267–288.

Young, Iris Marion. 2003. "The logic of masculinist protection: Reflections on the current security state." *Signs*. 29 (1): 1–25.

Notes

1 Throughout this chapter we use grief, sorrow, anguish, and pain interchangeably to mean an experience of intense sorrow caused by the loss of a loved one or similar trauma.

2 http://www.presidency.ucsb.edu/ws/?pid=24992 (last accessed March 13, 2014).

3 The U.S. role in Afghanistan is marked by support of several fundamentalist groups in order to orchestrate a pan-Islamic jihad against 'godless communism'.

4 "The problem here is not just internal to the life of the media, but involves the structuring effects that certain larger norms, themselves often racializing and civilizational, have on what is provisionally called 'reality'." (Butler 2009, 74).

5 Kaplan uses the term "mediated trauma" to identify the ways in which a traumatic event, such as 9/11, was mediated through television and print journalism, fictional dramas and literature.

6 This refers to research data collected between 2006 and 2008 in Afghanistan. For an overview of this research project see Fluri (2009).

7 In the introduction to *Homo Sacer*, Agamben defines ancient Greek terms for life: "zoē which expressed the simple fact of living common to all living beings (animals, men, or gods), and *bios*, which indicated the form or way of living proper to an individual or a group" (Agamben 1998, 1). He sets up these distinctions to critique the condition of modern "western" politics. "Western politics has not succeeded in constructing the link between *zoē* and *bios,* between voice and language, that would have healed the fracture. Bare life remains included in politics in the form of the exception" (Agamben 1998, 11). Agamben also identifies sacred life, *homo sacer*, which is made into "the object of aid and protection" (1998, 133). He continues to link humanitarian organizations "in perfect symmetry with state power, need. A humanitarianism separated from politics cannot fail to reproduce the isolation of scared life at the basis of sovereignty, and the camp" (1998, 134). (Also see, Fluri 2012.)

 8 Note, the U.S. military's counterinsurgency (COIN) manual identifies the concept of proportionality to be considered when civilian bodies may be injured or killed. "The principle of proportionality requires that the anticipated loss of life and damage to property incidental to attacks must not be excessive in relation to the concrete and direct military advantage expected to be gained" (Petraeus and Amos 2006).
 9 The Smithsonian was founded in 1846 as a U.S. government museum, which has grown into a research complex, which includes 19 museums and galleries, nine research facilities, and the national zoological park (http://www.si.edu, last accessed September 5, 2004). See Fried (2006).
10 The film about the Peter M. Goodrich Memorial Foundation is still in production, but can be viewed in its current form at http://www.axisofgoodmovie.com. Information about the Peter M. Goodrich Memorial Foundation can be found on their website, http://www.goodrichfoundation.org. The *Beyond Belief* film is available on Netflix and through the Beyond the 11th website, http://www.beyondthe11th.org.
11 Sally Goodrich named ABC Person of the Week http://abcnews.go.com/WNT/PersonOfWeek/story?id=1071393 (last accessed February 7, 2014). President Obama Honors Winners of the 2010 Citizens Medal: http://www.whitehouse.gov/the-press-office/president-obama-honors-winners-2010-citizens-medal (last accessed February 7, 2014).

3 The cost of a second chance

Life, death, and redemption among prison inmates and Thoroughbred ex-racehorses in Bluegrass Kentucky

Tamar V.S. McKee

In memory of Native Ivory (1984–2014)

In 1984, a New York City-based marketing executive, Monique Kohler, along with her riding instructor, Diana Pikulski, created what became the largest, nonprofit equine sanctuary in the world: the Thoroughbred Retirement Foundation ("TRF"). At the time, thousands of Thoroughbred racehorses were being sent to slaughter facilities in the United States[1] after their racing careers were over. The choice to send such horses to slaughter was a multi-faceted one, but pivoted around a fundamental acceptance that these horses were killable commodities that, according to capitalist logic, could and should be traded in one last attempt at making (or at least conserving) money. After living a life ontologically carved by such economic rationale – from the stallion fees paid upon successful procreation and birth, to sales earnings at yearling auctions, to winning race purses, to literally re-producing this cycle by becoming breeding stock—selling unprofitable horses to kill buyers who would then deliver them to slaughter was a last and fatal link in the chain of their commodification and exploitation. Incensed by the paradox of celebrating Thoroughbred racing in particular as the "sport of kings" one day, then the next sending them to a historically tabooed (cf: Sahlins 1976; Harris 1979) and highly controversial kind of death because of the suffering it brought to the horses (cf: Heller 2005; Stillman 2008), Kohler and Pikulski created the TRF to rescue Thoroughbreds—many times simply to just live the rest of their days out at pasture, so debilitated from racing were some of them that they could never be ridden again.

One of the first pastures the TRF horses found sanctuary in was at Wallkill Correctional Facility in upstate New York. The idea to house horses in prison pastures came from then-New York State Senator Howard Nolan, who suggested to Kohler that prisons with farm land might offer the space needed for the rescued horses. It came to pass that such prisons not only had the space, but also the labor (cf: Davis 2011) needed to care for the horses in the form of incarcerated men and women. This multispecies marriage of human labor and equine need soon became formalized as the TRF's "Second Chances" program, whereby both horses and humans were offered the opportunity to become rehabilitated from their broken pasts. Since its inception in 1984, the TRF's Second Chances programs have been established at prisons in nine other states—one of which being in Kentucky, which is the focus of this present essay.

For the horses, the notion of a "second chance" is understood by the TRF and its adherents as helping these horses recover from either a hard life lived on the track or from nearly being sent to slaughter after falling into abusive or neglectful care once their racing careers were over. "Give us your tired, your worn, your weary," an advertising poster for the TRF pleads on behalf of the horses. "Before a crippling injury or the auction killers rob him of his life, call the Thoroughbred Retirement Foundation." For the inmates, their second chance meant potentially redeeming their crimes and ensuing incarceration by not only acquiring post-parole employment skills in the form of equine care (and thus reducing their chance of returning to prison, a phenomenon known as "recidivism"), but by also forming relationships with the horses that inspire unprecedented responses of compassion and responsibility. "Even though the horse can't hug me back," one Second Chance student-inmate told me during an interview, "I can still feel that embrace when I wrap my arms around their neck. Or that head nudge he or she gives you when they vie for your attention. That's love. That's what the TRF help me find." Such insight further brings to mind Avery Gordon's writing on haunting, futurity, and how prisoners can defy the social death sentence of incarceration: these horses have the ability to help inmates become "impervious to the contingencies of institutionalized dehumanization and domination" that typified their experience of being criminalized and incarcerated (2011, 16).

With this context given, I turn to the larger questions this essay seeks to provoke, specifically in relation to the phenomenon I just outlined above: the rescue and redemption of human and equine lives that have been degraded, however variously, by institutionalized forms of domination and death. Once a life is rescued from death, what becomes of its so-called second chance? And what if this life at stake extends to both humans and nonhuman animals (Butler 2009; Kirksey and Helmreich 2010), and this death can be both socially constructed and biologically final (Gordon 2011)? How can the second chance of such lives be understood in a "redemptive" sense that is just as economically, culturally, and historically implicated, as it is motivated by moral, ethical, and/or religious beliefs (cf: Graeber 2011)? What else is entangled and emergent in multispecies relationships of rescue and redemption when we take a closer, critical look?

This essay engages with these framing questions because I am fundamentally interested in both examining the act of "rescue" as a conscious act of compassionate intervention for human animals and nonhuman ones, and complicating it beyond unquestioned and apolitical assumptions of its merit and effectiveness. "Decisions to extend life *for* humans or animals and decisions to curtail life are both notoriously controversial," writes Judith Butler (original emphasis), "precisely because there is no consensus on when and where decision should enter the scene" (2009, 20). Furthermore, what happens when a rescued life does not proceed onto an unquestionable path towards redemption? Why was such a life chosen to be rescued in the first place, and what might prohibit its re-flourishing? In this essay I will explore how culturally shaped, historically specific, and ontologically fraught rescue fundamentally is, and in doing so will tease out how inflected by economic capital and human power relations such compassionate acts (and their accompanying belief systems) can be as well. As such, this essay not only provides a critique of the act (and ideological discourse) of rescue, but exposes how precarious and grievable even rescued life can remain should "the context of social and political norms that frame the decision-making process" (Butler 2009, 21) not be realized and put to task.

In terms of cultural and historical specificity, this essay pivots around anthropological research I conducted in 2011 with prison inmates caring for Thoroughbred ex-racehorses at Blackburn Correctional Complex ("Blackburn") in Lexington, Kentucky. Over the course of four months, I interviewed ten male student-inmates participating in the TRF's Second Chances program there. This essay, however, is built only around one inmate's story, "Paul" (a pseudonym), and I do this out of conscious choice for two reasons. First, upon transcribing and reviewing my interviews with the men who participated in my study, I found that each interview alone was full of critical and illustrative information to impart and socio-cultural implications to analyze. While in other writings I have cross-analyzed these interviews (McKee 2014), for this particular essay I wanted to take the opportunity to focus solely on one particularly provocative interview in the method of writing life history as classically outlined by Behar (1990). In this way, I am not generalizing across many life stories, but telescoping on one and spending time and paying homage to the specific theoretical and narrative complexities of Paul's story and its larger implications.

In this way, Paul also acts as a "figure" in the sense that Donna Haraway defines it: "Figures collect people through their invitations to inhabit the corporeal story told in their lineaments. Figures are not representatives or didactic illustrations, but rather material-semiotic nodes or knots in which diverse bodies and meanings coshape each other" (2008, 4). Herein lies the second reason I choose to focus only on one man's story: by spending time on Paul's story alone we can better appreciate what and who exactly is collected and implicated in his second chance. In particular, I am interested in what his story tells us about how compassion and empathy is cultivated in a socio-cultural context that draws sharp divides between the criminal and the victim, the human and the animal, the killable and the saved. If, as Butler further states, "life requires support and enabling conditions in order to be a livable life" (2009, 21), what kind of life is livable when one inhabits what is considered the "wrong" side of the dividing line? And, furthermore, does life become more livable, supported, and enabled—*redeemed*—when it is rescued from such fatal distinctions, or does the mark of death and the conditions of killability that lead to it still haunt any second chance at life?

One major way in which I came to apprehend the phenomenon of rescue is through the concept of *redemptive capital* (McKee 2013). Redemptive capital is an analytic I created in response to what I saw happening between humans and horses in my research to help explore, (1) what economic, moral, and ethical criteria are used to determine whether or not a life is worthy of being saved in the first place—that is, what is too valuable to become killable, and (2) how emergent qualities in the rescued life remain under continuous economic, moral, and ethical re-valuation, and why. Redemptive capital is a tool to help tease out and identify the entanglement of capital and conscience, politics and ethics, in culturally and historically specific incidences of rescue not for the purpose of presenting a totally explanatory analysis, but to call out the circumstances continually creating the need for rescue in the first place. Redemptive capital's power lies in its ability to call forth and channel "specters or ghosts" that notify us "that what's been suppressed or concealed is very much alive and present, messing or interfering precisely with those always incomplete forms of containment and repression ceaselessly directed towards us" (Gordon 2011, 2). It just so happens that "the rescued" in this essay lie in the liminality of life, not death, as part of their haunting.

Ontological rupture

Discerning the redemptive capital of a life rescued from death begins with understanding how and why life (be it human or equine) comes to be threatened with death (be it social or biological) in the first place. In this case, I am interested in exploring "death" as something that is, simply put, just as biological as it is social. By biological, I mean the mortal extinguishing of life as animated within the body—such as when a captive bolt successfully hits its target and enters the brain of a horse, ideally ending all consciousness and ability to suffer; or when a little boy succumbs to the overcolonization of staph bacteria in his body because his parents cannot afford the antibiotics to treat the infection. These kinds of deaths (both of which are represented in this essay) are also understood socio-culturally too: in terms of the structural factors that precipitate mortal demise, as well as how death is understood, reckoned with, grieved or not considered grievable by certain communities. But I also consider death to be social in the way that outcasts, pariahs, or "fallen insiders," as Gordon (2011) calls them, are created according to fluctuating cultural systems of morality, punishment, inclusion and exclusion. Social death, then, is when one may still be biologically alive, but one has also been decidedly unmoored from one's previous social standing and ties to the point of losing the "support and enabling conditions" that make for a livable life, to re-invoke Butler (2009, 21). That is, one has been marked as socially killable – like criminals and prisoners. It is in this particular kind of death and the state of limbo that it indexes where I locate the seeds of redemptive capital, a state of being or "stage" that I call ontological rupture.

When the status and liveliness of something (here, horse and human) is undercut by imminent death, then an ontological rupture has occurred. Amidst all the crucial and causal entanglements that precipitate death, there is a way to locate the moment "when everything changes"—and it begins by evoking Van Gennep's 1977 *rites de passage* concept. In Van Gennep's rites of passage model, ritualistic change in one's social status occurs in three stages: separation, transition (Turner [1967] further codified it as "liminality"), and reincorporation (often also referred to as aggregation). Ontological rupture is akin to the specific phase of separation, in that the subject is cast out from one's "usual environment" (Van Gennep 1977, 82) or "previous world" (Van Gennep 1977, 175). Furthermore, key to understanding this notion of ontological rupture is that it creates the conditions for a kind of opportunistic liminality when death is not completed. That is, when all is not utterly lost (but at the critical point of "almost") and what is at stake, either success (salvation and redemption) or failure (sin and condemnation), could go either way. At such a moment is where the redemptive dynamic commences.

Turning now to Paul's story, let us consider how the notion of ontological rupture manifests in ethnographic detail:

I caught staph infection at a quarantine barn. I'd run down there during the day and treat all [the] *horses. Well, I get staph infection somehow. I didn't know what it was, just thought it was a swollen bug bite or something. Well, I went to the hospital and stuff and they said it was really contagious, and I was like "oh crap, I've been around my family members, my three year old son." All of a sudden we noticed this spot on the back of his leg, and it was staph infection. So we take him to the hospital and he stays two days at UK* [University of Kentucky] *hospital. He gets treated, everything's good, then he starts to go down. They're giving him more antibiotic. They take some blood tests and send him home because he's doing really good* [...] *I get a phone call the day after we bring him home from the doctor. He says, "I've got some bad news, Mr. _____, it is MRSA in his bloodstream. This is very serious." It was really, I mean – I'm a first time father, I get mad when somebody smacks a horse when they don't deserve it. So this is mine, I'm going to be very protective of it. I freaked out. And he called in a prescription medication, it was an oral antibiotic* [...] *The medical card wouldn't cover the oral antibiotic the next day when we was at the pharmacy. They wouldn't cover it because it was* [$300].[2]

During the time I knew him, Paul was a 24 year-old student-inmate in the TRF's Second Chances program at Blackburn in the fall of 2011. He came from a part of the Inner Bluegrass region of Kentucky he described as "country" in that, "my grandfather and stuff, they all worked on the horse farms," while as children "we all went to the same school" and passed the time "out in country, far away. Bonfires, a bunch of trucks." Paul grew up in a family with the labor identity as horse farm workers, be it in the foaling barn or out grooming yearling horses in the fields. While it tugged at him nostalgically, he also vocalized his frustration with the division of labor and accompanying hierarchal social status and treatment: "It used to be a farm owner would go up to a groomer and talk about the horse, the little things. Now it's just: you see a farm owner and you gotta keep your head down." If he wasn't "aggravated" by "this Irish boss, or this Australian boss," he particularly bemoaned the loss of housing for his fledgling family on the farm he worked because of "ten Mexicans that needed to live somewhere compared to one worker." Paul further chaffed: "I know it is ten workers to one, but I got a Social Security card. I'm not racist, my last name is [gives a common Hispanic last name], my dad's Mexican, but he worked his butt off to do it the right way."

He went on to explain: "I lost my job because I couldn't find a place. You only had a month to do it. How are you supposed to uproot and move a family in a month?" Due to the employment and housing convolutions of transnational migrant labor, ethnicity, and nationalism in the Bluegrass (cf: Buck 2001), Paul's value as a worker and ability to provide for his family eventually backslid into his taking dangerous, less-desirable jobs – such as working at the quarantine barn. As anthropologist Heide Casteñada et al. (2010, 489) characterize the type of work culture involved in the horse racing industry as, "unregulated, often dangerous, and characterized by informality," it is not just Paul's exposure to MRSA staph that is a consequence of this labor culture, but the cruel, arbitrary limits placed on his health care coverage as well.

> *So I am driving, it's late. 9:30–10. I was like, "I'm not going to lose my son," because I called everybody in my family and nobody would help. Everybody was giving me the runaround, thought I was lying because I didn't have no work they didn't think I would pay them back. I'd be damned if I let my son die for somethin' ... So I saw the [gun] on the floor, I grabbed it, went into the store and asked the lady. I said, "I'm not a bad guy, I just need the money." I counted out the money – I took [$325]. I told her I was sorry, they even had me on video and audio saying that. "This is for my son, " they have me sayin' that. "He's sick." I took the money. That morning I went to the pharmacy, paid [$300] dollars. I still had the receipt and change left over three days later when they came to pick me up because the lady recognized my eyes [...] My son was doing better, so I was like "screw it." I was old fashioned and confessed what I did. Everybody kept telling me I was so stupid for tellin'em that I did it because I could have gotten a better deal, whatever. But you can't lose who you are – yeah, I let a lot of people down, but you can't lose who you are. That's basically my story.*

Conventional, criminological thinking might identify the moment of Paul's ontological rupture as his arrest, inciting the process of criminal justice by removing him from the right to live "freely" with his son and wife. But what I am more concerned about is how and why Paul was actually torn from his usual environment and previous world before he decided to grab the "fake gun" that was "broken in half" and wield it like a real weapon in order to procure money he saw himself as having no other way of legally obtaining. In Paul's story about how he came to be incarcerated for robbing a liquor store to, in his explanation, pay for his son's antibiotic to fight off a MRSA staph infection, at what point do we identify ontological rupture? Was it the actual act of robbing the liquor store, or his confession to the crime, seen by his family members who refused to give him money in the first place as a "stupid" attempt at "old fashioned" honesty? Or was it the harsh sentencing the judge gave him—20 years—after the woman clerk he robbed from "gave a good speech" during her testimony? Or did it happen even before the crime was committed? When the deceiving "bug bite" was discovered and diag-nosed? When Paul had to take the quarantine barn job because there was no other work to be had? When it was decided what treatments would be covered on a "medical card" and what would not be in the United States?

Paul's ontological rupture continued to rip at the seam of his life as he was placed at Blackburn to serve his 20-year sentence, which he hoped to bring down to 12 years for good behavior because "I don't do drugs, or anything like that, so I might get leniency." His sentencing was particularly harsh both because of the specifics of his trial—the owner of the liquor store "knew the judge on a first name basis"—and because of the larger culture of penaliza-tion and system of incarceration of Kentucky. The factors that I go on to describe below should be read as structural forces that precipitate, as well as exacerbate, the phenomenon of ontological rupture.

Kentucky is an exceptional state through which to view U.S. incarceration because over the past ten years, "Kentucky has had one of the fastest growing prison populations in the nation" (Kentucky LRC 2011, 1). Furthermore, since 2000, while the prison population in "the U.S. state prison system as a whole" has only grown 13 percent, Kentucky's population boomed at 45 percent, incarcerating 1 out of every 92 adults as opposed to 1 out of 100 adults nationally (ibid.). Furthermore, during my time in the field, the cost of over-incarceration and the economy of social death it fostered was in crisis. From 1990 to 2010, Kentucky corrections spending had increased 214 per-cent, going from $140 million to $440 million; it was then projected that by 2020 "the state would need at least $161 million more on corrections to cover this growth," which ranged from the cost of providing beds to the purchase of bonds to cover construction (Kentucky LRC 2011, 6–8). Specific to Black-burn, with an annual operating budget of $8 million, 594 inmates are pro-vided "care, housing, custody, control, and governmental services jobs" within this minimum-security institution.

Furthermore, of these inmates, 58 percent are "black" and 41 percent are "white." In comparison to my study, two men self-identified as black while eight were white—and then men like Paul complicated such binary distinctions by being of European (white) ancestry with a stepfather from Mexico. While the racialization of incarceration was not a key question in my research, it came through in subtle but distinct ways during my interviews: from one man, "Darin," telling me he went to jail because some man "sealed his fate by calling me a nigger," to another, "Chris," telling me that he was here because "they need black men in jail," to Paul's aforementioned comment that he was not racist about the influx of Latino migrant workers on horse farms because he shared (at least through marriage) a similar cultural background and family name.

In addition to the factor of their perceived racial and cultural make-up, I also found other issues steered these men into being criminalized and then incarcerated: poverty, mental health, and substance abuse. In a state where punishment, instead of prevention and treatment, is foregrounded in the legal system, men who struggled with these issues were subsequently marked for imprisonment by them as well. For example, in addition to harsh sentencing for any drug-related crime, one additional main driver of Kentucky's inordinate incarceration rate is that, "Kentucky uses prison as opposed to probation or other alternative sentences at a much higher rater than most other states" (Kentucky LRC 2011, 7). Statistics from 2009 indicate that Kentucky courts sentenced 57 percent of all convicted felony offenders to prison, compared to a 41 percent national average (ibid.).

But in the midst of this overwhelming emphasis on discipline and punishment, an intervention of sorts happened for Paul: "When I came in [to Blackburn], I just saw a bunch of horses and had to come down. *It felt a little like an escape*" (my emphasis). It is in these last few words and the sense of unburdening they convey that we start seeing a tapering off of Paul's ontological rupture and separation from the life he once knew, and the beginning of what we might call his "rescue" – which in his particular story brings him back to horses ("you can't lose who you are"). But these are not the same Thoroughbreds he knew on the famed horse farms of Kentucky's Bluegrass. These are horses with their own stories of ontological rupture, rescue, and redemption that are told through partial paper trails of breeding registries, vet records, and sales receipts, as well as through the marks on their bodies (Barad 2003).[3] For Paul, the horse at Blackburn that converged with his story was Ivory.

"What story of Ivory's life would you tell?" I asked Paul during our interview in the classroom of the barn housing the TRF Second Chances program at Blackburn. Posters of equine anatomy and TRF educational material hung from the walls around us, while bookshelves overflowed with past copies of *The Blood-Horse*, the trade magazine for Thoroughbred horseracing, as well as annual stallion registry books and other equine-related literature that Linda, or "Ms. Dyer" as the men referred to her, the manager and instructor of the TRF program, used in teaching students about the ins and outs of working in the Thoroughbred industry. Paul sat at one of the student desks while I sat at the teacher's desk at the front and center of the room. Behind

Paul and in the back of the room, where she could still see out the door into the barn corridor beyond, sat Linda. Based on Blackburn safety and surveillance protocol, she had to remain present in the classroom while I interviewed the men. To my question, Paul replied:

> It's crazy. He's 27, so he's up there. His racing career, I don't know much about it but just that he's had a hard life and, I don't know how to really say it … He just keeps goin'. One day he'll stop, but we'll all stop.

What Paul couldn't tell me about Ivory's story I was able to discern through research on Ivory's partial paper trail, such as his pedigree and racing career (online via Equineline.com and Equibase.com), as well as his virtual sponsorship profile with the TRF. Ivory was born on March 18th, 1984, out of[4] a dam called "A Real Native" and by a stallion called "Poison Ivory." He emerged into this world as a bay (dark brown) colt and was registered as a gelding (a neutered male horse) in the state of New York under the racing name "Native Ivory" with The Jockey Club of North America. As far as his racing career went, what is exceptional is the duration for which he competed. Ivory is what you would call a "war horse," competing for approximately 12 years, running in 117 races and earning \$124,157[5]—as compared to many other Thoroughbred racehorses who are retired after their four-year-old season. This is common because such horses have either won enough prestigious races, called "stakes" races, to be considered valuable enough to breed – or because they have sustained some kind of injury that makes them either physically or monetarily unable to continue racing ("Give us your tired, your worn, your weary").

When a racehorse is retired from racing—but *not* for the purpose of breeding (which effectively keeps the horse in the "previous world" of the racing industry, just on the re-production end)—I argue that this is the moment of ontological rupture for these horses, as they lose not just their status but their whole *habitus* and reason they were brought forth in the world: to race and/or reinscribe the culture of racing through breeding. Unmoored from their original and ontological purpose in the world, former racehorses enter into a dangerous liminality where they are at the mercy of human interlocutors (what the TRF posters call the "auction killers") and their power to decide what is next for the horse. Without an intervention of rescue, this is when falling into relationships of abuse and neglect becomes more probable (if horses haven't already been victimized). As they are passed through "owner"[6] after owner, horses' monetary value and the regard for their well being and suffering (often referred to in the catchall term "welfare") can diminish until death becomes the remaining option in terms of making their life "worth it." This is when they are sent to slaughter. Or when the TRF steps in.

The Second Chances program at Blackburn was established in 1999, and one year later Ivory was retired there. Once at Blackburn, Ivory became known as the horse without a tail, as reflected in the TRF literature promoting him: "Native Ivory just takes your heart away as he has no tail," informs his profile page on the TRF's website. "He lost it in the starting gate and finished third!" As such, this missing tail reads as a lingering mark of his war horse campaign, and for someone like Paul he saw it as "unique" and gravitated towards the horse.

"What do you think about horse slaughter?" I went on to ask Paul.

> *First, I started workin' with horses, I used to joke and hear people talk about it on the farm and stuff … [Pause] I just don't see any purpose in it. If a horse is healthy, kind, there ain't nothin' wrong with the horse then why take it and kill it? It's senseless. I mean, if somebody's willing to take care of it, there should be more places like this. I mean, we just use'em then toss them aside. That's not right. I mean, horses gave us everything back in the past, this country was made on horses. It means we should show'em a little more respect than that.*

This shift in consciousness, from joking about sending horses to slaughter, to seeing the practice as "not right," is one salient transformation that the TRF Second Chances programs can foster in its student-inmates. In effect, it indexes a shift from accepting and reinscribing who is considered killable, to understanding why one should grieve and intervene instead.

Navigating liminality

At this point, the ontological ruptures for both Paul and Ivory have been discerned; now, we turn to the nature of their rescue, how it was instigated by an intervention, and yet how they still must navigate ongoing liminality due to the inherent precarity of life once it has lost its "sustaining conditions" (Butler 2009, 23) as well as the particularity of their redemptive potential. It is in this phase of rescue, when ontological rupture has happened but not fully succeeded, where we see the development and power of redemptive capital come to a fore. As I will now go on to explain, one reason why ontological rupture does not succeed in its complete erasure is because an "immediate rescue" takes place. That is to say, the slide into death is truncated because there is something in the condemned that is seen as worth saving and making an intervention, of granting the possibility of a second chance once the threat of death has been eased.

Essentially, that "something" is redemptive capital: the strategic *traits* seen in the condemned as initially worth saving. These traits then become the "stuff" by which the saved advance from one less-precarious social position to another. This "seeing," however, happens differently for each species based both on their attribution of agency (as in how consciously and effectively they can strategize their rescue) as well as according to the context of power relations between rescuers and the rescued, and the intentions of the redeemers for the redeemed. For example: for Paul, his immediate rescue happened when Linda finally accepted him into the program after his coming down to the farm "everyday for three weeks" looking for a job. What redemptive traits did Linda see in Paul that helped her make such a crucial decision? Was it his persistence, or the fact that he already came with prior equine experience? Or, in Gordon's terms, did Linda see a chance to further along "an integrity and fortitude that's impervious to the contingencies of institutionalized dehumanization and domination" (2011, 16)? Whatever it was, Paul's redemptive capital first manifested as traits possessed both prior to his social death sentence and in response to his desire to mediate his liminality and the accompanying state of servitude and punishment at Blackburn. As such, redemptive capital is both embodied (as in habitus) and emergent (relational and dynamic, if not "diffractive" [Haraway 1992] in its manifestation).

But these traits are not effective without their objective recognition and belief that they can help re-position someone. As such, Bourdieu's 1992 reconsideration of his ideas on "capital" becomes of use here in helping further clarify what is meant by redemptive capital and how the notion of "traits" comes into play. Paul's traits—persistence, prior knowledge and training – are not static attributes but "species of power (or capital) whose possession commands access to the specific profits that are at stake in the field" (Bourdieu and Wacquant 1992, 97). Sometimes it is a third party, such as Linda, who sees the species of capital that will work in a particular field or context (such as the educational and labor environment of the Second Chances program); and sometimes an "agent," as Bourdieu (ibid.) puts it, can discern what specific profits are at stake in the field and what s/he possesses (or can come to possess) to command access to them.

As such, for many of the men, not just Paul, the biggest draw down to the TRF farm was not necessarily the chance to work with horses and "escape" for a few hours each weekday, but that upon successful completion[7] of the program 90 days would be taken off their sentence. Thus, many men initially strategized their acceptance into the program in terms of quantitatively reducing their sentence.

Once "in," however, many of these men came to redeem their time in additional, more qualitative ways. "It makes me feel a bit of normalcy," Paul shared with me. "I'm just not patient, I mean, I'm learning that here," he continued. "So that's the main thing, and compassion. I've turned it towards my fellow man." Thus, as the men go through the Second Chances program, more redemptive capital emerges, often of the kind they did not anticipate: a sense of normalcy, patience, compassion, and love. (The question then becomes how this species of capital will be recognized beyond their liminal germination in the prison pastures of Blackburn, an issue I will address at the conclusion of this essay.)

By accepting him into the program, Linda intervened in the process of prison stealing away the "futurity" (Gordon 2011) and life from the imprisoned. By giving Paul a spot in the Second Chances program, Linda created the conditions in which Paul and other prisoners could "redeem time" while serving time, and therefore not internalize the "social death" that criminality and the temporal regime of prison can impose on someone (Gordon 2011, 15).

While Linda plays a major role in helping the men into and through the program, it is also their relationships with horses like Ivory that bring forth the more uncanny, unforeseen species of their redemptive capital. Sometimes this happens in a profoundly literal moment, as it did for Paul. As I was interviewing him and asking him about why Ivory was his favorite horse, Linda piped up, "He saved you!" I then asked, incredulously, "What happened?" Paul responded:

> *Yeah, he saved me today. I was checking out this other horse, and I'm having some trouble with my eyesight. I can't see anything over here* [indicates his peripheral vision] *and the alpha* [the dominant, most aggressive horse in the herd] *was coming up behind me to take a little nip. And I was doing something with Ivory and then all of a sudden he just took off and went straight*—[here he interjects to provide context] *Ivory's a wuss, he gets picked on by everybody—and for some reason he took on* [alpha horse's name indiscernible], *and he's scared to death of* [him] *every other day, but today … It was a good thing because his teeth were open, so it was kinda cool for him to look out.*

Paul then went on, without my asking him, to explain why he thought Ivory chose to look out for him that day. It appeared to be based on a previous care-oriented experience between the two of them:

> *He got kicked in the side and he had this big welt and it swelled real bad, and he was all standoffish and wouldn't come to the gate with the other horses so I was kinda looking out for him. And then all of a sudden, one day I'm sittin' there grooming horses, and he just comes up and puts his head on my shoulder. I guess he was tired or sick or somethin', and he just puts his head on my shoulder and just chills there a good ten minutes. Just wanted to be loved on. And ever since then he's always come straight to me and makes sure, I don't know … It's weird, I'd have a crappy day and he'll come right up to me, but any other time he's just chillin', waits for me to come right up to him.*

Because Paul looked out for Ivory when the horse was recovering from a particularly bad kick from another member of his herd, Paul interpreted Ivory's uncharacteristic behavior of putting his head on the man's shoulder in order "to be loved on" and, moreover, Ivory's protection of Paul from additional assault and injury, as the horse responding gratefully and with vulnerability to the man's care and concern. This kind of response conjures Despret's notion of "anthropo-zoo-genesis" whereby, "Both, human and horse, are cause and effect of each other's movements. Both induce and are induced, both affect and are affected. Both embody each other's mind" (2004: 115)—to which I would add that both embody each other's need to be loved and looked out for as well.

> *These horses help me, a lot. You get that contact—cause you don't get to see your family—so you get that contact, that closeness of another living thing that you can take care of that depends on you [...] It depends on you, and that's good to have in here. I mean, you got to look out for yourself, and you got to look out for someone else too.*

Saved from possible slaughter, abuse, and neglect, these horses are not inert "pasture ornaments" who simply live out their days grazing and being groomed. They are clearly active and responsive agents in dynamic relationships with men like Paul. Through their intra-actions (Barad 2003) with these men, the horses not only help discover and grow the redemptive capital of these humans, but their own redemptive capital is co-cultivated through such response. I see this happening in two ways. First, in the statement their lives make against the practice of horse slaughter (and the related problems of abuse and neglect); then, in what they bring out in the men.

While most of these horses are initially rescued because of one major salient trait—that they are registered Thoroughbred racehorses, which is made tangible and traceable via a tattoo of their Jockey Club registration number on their upper lip (McKee 2014)—once they are rescued, they also experience a liminal period of further trait assessment. This is when they come to reside in programs like Blackburn and enter into relationships with inmates. At first, many of them come with vices picked up from life "on track"—like biting and cribbing (wind sucking)—but as Linda pointed out to me, through the love of the men and, furthermore, because these horses are no longer treated like "products," their "personalities" emerge and vices subside. As these horses become with each other and with the inmates in different ecologies of care and relationships, they thrive in new and renewed ways: this is their redemptive capital. The more they come to live a livable life, the more they demonstrate the immorality of the precariousness they once faced: especially through the death threat of slaughter. Their sustained lives become a protest against the cruelty and suffering they once faced.

As such, the thriving of these horses also helps demonstrate and confirm the mission of the TRF: "the Thoroughbred Retirement Foundation offers a humane alternative to the dire possibilities that have long faced a great majority of ex-racehorses—neglect, abuse and slaughter. It is a place, built on love and caring, that is befitting such noble and deserving animals." In doing so, these horses also help the TRF as a non-profit organization to raise and secure money: "As a registered 501(C)(3) organization, the TRF receives no public funding and is entirely dependent on the generosity of private individuals," so reads the foundation's main page on its website. In this way, we see how the redemptive capital of these former racehorses demonstrates an entanglement of economics and morality; moral action needs economic resources, and to gain such funding, moral action must be proven possible.

In addition to the benefit these horses confer on the organization that cares for them, the thriving of their lives inflects the lives of the men. As men like Paul form relationships and have uncanny experiences with these horses, they are gaining redemptive capital in two ways. First in terms of the "cultural" species of capital that Bourdieu (1992) outlined, such as in the form of embodying skills and knowledge like how to care for Thoroughbred horses and perform farm-based work. This is the most celebrated form of capital that both the TRF and Blackburn promote for this program, often touting that men learn skills to make them employable upon parole. In this sense, redemptive capital also contains the "species" of social capital in that it can give men access to a social network that will recognize and sustain their employability—so long as the men can reciprocate by sustaining the social network in return (Bourdieu 1986).

These species of redemptive capital, however, are also the most problematic, for jobs in the horse industry of the Bluegrass were hard to come by during 2011 when the state was still reeling from the global economic recession of 2008–2009. Whereas in years past the small farms were the first to fold under trying economic times, "now even the big farms are doing it," Linda told me. Furthermore, while there have been some successful graduates from the Second Chances program—"there's been a lot of stories I heard," Paul told me, "one about an inmate that's now a farm manager, one that's working as a blacksmith, one that's doing good things at an equine hospital" – entry-level positions in the horse industry are characterized not just by their informality and potential danger (as I previously illustrated with Paul taking the job at the quarantine barn), many jobs are often part-time, on-call, or cash-paying only; *not* the full-time, taxable kind of jobs parolees are often required to have because it is assumed that part-time or cash paying jobs "are often associated with patterns that contribute to repeat offenses" (Bachi 2014, 12). "Due to these restrictions," Bachi laments, "many inmates lose the skills they have developed, and in many ways have come to love" (ibid.). Based on his participation in the TRF Second Chances program, will Paul be able to not only return to his profession in the horse industry, but do so from a more empowered position?

Questioning reincorportation

Such a question grows even more skeptical when we consider how former inmates must wrestle with what Philippe Combessie calls the "penal stigma," where the "dichotomous cleavage effected and materialized by the prison ... seeps through the walls and infects a wide range of social relationships" (2002, 535). That is to say, how will Paul and other men keep the stigma of incarceration from infecting their second chance upon release from prison? This last question begins to hint at the final level of redemptive capital, where the question of societal reincorporation comes into play now that a life has not only been rescued, but placed on a tentative path of redemption. From the above discussion, I have also already questioned how feasible this rein-corporation truly is, especially when the species of redemptive capital being cultivated (here, economic, cultural, and social) are not necessarily as power-ful and recognizable beyond the prison walls as idealized to be.

But there is that second form of redemptive capital still to be considered for the men in the Second Chances program, and it has to do more with culti-vating a "critical consciousness" (hooks 2004, 27) while imprisoned by "refusing the death sentence and its doom" and "to be treated as if one was never born, fated to a life of abandonment and spectrality" (Gordon 2011, 15). It is not necessarily the kind of redemptive capital that will absolve an inmate of his cost to the justice and corrections system of the state of Ken-tucky, nor necessarily of the trauma and shame brought to one's family and community by breaking the law, but the kind that might allow an individual to forgive himself and re-orient his habitus away from perpetuating hurt and crime as he comes to realize that he does not need to internalize a social death sentence.

An example of what I mean comes from the below passage from my inter-view with Paul:

> *Compassion, that's what I'll take from this program because the TRF not only takes in broken down horses but broken down men and it's that com-passion that I like about this program.*

To affect this kind of re-orientation of self and re-strategizing of one's posi-tion, it takes responding in the way that Haraway explores it, by meeting "the gaze of living, diverse animals and in response" becoming "undone and redone" (2008, 21). While in this particular passage she is confronting the conceit and intractability that has characterized the scientific study of and philosophical musing over nonhuman animals, the point that Haraway makes about coming undone and being redone by paying attention to the agency of an animal rings true in the case of men like Paul. These are men who are not only willing to meet the gaze of horses like Ivory, but be remade in the response they engendered in such an admission. Furthermore, as Haraway sees such response as also a moment of making new kinds of worlds that un-seat norms of violence and exploitation brought on by "militarized neoliberal models of world building" (2008, 3), the notion of student-inmates respond-ing to the horses in their care with new understandings of compassion sug-gests such other-world building—albeit on a microcosmic level that still has a world beyond the prison walls and pasture fences with which to reckon.

By bringing out the compassion in these men, by helping them to redeem time instead of being its servant, and helping them refuse the death sentence of imprisonment and cultivate instead critical consciousness, fortitude, and integrity, this is perhaps the most salient species of redemptive capital that these TRF horses offer—even if they cannot see the men through their transition back into society. Instead, horses like Ivory will remain at Blackburn, meeting and becoming with each student-inmate who passes through the Second Chances program. With each man, his story, and the redemptive capital he brings with him and that poises for emergence from him, these horses will shape and be shaped by their relationships with them, sometimes in copasetic ways (such as defending them against more aggressive horses) sometimes in frightening ways (such as being the target of such aggressive horses). Some men will be changed and use that transformation as their strategy to move beyond their subjugation to systems that perpetuate, in particular, labor exploitation and criminality; some will simply have 90 days taken off their sentence and be that much closer to the ideal of being released. Either way, the question remains: what will become of their redemptive capital once outside the prison walls—or does a crucial species of it remain back in the pastures of Blackburn?

References

Bachi, Keren. 2014. "An Equine-Facilitated Prison-Based Program: Human-Horse Relations and Effects on Inmate Emotions and Behaviors." Ph.D. dissertation, City University of New York.

Barad, Karen. 2003. "Posthumanist Performativity: Toward an Understanding of how Matter Comes to Matter." *Signs* 28 (3): 801–831.

Behar, Ruth. 1990. "Rage and Redemption: Reading the Life Story of a Mexican Marketing Woman." *Feminist Studies* 16 (2): 223–258.

Blackburn Correctional Complex. "About BCC." http://corrections.ky.gov/depts/AI/BCC/Pages/AboutBCC.aspx (accessed September 8, 2014).

Bourdieu, Pierre. 1986. "The Forms of Capital," In *Handbook of Theory and Research for the Sociology of Education*, edited by. J. Richardson, 241–258. New York, New York: Greenwood.

Bourdieu, Pierre and Loic J.D. Wacquant. 1992. *An Invitation to Reflexive Sociology.* Chicago, Illinois: The University of Chicago Press.

Buck, Pem Davidson. 2001. *Worked to the Bone: Race, Class, Power, and Privilege in Kentucky.* New York: Monthly Review Press.

Butler, Judith. 2009. *Frames of War: When is Life Grievable?* London: Verso.

Cassidy, Rebecca. 2002. *Sport of Kings.* Oxford: Oxford University Press.

Casteñada, Heide, Nolan Klein, and Nathaniel Dickey. 2010. "Health Concerns of Migrant Backstretch Workers at Horse Tracks." *Journal of Health Care for the Poor and Underserved* 21 (2): 489–503.

Combessie, Phillippe. 2002. "Marking the Carceral Boundary." *Ethnography* 3 (4): 535–555.

Davis, Angela. 2011. *Abolition Democracy: Beyond Empire, Prisons, and Torture.* New York: Seven Stories Press.

Despret, Vinciane. 2004. "The Body we Care for: Figures of Anthro-Po-Zoo-Genesis." *Body & Society* 10 (2): 111–134.

Gordon, Avery F. 2011. "Some Thoughts on Haunting and Futurity." *Borderlands* 10 (2): 1–21.

Graeber, David. 2011. *Debt: The First 5,000 Years.* Brooklyn, NY: Melville House.

Kirksey, S. Eben and Stefan Helmreich. 2010. "The Emergence of Multispecies Ethnography." *Cultural Anthropology* 25 (4): 545–576.

Haraway, Donna J. 2008. *When Species Meet.* Minneapolis: University of Minnesota Press.

——1992. "The Promises of Monsters: A Regenerative Politics for Inappropriate/d Others," In *Cultural Studies*, edited by Lawrence Grossberg, Cary Nelson and Paula A. Treichler, 295–337. New York: Routledge.

Harding, Susan. 1987. "Convicted by the Holy Spirit: The Rhetoric of Fundamentalist Baptist Conversion." *American Ethnologist* 14 (1): 167–181.

Harris, Marvin. 1979. *Cultural Materialism.* Walnut Creek, CA: Altamira Press.

Heller, Bill. 2005. *After the Finish Line: Racing to End Horse Slaughter.* Irvine, California: i5 Press.

hooks, bell. 2004. *We Real Cool: Black Men and Masculinity.* New York: Routledge.

Kentucky Legislative Research Commission. 2011. "Report of the Task Force on the Penal Code and Controlled Substances Act." S.11RS-506, Reg. Sess., at 1

available at http://www.lrc.ky.gov/lrcpubs/rm506.pdf. (accessed December 4, 2014).

Maurstad, Anita, Dona Davis, and Sarah Cowles. 2013. "Co-being and Intra-Action in horse–human Relationships: A Multi-Species Ethnography of be(Com)Ing Human and be(Com)Ing Horse." *Social Anthropology* 21 (3): 322–335.

McKee, Tamar. 2014. "Ghost Herds: Rescuing Horses and Horse People in Bluegrass Kentucky." Ph.D. dissertation, University of British Columbia.

——2013. "Redemptive Capital: An Ethnographic Look at Human-Horse Rescue Relationships." *INK – Ideas, Numbers, Knowledge* 2 (2): 14–16.

Sahlins, Marshall. 1976. *Culture and Practical Reason.* Chicago, IL: The University of Chicago.

Stillman, Deanne. 2008. *Mustang: The Saga of the Wild Horse in the American West.* New York, New York: Houghton Mifflin Company.

Thoroughbred Retirement Foundation. "Native Ivory." http://www.trfinc.org/c42/c43/Native-Ivory-c70.html (accessed June 26, 2014).

——"Main Page."http://www.trfinc.org (accessed June 26, 2014).

Turner, Victor. 1967. *The Forest of Symbols.* Ithaca, NY: Cornell University Press.

Van Gennep, Arnold. 1977. *The Rites of Passage.* New York: Routledge.

Notes

1 Equine slaughter has since been provisionally banned (in 2007) and reinstated (in 2011) in the United States due to a variety of legislative action (McKee 2014, 212–213).

2 I changed the amount of money described to me as needed to pay for Paul' son's medication, as well as the ensuing amount stolen, in an effort to further conceal any traits that might lead to identification of Paul's real identity.

3 As Barad writes in reference to her concept of "agential intra-action" (which implicitly informs the epistemological stance of this essay) and the idea of "marks left on bodies":

> Agential intra-actions are causal enactments. Recall that an agential cut effects a local separability of different "component parts" of the phenomenon, one of which ("the cause") expresses itself in effecting and marking the other ("the effect"). In a scientific context this process is known as a "measurement."

(Indeed, the notion of "measurement" is nothing more or less than a causal intra-action.) Whether it is thought of as a "measurement," or as part of the universe making itself intelligible to another part in its ongoing differentiating intelligibility and materialization, is a matter of preference. Either way, what is important about causal intra-actions is the fact that marks are left on bodies. Objectivity means being accountable to marks on bodies.

(2003, 824)

4 In the focal language of recounting bloodlines in the Thoroughbred racing world, one says that a horse is "by" a certain stallion and "out of" a certain broodmare. It connotes a bygone, implicit assumption that stallions are the main creators of horses, while mares simply serve as vessels through which foals pass. See Cassidy (2002).
5 In the focal language of the Bluegrass horse people in my study, particularly those who rescue former racehorses, a horse with such a racing career is called a "war horse" because their racing campaign persisted for so long (over 50 races) and made over $50,000 in the process. These horses are exceptional and celebrated subversively as such in juxtaposition to the more mainstream phenomenon of horses running just a handful of races for three years, yet making millions of dollars.
6 I flag the word "owner" to raise two conditions: first, to indicate that I do not take the relationship between human and horse to be universally and innately one of ownership but rather, and second, that to "own" a horse (or any creature, for that matter) is culturally constructed, historically contingent, and relies on societal acceptance and sanction of such bio-power relations.
7 Such as passing a 250-plus question exam, receiving a certificate of completion and 16 hours of prison educational credit.

4 The administration of death

Killing and letting die during the Cambodian genocide

James A. Tyner

Mam Mot's black, close-cropped hair is graying.[1] Now in his early fifties, Mot reflects back on his life and the hardships he endured as a young man. He lived through the violence that plagued Cambodia during the years 1975–1979—a horrific chapter in his country's history that witnessed upwards of two million deaths. His younger brother, Hun, was one such casualty. Suffering the pangs of malnutrition, Mot's brother gathered a coconut that had fallen to the ground. Under the regime of the Communist Party of Kampuchea (CPK; also known as the Khmer Rouge), such an action was considered 'theft' against the state. Punishment was swift and harsh; the young man was executed.

Hun was killed at, or near, Ta Sek Security Center, located in Kampong Som Province. Today, no visible marker remains of the former prison or of the unmarked mass grave in which Hun was buried; the lands have long since been converted to rice fields.

The death of Hun was far from exceptional. During the Cambodian 'genocide',[2] approximately half of those who died perished from starvation, disease, exhaustion, and exposure; the remainder were directly killed, most via hastily conducted executions in isolated copses of trees or dense jungle. No ritual burials or funeral practices were permitted; corpses were disposed in unmarked mass graves. What are we to make of these deaths? Why did so many people die from preventable conditions (i.e. starvation and disease) and why were so many others executed in an attempt to change those conditions? And why were these deaths unremarked, the bodies left untended in anonymous mass graves?

It is commonplace to write-off CPK policy as irrational, chaotic, or simply non-existent; that policies resulted haphazardly from 'brain-storming sessions' or were 'plucked from the sky' (Himel 2007; Bultmann 2012). Indeed, there is a tendency, as Vickery (1984, 39) laments, for scholars to uncritically presume that CPK policies were simply "perverse and had no rational basis in either economic or political necessity." McIntyre (1996, 749), for example, declares that the CPK "eschewed administrative apparatuses and bureaucracy." Certainly, many policies were hastily conceived and found wanting in detail. However, this does not, in total, indicate a lack of foresight in planning or of bureaucratic oversight.

Much has been made also of the CPK's supposed romanticism of the Angkor Empire (c. 900–1400 CE). Winter (2007, 44), for example, explains that the Khmer Rouge's "idealization of Angkor's social and economic foundations defined the parameters of an agrarian utopia" and that "urbanization and industrialization were the source of many of Cambodia's ills and failures." Consequently, Winter (2007, 44) surmises that the CPK sought to "revert to an agrarian-based economy." Maguire (2005, 36) is more blunt in his assessment, declaring simply that CPK governance was an "experiment in 'Stone Age' communism."

It is simply not the case that the CPK attempted to revert to some agrarian utopia—despite *limited* political rhetoric to the contrary. CPK policies indicate a commitment to increased agricultural productivity as a means of building industry. Their intent was not—contra many superficial accounts—to turn back the pages of time to an earlier epoch, but instead to produce a modern, industrialized economy unparalleled in human history. Emphasis was placed also, paradoxically, on social improvements—a point that seems contradictory in the light of the subsequent mass violence. However, such contradictions disappear when one acknowledges that the CPK rationalized their management practices on the utilitarian assumption that some lives were more important than others; and that (some) life must be left to die in order that others may live.

As recent scholarship indicates, the CPK was exceptionally pragmatic and calculative in its decision-making; violence, in fact, was highly administered. For this reason, it is more appropriate to consider the mass violence not as irrational or chaotic, but rather as a form of *administrative violence* (Tyner 2014a; Tyner and Devadoss 2014). Indeed, a reconfiguration of the Cambodian 'genocide' as exemplary of administrative violence is crucial, for it directs attention to the most fundamental of all questions regarding political sovereignty: the determination, the calculation, of who may live and who must die.

In this chapter I take seriously the problem of what makes a livable life and a grievable death; that certain lives are 'made kill-able' by their positioning in social hierarchies of dominance; and that grievability and killability are governed closely by the economic logics that work to obscure important moral frameworks and ethical social relations. To this end I develop three points with respect to the economies of violence in general and the mass violence of Cambodia specifically. First point: the moment of killing, but let us say violence, is historically, geographically, and morally conditioned; that is, violence is not as it appears; violence is neither self-evident nor given. Violence (and killing) must be theorized as not having a universal quality but as something produced by, and producing, social-spatially contingent modes of production (Tyner and Inwood 2014). By extension, to better ascertain the scale and scope of violence in Democratic Kampuchea—as Cambodia was renamed by the CPK—it is necessary to resituate our understanding of 'violence' within the parameters of CPK political-economy.

Second point: all life-forms, as Butler (2004) observes, share the same vulnerability to death. But where Butler finds in our shared mortality the possibility of solidarity, I find the further subsumption of life to calculated political and economic decisions. All life is conditioned by the certainty of death; the occasion of that death is less certain. To this end, recent years have witnessed an efflorescence of writings on the subject of premature death. Gilmore (2002, 16) for example forwards the notion that premature death follows from the application of violence. It is necessary, however, to acknowledge that premature death is a bio-political and bio-economic concept, one that is intimately bound to the modernist ordering of life that dominates our contemporary understanding of both bodies and populations (Tyner 2014b). As detailed below, within Democratic Kampuchea the CPK evinced a notable indifference to life; this developed, I argue, not because of some abstract callousness to life itself, but rather because of a concrete, materialist understanding of the necessity for increased economic productivity.

Third point: The taking of life must not be limited solely to the physical act of killing, but expanded to encompass the disallowal of life—the letting die of some bodies as opposed to the making live of others. For it is my argument that particular modes of production that are predicated on production for exchange—of which capitalism is but one of many forms—letting die, or the potential of letting die, is structurally imposed; and yet, because of particular and dominant abstractions of violence, the prevalence of letting die remains obscured. To this end, I argue that the economic system imposed by the CPK was one of production for exchange. More specifically, I maintain that, rhetoric aside, the CPK revolution was neither Marxist, socialist, nor communist; and that the economic system planned and implemented by the Khmer Rouge was an exploitative system of production for exchange (Tyner 2014d). This argument is crucial, for it provides the foundation for an understanding of both the economics of killing and of the seeming indifference to life as evinced by the CPK between 1975 and 1979.

In the remainder of this chapter I take these points in reverse order, beginning with the philosophical distinction between killing and letting die and the 'indifference' to life intrinsic to economic systems of production for exchange. Next, I document the modernist ordering of life under the CPK with particular emphasis on the establishment of an economic system of production for exchange. In the penultimate section I highlight how violence within Democratic Kampuchea was mortally conditioned through administrative practice.

Production for exchange and the indifference to life

Philosophers and medical ethicists have long contemplated the moral difference between 'killing' and 'letting die'. As Green (1980, 195) explains, "killing and letting die are frequently taken to differ in that they respectively involve doing something to cause death and doing nothing to prevent death; and it is usually supposed that, if the distinction has moral significance, it is because it is worse to kill than to let die." Such an argument is false, however, because it fails to consider the underlying social relations that inform 'doing nothing'. By way of analogy, consider the workings of a formal labor market. We are told that in the market—conditioned by the 'hidden hand' of supply-and-demand—workers are 'free' to participate in paid employment; and that workers receive a fair day's wage for a fair day's work. Marx of course challenged this surface appearance, calling attention to the exploitative social relations that are foundational to market dynamics. A similar fetishism is at play in many narratives of 'letting die', namely that letting die is considered an inaction and therefore agent-less. In actuality, the supposed inaction of letting die is a conservative action; it is a choice to do nothing when one otherwise could have acted. That 'letting die' is generally not considered a form of violence is, I argue, symptomatic of the dominant abstraction of violence as a physical, intentional, act (cf. Tyner 2014c).

Here, I reconsider violence—and specifically, the act of letting die—from a materialist standpoint. Stated simply, a materialist conception of violence begins, following Marx and Engels (1998, 36–37) "with real individuals, their activity and the material conditions of their life." Such a beginning is neither arbitrary nor deterministic, but rather predicated on what Marx and Engels (p. 37) term the "first premise" of all human history, namely "the existence of living human individuals." This is especially salient, given our common-sense understanding of violence as any action or inaction that threatens human fulfillment or survivability. Consequently, it is imperative to understand how humans (in this case) satisfy basic needs (e.g. food, water, shelter, clothing), for any given society will have its own 'unique' way of satisfying (producing) these material needs, whether by self-production, trade, barter, exchange, or theft. In anticipation of later arguments, the Communist Party of Kampuchea initiated a particular mode of production in an attempt to satisfy specific conditions of vital existence. How these conditions were satisfied goes a long way in understanding the scale and scope of violence that transpired.

A materialist understanding of violence directs attention first to the conception of *production in general*. As outlined by Marx (1990, 283):

> Labor is ... a process between man [*sic*] and nature, a process by which man, through his own actions, mediates, regulates and controls the metabolism between himself and nature. He confronts the materials of nature as a force of nature. He sets in motion the natural forces which belong to his own body, his arms, legs, head and hands, in order to appropriate the materials of nature in a form adapted to his own needs. Through this movement he acts upon external nature and changes it, and in this way he simultaneously changes his own nature.

In this quote nature *appears* as something external to human activity; and such a presumption could possibly lead one to conclude that Marx conceived of nature as something to be appropriated and mastered by humans. Thus, as

Neil Smith (2008, 54) writes, humans are born with certain natural needs, such as food, water, and shelter, and they are born into a world where nature provides, either directly or indirectly, the means for fulfilling these needs. However, a reconstructed Marxist conception of nature, as Smith (2008, 55) elaborates, is dialectical. Marx presupposes a general unity of 'nature' with 'society', one that is derived from the concrete activity of natural beings, produced in practice through labor (Smith 2008, 55–56).

In his reading of Marx, Smith (2008) identifies a fundamental transformation between *production in general* and *production for exchange*—specifically, those economic systems predicated on the commodity-form of production. Commodities, following Marx, are not 'things' but rather 'relations', foremost being the relationship between 'use value' and 'exchange value'. On the one hand, commodities, as products of human (and animal) labor, possess some useful quality for people and, on the other hand, have exchange value, in that one commodity may be exchanged for another commodity. Under systems of exchange, however—and unlike barter systems—commodities are not simply exchanged. As Marx (1990, 138) writes, these "are only commodities because they have a dual nature, because they are at the same time objects of utility and bearers of value." Within an economic system predicated upon exchange, commodities are not exchanged according to their degree of usefulness; rather, they are exchanged based on the premise—and promise—of the accumulation of surplus value.

Dominant economic systems (e.g. modes of production) profoundly shape—but do not determine—calculations of violence (Tyner and Inwood 2014). In systems of production for exchange, such as capitalism, the inner logics of the commodity form are crucial to understand these calculations. For given that "the commodity form reifies and objectifies social relations by subsuming them to a commodity-economic logic," it follows that the accumulation of wealth for its own sake will be determinate of a particular market-logic" (Albritton 2007, 22). This logic is characterized by a value system predicated on *indifference.* In other words, rather than focusing on 'difference' as the basis of societal inequalities and the economics of killing (or letting die), it is necessary to engage in the exploitative logic of indifference.

Within systems of production for exchange, it matters little what is produced—as long as surplus value may be accumulated. Marx refers to this as 'indifference to use value'. Faced with seemingly indifferent choice, how then are vital decisions made? All else being equal, the choice is straightforward. Preference is exhibited toward those products that will generate the most profit; equally important are geographic questions of economic opportunity (e.g. comparative advantage). What is most important in this 'trade-off' of production is that the concept 'indifference to use value' contains within it its own inner contradictions, that is, a unity of opposites between 'indifference' and 'preference'. Restated, systemic to the concept 'indifference' is the concept 'preference'. To be indifferent to something is, at one level, to exhibit a non-preference. However, faced with a choice—to which one may be initially indifferent—one must still make a decision.

At this point I may be accused of straying far-and-wide from the general question of violence and, specifically, the violence meted by the Khmer Rouge. However, as I argue in the following section, economic systems of production for exchange—and the systemic indifference to use value—imparts a particular configuration of violence and the calculation of who may live and who must die. For I argue that the valorization of surplus within systems of production for exchange is enjoined by an indifference to life. With specific reference to capitalism, for example, Marx (1990, 376) explains that "capital asks no questions about the length of life of labor-power. What interests it is purely and simply the maximum of labor-power that can be set in motion in a working day. It attains this objective by shortening the life of labor-power, in the same way as a greedy farmer snatches more produce from the soil by robbing it of its fertility."

"The driving motive and determining purpose of [exchange] production," Marx (1990, 449) argues, "is the self-valorization of capital to the greatest possible extent, i.e., the greatest possible production of surplus-value, hence the greatest possible exploitation of labor-power by the capitalist." But just as the "werewolf-like hunger for surplus-labor" (Marx 1990, 353) was hidden by the fetishizing of the 'free' market, so too is the violence intrinsic to capitalism hidden. For violence under production for exchange entails not only the direct, interpersonal force required to appropriate land and the means of production from the many to privilege the few; violence is also systemic and structural, built into the very foundation of socio-economic relations. This violence, I argue, is founded in the contradiction that workers are both producers and consumers; this, under production for exchange, creates the structural conditions of heightened vulnerability and suscept-ibility to premature death as seen in Cambodia.

The unity of production and consumption highlights an especially impor-tant contradiction inherent in production for exchange systems—a contra-diction that is manifest in the tendency to 'let die'. Owners of the means of production, for example, strive to minimize labor costs in order to accumulate greater profits—the so-called *minimum wage*. Marx (1990, 1067) explains that the minimum price paid (the wage) is that of "the means of subsistence that is customarily held to be essential in a given state of society to enable the worker to exert his [*sic*] labor-power with the necessary degree of strength, health, vitality, etc. and to perpetuate himself by producing replacements for himself." In other words, concrete wages are determined abstractly, calculated on the basis of market-logics that determine the least cost necessary to keep workers and the next generation of workers alive.

This tendency, however, is hidden within the workings of the formal waged-labor market. The 'wage' appears as something that results from an equal exchange between employer and employee. As the saying goes, worker's receive a 'fair day's wage for a fair day's work'. Marx details that this is anything but the case. In a well-known—but particularly apt—section of *Capital*, Marx (1990, 342) writes: "capital has one sole driving force, the drive to valorize itself, to create surplus-value, to make its constant part, the means of production, absorb the greatest possible amount of surplus labor. Capital is dead labor which, vampire-like, lives only by sucking living labor, and lives the more, the more labor it sucks. The time during which the worker works is the time during which the capitalist consumes the labor-power he has bought from him."

Through the generation of both absolute and relative surpluses, workers are necessarily exploited in the production process. Moreover—and this is key— workers must still purchase their means of subsistence from *other owners of the means of production*. As Marx (1990, 717) explains, "the capital given in return for labor-power is converted into means of subsistence which have to be consumed to reproduce the muscles, nerves, bones and brains of existing workers, and to bring new workers into existence."

In actuality, workers may supplement their income through other means. Workers for example can participate in the informal market (i.e. doing odd jobs 'under the table'); they might also grow vegetables in their backyards. It should be clear, however, that many of these ancillary activities may (and frequently are) made illegal; in Democratic Kampuchea, for example, the private tending of vegetable gardens or the hunting of animals was often considered a capital offense. Within production for exchange, therefore, it is not simply that some are denied access to the means of production; it is also that some are denied access to the means of subsistence, or rather, life itself. It is this unequal vulnerability, this precarity which lays the foundation for a calculation of who may live and who must die under systems of production for exchange.

Surplus production under the Khmer Rouge

It is taken as given that rice would become the pivot upon which CPK agri- cultural policy hinged. Such an uncritical presumption, however, overlooks the calculations made by high-ranking Khmer Rouge cadre. Recognition of the entirety of CPK policy indicates that planning—albeit unrealistic in terms of quotas, among other factors—was very much present. One would be remiss to discount the decision-making capabilities, for the *economic* choices made by the CPK provide the foundation for subsequent understandings of the ensuing wide-spread violence. In other words, the killing and letting die of upwards of two million men, women, and children occurred not because Democratic Kampuchea was a lawless, chaotic terror state; rather, the vio- lence resulted because of *coherent* administrative assessments (cf. Tyner and Devadoss 2014).

An emphasis on the production of rice aligns with well-established *market principles*. In the CPK's (1988a, 48) Four-Year Plan, for example, it was determined that "to "transform our land, which is our most important resource, so as to produce harvests rapidly" it would be necessary to "fight in the field of agriculture because we have agricultural resources. We'll move to other fields when the agricultural battle is finished." Rather than promoting agriculture in some pale imitation of previous empires, the CPK calculated that this was the most appropriate path towards a modernized, industrial state. The report (p. 48) continues: "We stand on agriculture as the basis, so as to collect agricultural capital with which to strengthen and expand industry."

David Chandler (1988, 37), in his interpretation of this document, acknowledges that "sensibly enough, the [Four-Year plan] argues that exports of agricultural products, rather than minerals or manufactured goods, could best provide the income needed by DK for autarchic economic growth." However, Chandler appears to miss the larger picture. Crucial here is Chandler's characterization of the CPK as autarchic. To be sure, numerous CPK documents identify self-determination and self-reliance as economic (and political) objectives. Such aims, however, mirror those of most sovereign states, namely the desire to be free from economic domination by other states. Presently, as a case in point, many politicians—and petroleum corporations— in the United States of America are clamoring for an intensified domestic energy policy so as to minimize dependence on 'Middle East' oil. One would be hard-pressed, however, to find any depiction of US energy policy as autarchic. My point is simply this: Remove the political rhetoric of the CPK from our analytic lenses and we find a policy guided not by 'Stone Age Communism' but instead by *capitalist* doctrine (cf. Tyner 2014d).

For some readers it will appear anathema to describe the Communist Party of Kampuchea—and the Khmer Rouge revolution—as anything but communist. And yet, the parameters of key policy documents, including the Four-Year plan, suggest otherwise. As Chandler identifies—but glosses over—the CPK requires goods (i.e. commodities) to *export* in order to gen- erate *income* for economic growth. A policy based on exports, I suggest, is counter to the conclusion that Democratic Kampuchea was to be autarchic. Moreover, the decision-making evinced in the Four-Year plan indicates that CPK leaders made calculations based on their country's *comparative advantage*. At this level, I would argue that the CPK was largely indifferent to use-value but recognized a distinct advantage in agriculture, specifically rice. Indeed, the Four-Year plan (p. 46) makes clear that Democratic Kam- puchea's "natural characteristics have given us great advantages compared with China, Vietnam, or Africa."

The CPK rhetorically described their society as communist. Such claims, as we have seen, have subsequently been uncritically adopted by many his- torians of the 'genocide'. As prima facie evidence, both the CPK and later historians point to the abolition of currency and domestic markets, the elimination of private property, and the creation of agricultural communes. Similarly, the use of central planning in the production and distribution of goods and services is held as exemplary. A class analysis, however, indicates that the political economy of Democratic Kampuchea—similar to the Soviet

Union—was a particular form of capitalism and not socialism or communism (Resnik and Wolff 1994, 9). As Richard Wolff (2012, 104) explains, "what defines an economic system ... is not primarily how productive resources are owned nor how resources and products are distributed. Rather, the key definitional dimension is the organization of production. More precisely, the definitional priority concerns how the production and distribution of the surplus are organized."

Within Democratic Kampuchea, *privatized* forms of capitalism were indeed eliminated—violently so. Most banks were destroyed; land-owners were executed. And yet, under a system of production for exchange developed by the CPK, *collectivized* workers remained exploited, their surplus labor appropriated for state use. Recall again Marx's well-known discussion of commodity exchange. Marx (1990, 188) writes, "Because all commodities, as values, are objectified human labor, and therefore in themselves commensurable, their values can be communally measured in one and the same specific commodity, and this commodity can be converted into the common measure of their values, that is into money." Consequently, the "process of exchange is ... accomplished through two metamorphoses of opposite yet complementary character—the conversion of the commodity into money, and the re-conversion of the money into a commodity" (Marx 1990, 200). This is illustrated in Marx's well-known form: 'Commodity-Money-Commodity', or simply C-M-C. The first transformation, C-M, represents the conversion of a commodity into money (i.e. the act of selling), while the second transformation, M-C represents the conversion of money into a commodity (i.e. the act of buying). Hence, this single process is two-sided: from one pole, that of the commodity-owner, it is a sale, and from the other pole, that of the money-owner, it is a purchase (Marx 1990, 203).

This simple model of circulation *would appear* to bear little resemblance to the practices of the Khmer Rouge. As part of its overall goal of achieving economic autonomy independence the CPK championed self-sufficiency and self-reliance, both of which would suggest, based on Chandler's interpretation, a policy of economic autarky. However, as explained in its 'Four-Year Plan', developed between July 21 and August 2, 1976, the CPK identified two economic objectives. The first was "to serve the people's livelihood, and to raise the people's standard of living quickly, both in terms of supplies and in terms of other material goods" (CPK 1988a, 51). This was to be accomplished through the satisfaction of a second objective, namely to "seek, gather, save, and *increase capital* from agriculture, aiming to rapidly expand our agriculture, our industry, and our defense rapidly" (CPK 1988b, 51; emphasis added).Therefore, to achieve *industrial* self-sufficiency—including both light and heavy industry—the CPK decreed that they would "only have to earn [foreign] capital from agriculture" (CPK 1988b, 96).

Capital, as we have seen, was to be generated through the cultivation of rice. This is clearly illustrated in a series of remarks prepared and delivered by Pol Pot to a special meeting of the CPK 'center' during August 21–23, 1976.

Here, Pol Pot considers "the production of rice as it is related to rice fields."
He explains:

> We have greater resources than other countries in terms of rice fields.
> Furthermore, the strength of our rice fields is that we have more of them
> than others do. The strength of our agriculture is greater than that of
> other countries in this respect. ... It is the Party's wish to transform
> agriculture from a backward type to a modern type in ten to fifteen years.
> A long-term strategy must be worked out. We are working (here) on a
> Four-Year Plan in order to set off in the direction of achieving this 10–15
> year target.
>
> (CPK 1988b, 131)

Thus it was determined by the CPK that Democratic Kampuchea would need
to *triple* annual rice production, to a national average yield of three tons per
hectare. Only by attaining such a surplus could the CPK raise sufficient rev-
enues to obtain necessary goods and commodities from abroad.

The CPK identified the necessity of both capital accumulation and foreign
trade. With the abolition of money this seems problematic at best.[3] Following
the simple model of circulation, C-M-C, commodities are exchanged (sold)
for money; that money is then used to purchase additional commodities.
Clearly this was not the model developed by the Khmer Rouge. Indeed, historical reconstructions would seem to indicate a system of barter, along the
lines of C-C, whereby the CPK would exchange rice, for example, for textiles,
medicines, and other commodities not available in Democratic Kampuchea.
And indeed, documentary evidence remains of vast shipments of rice exported to China, Yugoslavia, Madagascar, and Hong Kong. To give but one
example, between January and September 1978 the Khmer Rouge exported
29,758 tons of rice to China, valued at US$5,911,833.[4]

To leave the CPK's economy at this surface level is unsatisfactory, for it
risks losing sight of the specific mechanisms introduced to generate *surplus*
capital. One is tempted, for example, to conclude that 'surplus' capital was
simply derived from increased rice production; that the 'surplus' identified
by the CPK was not 'surplus' from a Marxist understanding but merely
additional rice to be traded with foreign governments. Surplus-value, as
opposed to simply surplus (i.e. excess quantities) is a defining feature of
capitalism and thus sounds discordant with the Standard Total View of
Democratic Kampuchea. I maintain, however, that the CPK did explicitly
attempt to realize surplus-value through a system of production for exchange
and the exploitation of its population.[5]

Surplus-value is generated through the exploitation of labor-capacity and
assumes two basic forms: absolute surplus-value and relative surplus-value.
Within Democratic Kampuchea, initially the CPK devised a means to generate *absolute* surplus-value. Increased rice surpluses were obtained through
the use of forced labor and the extension of the working day—structural

conditions that led to widespread exhaustion and death. However, there are physical limits to the amount of capital accumulated in the process, limits I argue the Khmer Rouge overcame by the generation of a form of *relative* surplus-value.

For Marx, it was not 'necessary' labor time that defined labor-power's value; rather it was *socially necessary labor time*. Understood by Marx (1990, 129) as "the labor-time required to produce any use-value under the conditions of production normal for a given society and with the average degree of skill and intensity of labor prevalent in that society," a consideration of socially necessary labor time transfers the level of argument from any individual capitalist to society as a whole. This is possible because, as Fine and Saad-Filho (2010, 38) explain, the "production of relative surplus value depends critically upon all capitalists, since none alone produces a significant proportion of the commodities required for the reproduction of the working class."

Simply put, an increase in average productivity increases the average number of commodities produced per unit of time; it thereby decreases the amount of socially necessary labor time required for the production of a single commodity and, hence, the value of each commodity (Postone 1993, 193). With an increase in the productivity of labor—through refinements of the division of labor or the introduction of machinery—the value of labor-power falls and the portion of the working day necessary for the reproduction of that value will be shortened. Capital thus "has an immanent drive, and a constant tendency, towards increasing the productivity of labor, in order to cheapen commodities and, by cheapening commodities, to cheapen the worker himself [*sic*]" (Marx 1990, 436–437).

How then did the CPK foster the accumulation of *relative* surplus-value in the absence of currency? It was accomplished, I argue, by the substitution of food rations for wages. Beginning in 1976 the CPK initiated an elaborate system of food rations; this is widely documented and routinely cited as a contributing factor to the hundreds of thousands of deaths resultant from famine. However, these accounts largely fail to consider the economic implications of the CPK system. The specific allocation of food rations warrants attention, for it provides a quantitative insight into the qualitative distinctions made by the CPK. Consider, for example, the CPK proposed policy that from 1977 onwards, "the [food] ration for the people will average … 312 kilograms of rice per person per year throughout the country" (CPK 1988a, 51).[6] More specifically, a four-fold system was devised to distribute food rations based on type of work-force.[7] Those workers classified in the No. 1 system would be allocated three cans of rice per day; those in the No. 2 system, two-and-one-half cans; No. 3, two cans, and No. 4, one-and-one-half cans. This numeric system refers to the type of labor involved; those people performing the heaviest manual labor, in principle, were to receive the highest rations. The lightest tasks, performed by the elder or the sick, received the smallest rations. Pregnant women, or women who had just given birth, were at times given higher rations.[8]

Figure 4.1 Harvesting rice in Democratic Kampuchea. Photograph courtesy of the Documentation Center of Cambodia.

In short, the CPK calculated an amount of rice based on the *socially necessary labor time* required to plant and harvest rice. Thus, in its Four-Year plan the CPK calculated that the average amount of rice production would increase from 245,000 tons in 1977 to 462,000 tons in 1980; this would, according to their estimates, result in a gain of US$121,000,000 over the four year period. To meet these objectives, however, workers were to remain vigilant in their revolutionary zeal and, with the 'proper' consciousness, increase productivity.[9] Crucially, the amount of rations to be allocated for worker consumption was to remain at 320,000 tons per annum (CPK 1988a, Table 2). In other words, it was assumed that as productivity increased, and workers became more efficient, there was no need to increase the amount of food rations allocated.

Consequently, both absolute and relative surplus-value was in theory to be generated through the establishment of food rations. What is crucial to emphasize is that under communism (in general) products of surplus labor are received collectively by these same workers (cf. Resnick and Wolff 1988, 19). Within Democratic Kampuchea, designated state officials—persons other than the producers—appropriated the products of worker-labor (Resnik and Wolff 1994). One readily sees the class-structure of an exploitative economic system of exchange. Private property *was* abolished—but crucially, the people were still separated from the means of production; they owned neither land nor tools. More importantly, however, workers did not collectively appropriate their own surplus labor and distribute it according to collective need; rather state functionaries appropriated the surplus and exchanged it for commodities on the global market. At this point, Democratic Kampuchea begins to appear less like a 'communist' state and more like a nascent capitalist state (cf. Resnick and Wolff 1993, 1994).

The generation of agricultural surpluses by the CPK therefore was to be achieved by a state-led and bureaucratically run process of 'primitive accumulation' (Tyner 2014a, 75). Peasants were violently dispossessed from their land and from most other means of subsistence. The gathering of fruits and vegetables from 'common lands' was re-cast as theft—a traitorous offence. Such is the economic foundation of much direct (i.e. executions) and indirect (i.e. malnutrition, starvation) violence that characterized Democratic Kampuchea. It is necessary, however, to elaborate on these conditions, for it is my argument that CPK policy indicates a basic political-economic objective of complete subsumption to the commodity-form as manifest in food-rations. Consequently, the various practices imposed and enforced by the CPK, such as the institution of communal dining, the prohibition of subsistence-means of production, the establishment of collectives and work-camps, reveal not simply the creation of a 'terror state' but rather the means to ensure compliance with the emergent mode of production based on the exchange of agricultural surplus. It was this system of exchange—and a greater indifference to use value—that consigned two million people to premature deaths.

As theorists and critics of capitalism—including both Adam Smith and Karl Marx—have long observed, capitalists usually cannot consign their laborers to a premature death. Marx (1990, 348) averred that the health and fitness of the working class is often a matter of considerable state interest. Smith (2004, 57) likewise surmised that "a man [*sic*] must always live by his work, and his wages must at least be sufficient to maintain him." It is often necessary, therefore, for both the 'state' and the owners of the means of production to limit the exploitation and degradation of the living worker, if only to facilitate the (re)production of the next generation of workers (Tyner 2014c, 42).

How though might a thoroughly commodified system of production for exchange look? Albritton (2009, 37) provides a particularly apt summary of life and death under such conditions:

> A completely commodified labor market would be managed completely by the wage rate, which in turn is a result of the supply of and demand for workers. A large supply of workers relative to demand will lead to lower and lower wages. If this situation continues, wages will eventually fall below bare physical subsistence and workers will die off, until their supply shrinks enough to once again push wages to a level at or above subsistence.

A pure, completely commodified capitalist labor market, in other words, would necessarily operate on the basis of letting die a certain portion of workers (Tyner 2014c, 42).

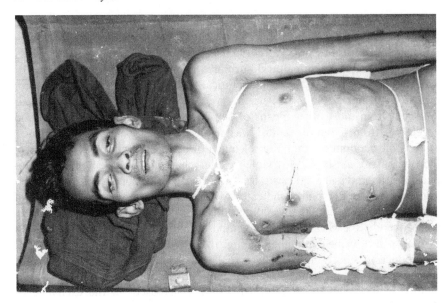

Figure 4.2 Corpse of man tortured and killed at S-21 Security Center. Photograph courtesy of the Documentation Center of Cambodia.

Such a scenario has profound implications for understanding the mass violence that gripped Democratic Kampuchea. For although Democratic Kampuchea was not economically dependent upon formal labor markets, I maintain that it was a thoroughly commodified society. Violence was structurally constituted through a reduction of the necessary conditions for survival, as the more communist-sounding term 'ration' was substituted for the more capitalist-sounding 'wage' (Tyner 2014a, 75; Tyner 2014d). Regardless of terminology, however, whether wage or ration, the end-point was the same: laborers were denied access to the means of production; and through overwork and the prohibition of alternative means of subsistence, both agricultural surplus and fatalities ensued. Those who resisted, or sought to supplement their meagre rations, were subject to direct violence in the form of imprisonment, torture, and execution.

Within Democratic Kampuchea life or death decisions hinged on whether any given man, woman, or child was perceived as having 'use-value' (Tyner 2008, 160). Indeed, the Khmer Rouge's oft-used saying 'If you live there is no gain. If you die there is no loss,' approaches this bio-economic conception. The phrase speaks to the liminal position of life itself; it speaks also to the indifference endemic to an economic system predicated on the privileging of exchange-value over use-value. All life, in the abstract, was inconsequential beyond its immediate labor-capacity. The CPK regime, in this sense, was totalizing, in that the persecution of people was not limited to 'racial' or 'religious' groupings, but rather conditioned by one's relationship to the dominant mode of production.

Throughout Democratic Kampuchea, all citizens were potentially equal in death. The new society was predicated on rhetoric of equality: a communist ideal that premised class division would be rendered obsolete through the elimination of private property and the abolition of currency. In a brutal irony, however, the physicality of mass graves *appears* to conform to this ideal; that the anonymous burials negated differences; that even in death, all became equal. However, mass graves reveal more than they appear, for mass graves demonstrate concretely the indifference to life (Tyner 2014a).

Within Democratic Kampuchea life was utilitarian. A person's value was measured by his or her ability to contribute to the Party, the State, and Revolution. And as politicized life, any life that ceased to have relevance—value—became expendable. In short, laborers were susceptible either to direct forms of killing or more indirect means. During the reign of the Khmer Rouge, all people were reduced to that of surplus population; indifferent bodies were judged and valued by their capacity to labor. And one's qualitative capacity for labor often meant the quantitative difference between life and death (Tyner 2014a).

The CPK permitted no funerary practices and no individualized burials. The anonymity of death therefore speaks to the broader administration of death. For as Butler (2004, 34) notes, the presence of an obituary, for example, indicates that "there would have had to have been a life, a life worth noting, a life worth valuing and preserving, a life that qualifies for recognition." The unmarked and unremarked deaths that constitute Cambodia's mass violence serve as silent witnesses to the calculations and valuations

Figure 4.3 Khmer Rouge soldiers. All were considered qualitatively equal in life and in death.

of life under the CPK. Death for the Party was not grievable, precisely because life was valued instrumentally. Living bodies were adjudged on their potential labor-capacity; dead bodies were by-products.

Conclusions

According to Cartwright (1996, 354), a plausible account of killing and letting die may be that one kills someone if one initiates a causal sequence that ends in one's death, whereas one lets another die if one allows an already existing casual sequence to culminate in that person's death. In effect, Cartwright is addressing the broader context, or conditions, that may result in death. And indeed geographers have addressed at length these conditions, for they fall under the rubric of structural violence. From this perspective, states (should) have a moral and legal responsibility for the creation of conditions that lead to starvation, malnutrition, or exposure to pollutants. Within the context of the Cambodian 'genocide', therefore, it is possible to argue that those social and environmental conditions that led to famine, disease, exhaustion, and exposure were the direct result of specific, calculated practices undertaken by the CPK. The collectivization of agriculture; the extreme rationing of foods; the mandatory dawn-to-dusk work hours: these were the conditions that made premature death possible.

Ironically, paradoxically, these practices—the collectivization of agriculture, the establishment of labor camps, and even the use of food rations—were enacted *to foster life*. A stated objective of the CPK's Four-Year Plan (1988a, 51), for example, was to "produce rice for food to raise the standard of living of the people." Likewise, the (re)establishment of hospitals, pharmaceutical factories, and other health-related practices indicate not so much a complete disregard on behalf of the CPK for the lives of its citizens (cf. Tyner 2012), but rather a more nuanced interpretation—and calculation—of citizenship.

It is too simplistic to paint Democratic Kampuchea as a 'terror state' or to minimize the economic planning of the CPK because of unrealistic expectations. It is also unhelpful to mistake political rhetoric for actual practice. In this chapter I have argued that the killing and letting die of millions of men, women, and children in Democratic Kampuchea resulted not from a lack of planning but rather from a surfeit of administrative calculations. Moreover, the two are conjoined, in that direct violence—the killing of people in the form of execution—was predicated more so on the necessity to ensure compliance with an economic system based on dispossession and exploitation than it was because of abstract generalities such as 'evil' or vulgar characterizations of 'Stone Age Communism'.

References

Albritton, Robert. 2007. *Economics Transformed: Discovering the Brilliance of Marx.* London: Pluto Press.
——2009. *Let Them Eat Junk: How Capitalism Creates Hunger and Obesity.* New York: Pluto Press.

Bultmann, Daniel. 2012. "Irrigating a socialist utopia: Disciplinary space and population control under the Khmer Rouge, 1975–1979." *Transcience*. 3: 40–52.

Butler, Judith. 2004. *Precarious Life: The Powers of Mourning and Violence*. London: Verso.

Cartwright, Will. 1996. "Killing and letting die: A defensible distinction." *British Medical Bulletin*. 52: 354–361.

Chandler, David. 1988. "Introduction to 'The party's four-year plan to build socialism in all fields, 1977–1980.'" In *Pol Pot Plans the Future: Confidential Leadership Documents from Democratic Kampuchea, 1976–1977*, edited by David Chandler, Ben Kiernan, and Chanthou Boua, 36–43. New Haven, CT: Yale University Southeast Asia Studies, Monograph Series 33.

Communist Party of Kampuchea [CPK]. 1988a. "The party's four-year plan to build socialism in all fields, 1977–1980," translated by Chanthou Boua. *In Pol Pot Plans the Future: Confidential Leadership Documents from Democratic Kampuchea, 1976–1977*, edited by David Chandler, Ben Kiernan, and Chanthou Boua, 43–119. New Haven, CT: Yale University Southeast Asia Studies, Monograph Series 33.

——1988b. "Preliminary explanation before reading the plan, by the Party Secretary," translated by David Chandler. *In Pol Pot Plans the Future: Confidential Leadership Documents from Democratic Kampuchea, 1976–1977*, edited by David Chandler, Ben Kiernan, and Chanthou Boua, 120–163. New Haven, CT: Yale University Southeast Asia Studies, Monograph Series 33.

Fine, Ben and Alfredo Saad-Filho. 2010. *Marx's 'Capital'*, 5th edition. New York: Pluto Press.

Gilmore, Ruth W. 2002. "Fatal couplings of power and difference: Notes on racism and geography," *The Professional Geographer*. 54: 15–24.

Green, O.H. 1980. "Killing and letting die." *American Philosophical Quarterly*. 17: 195–204.

Himel, J. 2007. "Khmer Rouge irrigation development in Cambodia," *Searching for the Truth*, Special English Edition, First Quarter: 42–49.

Maguire, Peter. 2005. *Facing Death in Cambodia*. New York: Columbia University Press.

Marx, Karl. 1990. *Capital, Volume 1*, translated Ben Fowkes. New York: Penguin Books.

Marx, Karl and Friedrich Engels. 1998. *The German Ideology including Theses on Feuerbach and Introduction to the Critique of Political Economy*. Amherst, NY: Prometheus Books.

McIntyre, Kevin. 1996. "Geography as destiny: Cities, villages and Khmer Rouge Orientalism," *Comparative Studies in Society and History*. 38: 730–758.

Postone, Moishe. 1993. Time, Labor, and Social Domination: *A Reinterpretation of Marx's Critical Theory*. Cambridge: Cambridge University Press.

Resnick, Stephen and Richard Wolff. 1988. "Communism: Between class and classless," *Rethinking Marxism* 1: 14–42.

——1993. "State capitalism in the USSR? A high-stakes debate," *Rethinking Marxism* 6: 46–68.

——1994. "Between state and private capitalism: What was Soviet 'socialism'?" *Rethinking Marxism* 7: 9–30.

Smith, Adam. 2004. *The Wealth of Nations*. New York: Barnes & Noble.

Smith, Neil. 2008. *Uneven Development: Nature, Capital, and the Production of Space*, 3rd edition. Athens: University of Georgia Press.

Tyner, James A. 2008. *The Killing of Cambodia: Geography, Genocide and the Unmaking of Space.* Aldershot, UK: Ashgate.

——2012. "State sovereignty, bioethics, and political geographies: The practice of medicine under the Khmer Rouge," *Environment and Planning D: Society and Space* 30: 842–860.

——2014a. "Dead labor, landscapes, and mass graves: Administrative violence during the Cambodian genocide." *Geoforum* 52: 70–77.

——2014b. "Population geography II: Mortality, premature death, and the ordering of life," *Progress in Human Geography* DOI: 10.1177/0309132514527037

——2014c. "Dead labor, homo sacer, and letting die in the labor market," *Human Geography* 7: 35–48.

——2014d. "Violence, surplus production, and the transformation of nature during the Cambodian genocide," *Rethinking Marxism* 26: 490–506.

Tyner, James A. and Christabel Devadoss. 2014. "Administrative violence, prison geographies and the photographs of Tuol Sleng Security Center, Cambodia." *Area* 46: 361–368.

Tyner, James A. and Inwood, Joshua. 2014. "Violence as fetish: Geography, Marxism, and dialectics." *Progress in Human Geography* DOI: 10.1177/0309132513516177

Vickery, Michael. 1984. *Cambodia, 1975–1982.* Chiang Mai, Thailand: Silkworm Press.

Winter, Tim. 2007. *Post-Conflict Heritage, Postcolonial Tourism: Culture, Politics and Development at Angkor.* New York: Routledge.

Wolff, Richard. 2012. *Democracy at Work: A Cure for Capitalism.* Chicago: Haymarket Books.

Notes

1 Mam Mot is a pseudonym. Interview with author, July 2013.
2 Much scholarly debate has addressed the question of whether the mass violence that occurred in Cambodia between 1975 and 1979 was *genocidal*. To indicate the still-contested nature of this significant legal question, I utilize 'scare quotes' throughout this chapter.
3 It should be noted that some CPK cadre proposed to re-introduce currency; and that new monies were actually printed. The re-introduction of currency, however, never materialized and those who championed this economic course-of-action were largely executed.
4 Document Number 'D23948' on file at the Documentation Center of Cambodia, Phnom Penh.
5 For a more complete discussion, see Tyner (2014d).
6 This translates into approximately 0.85 kilograms per day.
7 The 'cans' used for measurement were most often Nestle's condensed milk cans; each can could contain approximately 200 grams of rice.
8 Moreover, detailed work-schedules were devised—although not necessarily implemented—that determined how many days of work were required, and for how many days, for society as a whole. In this way, the CPK determined the average amount of surplus that could be produced for the country as a whole.
9 It should not be overlooked that many capitalists in North America, Europe, and elsewhere make these same demands—but with different terminology—of their own workers. In the United States of America, for example, demands for worker-productivity are usually couched in a hyper-patriotism and is supplemented with the exhortation to 'buy American'.

5 Is the Puerto Rican parrot worth saving?

The biopolitics of endangerment and grievability

Irus Braverman

[We must] increase investment in biodiversity conservation by at least an order of magnitude. ... Nevertheless, the total costs are small relative to the value of the potential goods and services that biodiversity provides, e.g., equivalent to 1 to 4 percent of the estimated net value of ecosystem services that are lost per year, estimated at 2 to 6.6 trillion dollars. More prosaically, the total required is less than 20 percent of annual global consumer spending on soft drinks.

(McCarthy et al. 2012, 949)

Between 1999 and 2009, 17.2 million dollars were spent by state and federal agencies toward the conservation of the Puerto Rican parrot (*Amazona vittata*)—an amount exceeding that spent on any other parrot species (USFWS 2012) and on the majority of birds—but a miniscule of the daily expenditures of consumers on soft drinks. What do these figures teach us about the hierarchies of life on this planet? What is more grievable, Pepsi™ or parrot?

The Puerto Rican parrot stands approximately one foot tall, with bright green feathers, a coal black eye surrounded by white, and red face markings (Figure 5.1). The only parrot endemic to Puerto Rico, this bird went from an estimated one million birds prior to European colonization, to between 200 and 250 in the mid-1950s (Vélez, interview). The major reason for the bird's decline is loss of habitat and deforestation: the bird relies on old or decaying trees for nest cavities to rear its young, and 90 percent of Puerto Rico was deforested by the mid-1950s (White et al. 2014, 14). The remaining parrot population was confined to the Luquillo Mountains of northeastern Puerto Rico.

By 1973, the total population of the species numbered only 13 birds, placing it on the brink of extinction by any criteria. At this point, a decision was made to start a breeding population in captivity. "It was a big risk," recalls Jafet Vélez, Iguaca Aviary Manager at Luquillo for the USFWS (interview). To minimize the risk, the team selected eggs and chicks, rather than breeding age adults, and took eleven of those into captivity. All of the captive birds to date are descendants of these eleven founders (Vélez, interview). The first breeding population was established at the Luquillo (now Iguaca) Aviary near the El Yunque Peak in the Caribbean National Forest in 1973. A second

Figure 5.1 A Puerto Rican parrot feeds in a flight cage, Iguaca Aviary, El Yunque
Forest, Puerto Rico. Photo by author, January 14, 2013.

breeding population was established in the José Vivaldi Aviary at Rio Abajo
in 1993. During the first three years, 34 captive-reared birds were released; 20
or so died, mostly due to predation by red-tailed hawks (*Buteo jamaicensis*).

At first, the captive breeding program produced one to three chicks per
year. But by 2000, biologists had become relatively successful at producing
parrots in captivity and by 2014, captive breeding produced between 75 and
100 chicks per year (White et al. 2005, 424). What accounts for this incredible
success is El Yunque's intense reliance on experiments with a closely related
bird: the Hispaniolan Amazon (*Amazona ventralis*) of the Dominican
Republic. Unlike the Puerto Rican parrot, the Hispaniolan is not listed as
endangered and has therefore served as a convenient surrogate for experimentation (White, interview). From 1997 to 1999, 49 Hispaniolan parrots
were released in the Dominican Republic. At first many died, but through
experimentation, a team of scientists learned that the parrot requires both
pre- and post-release management to thrive in the wild, including flight
training before release, acclimation to release sites, and food supplementation
(Collazo et al. 2003). As a result of these findings, for their initial releases
in El Yunque, the Puerto Rican parrots were held for at least four months in
large flight cages before being transferred to acclimation cages at the release

site. Additionally, one month prior to their release, the parrots were allowed to adjust to their surroundings while undergoing a three-phase training to recognize hawks and other threats. Using progressively stronger stimuli—first, a hawk call and a silhouette of a hawk moving in the sky above the cage, then an actual fly-over by a trained hawk, and finally a hawk attacking a tethered (protected) Hispaniolan for the caged parrots to see—the researchers sensitized the parrots to the sights and sounds of hawks. After this experimentation, 84 percent of the parrots showed increased vigilance that would, so the experts hoped, help them survive in the wild (White et al. 2014, 112).

To optimize genetic diversity, the parrots are routinely moved between the wild and captive populations in each aviary as well as between the two aviaries. Olivieri explains: "We move chicks and eggs from one population to another" (interview). For example, infertile wild birds are given captive eggs to foster (Olivieri and Valentin, interviews), and Hispaniolans with a track record of success as foster parents raise eggs from Puerto Rican parrots that have recently laid eggs but have not proven successful at laying fertile eggs, impelling the endangered parrots to lay another clutch, and thus doubling their chance of successful reproduction for the year (Vélez, interview). In addition to knowing, tracking, and monitoring the Puerto Rican parrots to the finest detail, a computer program also recommends their optimal pairing (Vélez, interview).

In 2014, there are 300 parrots in Puerto Rico, 58 to 80 of them living in the wild (Serrano 2012). At the same time, an estimated 225 hawks live within the El Yunque forest, giving it the highest hawk population density in the western hemisphere—and a persistent threat to the released parrots. The red-tailed hawks are legally protected under the Migratory Bird Treaty Act. To negotiate the conflict between the Migratory Act and the Endangered Species Act, a permit was granted through the Migratory Bird Treaty Act that allows the US Fish and Wildlife Service (USFWS) to "take" (in this case, kill) up to 24 hawks a year to protect vulnerable parrots. In the words of one of the program's managers: "[We] carefully monitor fledglings at nest sites when they are most vulnerable and shoot hawks that seem to be about to prey on them. ... The [adults] have survived for many years so they know how to evade the red-tailed hawk, but the babies—they don't" (López-Flores, interview). "We only take it [the hawk] when one of those animals [are] going to take a parrot," another of the program's managers explains (Muñiz, interview).

The parrot–hawk conflict is duplicated across conservation projects around the world and is often a characteristic component of this kind of work—namely, engaging in killing in order to make live. Under this as well as so many other conservation projects, species lives that matter less are made killable in the service of the life of the grievable species. The story of the Puerto Rican parrot's conservation also demonstrates the complex and overlapping legal and economic regimes and the hyperregulation of endangered life. It shows the differential treatment between lives that matter more and are thus funded more generously and assigned higher protection levels (endangered parrots, and fledglings in particular), and those that matter less and are thus less protected (the Hispaniolans and the red-tailed hawks). The species conservation paradigm, while centered on affirmative "make live" projects for threatened species, is thus inevitably a story of violence and death for the not (or less) threatened ones. The threat of extinction is not only a subject of grief but also a motivation to "make live."

A few words on the structure of this chapter. After a brief discussion of the project of governing species through the act of listing, I examine the list as a biopolitical technology and its application to nonhuman animals. Next, I focus on the "mother" of all threatened species lists—the IUCN Red List—and its economic dimensions. Finally, I discuss interrelated incentives such as the lists of the Alliance for Zero Extinction (AZE) and the Evolutionarily Distinct and Globally Endangered (EDGE) of the Zoological Society of London. The ethnographic focus of this chapter conveys the biopolitical paradigm that lies at the heart of species conservation and its underlying economic, regulatory, and ethical convictions.

Governing species

As the Puerto Rican parrot example shows, the act of listing threatened species impacts the life and death of actual, embodied animals. While recognizing these functions and effects on the individual level, this chapter focuses on the management of life at the level of the biological *species*, what Foucault refers to as biopolitics, as distinct from (yet entangled and coproduced with) anatomo-politics (Foucault 1990). In other words, I examine how the practices of assessing and listing nonhuman species translate into particular knowledges of species, as connected with, yet distinct from, knowledges of individual animals and populations. I also explore how economic logics intersect and impact such knowledges.

The project of governing species sits somewhere between that of governing individuals and that of governing statistical populations—and corresponds with both (Braverman 2015, 196). Unlike Foucault's abstract population (which, I should point out, is different from the understanding of a population in the conservation context, typically as a unit smaller than a species), a species has a face and a context; it is situated—as becomes clear from the narratives of conservation experts. Put differently, thinking and governing through species regimes enables both an abstraction—a grid over the Linnaean kingdoms (Foucault 1970)—and an embodiment: a personification of ecosystems, habitats, and populations. Since humans understand themselves primarily as a species and therefore both relate to, and differentiate themselves from, other species—it is important to critically examine this lens and the work that it performs in the world (ibid.).

For conservation scientists, the species is the foundational ontological unit for knowing and calculating life, or viability (Braverman 2014; 2015; Sandler 2012). Biermann and Mansfield reflect on the perspective of conservation experts that: "Managing individual nonhuman lives is meaningless in responding to the crisis of biodiversity loss; individual lives acquire meaning only when they advance the long-term well being of the broader population or are essential to sustaining key biological processes, especially evolution" (2014, 264). According to this way of thinking, the death of an individual gains meaning and grievability status according to the level of endangerment of the species: once on the brink of extinction, for example, the individual becomes larger than a singular life, and her or his death is therefore more grievable than a singular death: it becomes the death of a life form, the death of nature (Braverman 2015, 231). While many scholars theorize grievable life in the context of the individual, this project importantly documents the ways in which grievability occurs at the scale of the species. What does it mean for *Homo sapiens* to grieve the loss of a nonhuman species? How might this type of grief differ from a sense of grief about the loss of biodiversity more generally? And what role does grief play in differentiating between species and creating a hierarchy of grievable life, whereby certain species get legal protection and financial support—but others do not?

Alongside the affirmative "make live" emphasis of threatened species lists, the deaths of so many other life forms who are not rare, charismatic, or visible enough to warrant the "threatened" designation fall outside the range of protections established by the list, or outside the list altogether (Braverman 2015, 229). Such life forms are effectively "list-less": incalculable, unmemorable, and thus killable. Toward the end of this chapter, I argue that the conservation value of a species is defined through its inclusion and rank in an increasing number of lists and that the power of such lists is constantly eroded as new lists take their place in defining what is even more threatened, endangered, or extinct.

Foucault refers to the project of differentiating between what must live and what must die as "racism," as I shall explain shortly. This chapter provides a more nuanced reading of Foucault's 'racism,' and how it extends to nonhuman animals. It points to the speciesism in Foucault's framing of biopolitics and racism, putting forward a discussion of these concepts that is anti-speciesist. Specifically, my project illuminates the immense regulatory and economic powers of threatened species lists and their heightened focus on, and differentiation of, life. I argue that in addition to reinforcing the biopolitical differentiation between perceivably distinct nonhuman species, threatened species lists also reinforce the biopolitical differentiation between human and nonhuman species, with the human never being subject to the threatened list. Such a differentiated, or 'racial,' treatment of the life and death of species through their en-listing, down- and up-listing, multi-listing, and un-listing translates into the positive protection and active management of nonhumans. Threatened species lists are thus biopolitical technologies in the battle against biological extinction. Listing threatened species becomes a way to affirm—and justify—that life which is more and most important to save.

While an increasing portion of biopolitical work is centered on thanatopolitics or necropolitics, my project brings into focus an affirmative biopolitics

(Braidotti 2013; Rutherford and Rutherford 2013, 426), namely "the ways in which biopolitics can be more about life than death, about inclusion rather than exclusion" (Rutherford and Rutherford 2013, 429). What happens to those list-less lives that fall outside the realm of the threatened list does not figure within this account, which focuses instead on the viability of the listed. But such a focus on the affirmative does not entail a disavowal of death. Quite the contrary, as Biermann and Mansfield argue, "to *make live* does not mean to avoid death altogether but to manage death at the level of the population. In a biopolitical regime, death is transformed into a rate of mortality, which is open to intervention and management. This transformation erases the fact that not all life is equally promoted" (2014, 259). For the list-less, the rule is typically the non-application of protection and the phasing out of support, although it can include much more explicitly sovereign methods when pertaining to certain species, especially those that threaten the purity of the listed (e.g. Gila and rainbow trout or crested and marine toads; Braverman 2015, 27, 107). But while the Red List's redness is intended to alert us of the dire state of those species that are listed as threatened and to the intensified management of their mortality rates, it fails to alert us of those species and individual animals who have been marginalized in the process of saving the chosen ones (Braverman 2015).

The biopolitics of species conservation

Michel Foucault's concept "biopower" helps make sense of conservation's extensive use of species ontology and the focus on calculations of rarity in practices of listing life. In the pre-modern period, sovereign power was characterized by the "the right to decide life and death," that is, the right to *take* life or *let* live (Foucault 1990, 135–6). Foucault argues that this ancient right has been replaced by a "power to *foster* life or *disallow* it to the point of death" (1990, 138). He defines this new "power over life"—which he sees as emerging in the eighteenth century with the development of bourgeois society and capitalism—as "biopower." In his words: "Power would no longer be dealing simply with legal subjects over whom the ultimate dominion was death, but with living beings, and the mastery it would be able to exercise over them would have to be applied at the level of life itself; it is the taking charge of life, more than the threat of death, that gave power its access even to the body" (1990, 142–3). Power, Foucault argues, no longer has death as its focus, but rather the administration of the living: "Such a power has to qualify, measure, appraise, and hierarchize, rather than display itself in its murderous splendor" (1990, 144).

Although Foucault uses the term biopower to describe the project of governing *human* bodies, populations, and life (see also Rabinow and Rose 2006; Rose 2001), my work draws on growing scholarship that expands this notion to the governing of nonhuman animal species and populations (Friese 2013; Haraway 2008; Rutherford and Rutherford 2013; Shukin 2009; Wolfe 2013).

Within this scholarship, limited attention has been paid to the role of race in the biopolitical differentiation of nonhuman life (but see Biermann and Mansfield 2014, 261).

Foucault refers to the break between the livable and killable as "racism." According to this definition, the death of the other improves life as a whole. In other words, death is a means to foster life. Foucault writes: "racism justifies the death-function in the economy of biopower by appealing to the principle that the death of others makes one biologically stronger insofar as one is a member of a race or population, insofar as one is an element in a unitary living plurality" (2003, 258). He continues: "The enemies who have to be done away with are not adversaries in the political sense of the term; they are threats, either external or internal, to the population" (2003, 256).

The project of racism, as Foucault defines it, is crucial for explaining the distinction between list-less and listed life. The source of the difference between human- and nonhuman-focused lists is evident when examining them through a biopolitical lens: according to Foucault, only (certain) humans are privileged with political life. Animals and plants, along with all that is considered natural or wild, are relegated to the realm of biological life—namely, that which is killable. By contrast, this chapter applies the distinction between biological and political life also to the nonhuman context. I argue that through their listing as threatened, certain species' lives are elevated to a political status, while the rest (initially at least, the unlisted) remain biological, or mere, life (Braverman 2015).

Unlike for Foucault, however, in the context of threatened species management, the "list-less" population is ostensibly that which is *not threatened*, and not necessarily that which threatens. Rather than posing a biopolitical threat to the flourishing of listed populations, certain list-less populations simply remain killable, whereas the threatened ones are elevated into a grievable status. However, certain list-less species are downgraded to the category of "invasive," "hybrid," or "nuisance," posing a more typically biopolitical threat to the purity of the protected species. These inter-species threats become subject to forms of control by humans, such as elimination or purity management (Braverman 2015). Threatened species lists are about creating, calculating, and re-performing that line between nonhuman lives that are killable and those lives that must be cultivated and that are grievable.

The IUCN Red List for Threatened Species™

IUCN's Red List is the first modern comprehensive global attempt at listing threatened species. The IUCN has been producing Red Data Books and Red Lists since 1963 (Lamoreux et al. 2003, 215). Despite the insistence on the part of many IUCN scientists that the Red List is not prescriptive (Hoffmann, interview), all agree that it has had profound influence on conservation practices and practitioners around the world (Possingham et al. 2002; Rodrigues et al. 2006). Specifically, the Red List has inspired the development of numerous national and regional red lists and functions as an important source for the Convention on International Trade in Endangered Species of Wild Fauna and Flora (CITES)—a powerful international convention on trade (Miller 2013) that determines whether and how trade in certain species will be regulated.

The Red List is by far the most influential and widely used method for evaluating global extinction risk. It has been in use for five decades, and has evolved during this period from a subjective, expert-based system lacking standardized criteria to a uniform rule-based system (Miller 2013, 195; Mace et al. 2008). The IUCN revised its risk-ranking system into data-driven quantitative criteria in 1994 and finalized these categories and criteria in 2001 (IUCN 2001a; see also Mace et al. 2008). The current system is designed to provide "a standardized, consistent, and transparent method for assessing extinction risk, thereby increasing the objectivity and scientific credibility of the assessments" (Miller 2013, 195).

The Red List classifies taxa into nine categories: Extinct, Extinct in the Wild, Critically Endangered, Endangered, Vulnerable, Near Threatened, Least Concern, Data Deficient, and Not Evaluated (IUCN 2001b). The system consists of one set of criteria that are applicable to all species and that measure the symptoms of endangerment (but not the causes). The three IUCN Red List threatened categories are Critically Endangered, Endangered, and Vulnerable. Five criteria, listed A through E, are used to categorize a taxon within these threatened categories. Although the other categories are formally listed, they are not assessed in the same manner, hence being "less" listed, or "list-less." The threatened criteria are: A) a reduction in population size; B) a small, reduced, fragmented, or fluctuating geographic range; C) a decline in size of an already small population; D) a very small or restricted population; and E) a quantitative analysis indicating the probability of extinction. To be listed as Critically Endangered, for example, a species must decline by 90 percent or more, cover less than $100km^2$, or consist of fewer than 50 mature individuals (IUCN 2001b). A species need only satisfy one criterion to be listed. Each of these categories contains a list of species, which can be traced in the Red List's online database, with one exception: the category of Not Evaluated includes no taxa (IUCN 2013a), literally establishing a list-less life. List-less, because when a species is not evaluated, it is devoid of human protection, thereby remaining mere life. Generally speaking, then, the further the species is ranked away from the Extinct category, the more unseen it is from the list's perspective and the more killable it is, and vice versa.

Watson says generally about the rigid criteria of the Red List, and of threatened lists more generally, that: "At the end of the day, all listings are arbitrary: they're not driven by the laws of physics, they're actually created … by humans trying their best to develop the most appropriate categories according to the best available knowledge" (interview). Yet alongside its reliance on fixed and rigid standards, the Red List also enables flexibility and change. Accordingly, the number of species listed in each category changes

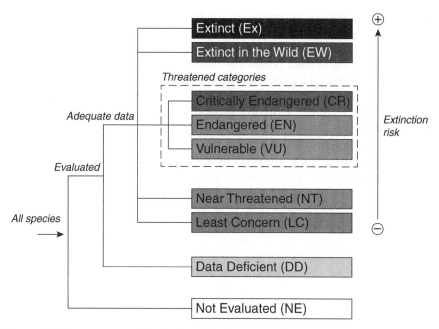

Figure 5.2 The structure of the IUCN Red List Categories, reprinted from http://www.
iucnredlist.org/static/categories_criteria_3_1. Source: The IUCN Red List
of Threatened Species © IUCN.

every time it is updated (on the books, every five years). This is a result of
various factors, including species being assessed for the first time, species
being reassessed and moved into a different category of threat, and taxonomic
revisions. The IUCN distinguishes genuine (namely, real changes in threat
levels) from non-genuine (namely, technical changes in threat levels that result
from error, taxonomic revisions, or changes in threshold definitions) reasons
for revising the listing (IUCN 2013b). The ever-changing nature of the list
makes it even more powerful, as no protection, or un-protection, is ever fixed
or settled and thus there is constant reliance on the listing process.

In its aspiration to comprehensiveness, simplicity, comparability, con-
sistency, objectivity, and credibility, the Red List is a perfect example of the
effectiveness of the list as a biopolitical technology. By 2013, the IUCN Species Survival Commission network—which is comprised of thousands of scientists and experts from around the world—evaluated the global threat status
of 71,576 species of animals, plants, and fungi (IUCN 2013c). The aim: to
assess and appropriately categorize every living species (IUCN 2001b). Mike
Hoffmann clarifies, accordingly, that the Red List of Threatened Species is in
fact not just about threatened species, but about *all* species. "You can't talk
about the status of biodiversity globally unless you've assessed everything," he
says. Nonetheless, he is first to admit that "we have lots of biases," explaining
that the system is "still very much biased towards vertebrates" and that

"plants, fungi, and invertebrates are underrepresented" (interview). "We've got a long way to go," he says about the current state of the Red List.

Generally, the assumption is that the simpler the categories and criteria, the more they can be applied across the board to the various taxa on the list. Indeed, the criteria and categories "are designed to apply whether you are a mammal or a bird or a fungus or a plant or whatever you are" (Hoffmann, interview). For example, Criterion D requires a threshold of fewer than 50 mature individuals (IUCN 2001b); this number applies to all taxa, from fungi to whales. The application of scale in the IUCN criteria of geographic range (Criterion B) surfaces the problems of this "one size fits all" approach. The IUCN cautions that: "The choice of scale at which range is estimated may thus, itself, influence the outcome of Red List assessments and could be a source of inconsistency and bias. It is impossible to provide any strict but general rules for mapping taxa or habitats; the most appropriate scale will depend on the taxon in question, and the origin and comprehensiveness of the distribution data" (IUCN 2001b).

Nonetheless, the central idea of the Red List "was to come up with one system that is applicable across all taxa, and you can therefore make *comparisons* across your different taxonomic groups" (Hoffmann, interview). In addition to the heightened comparability between different taxa, the Red List provides comparability within a particular taxon over time. It makes possible grand calculations such as this one: "On average, 52 species of mammals, birds, and amphibians move one category closer to extinction each year"; or this: "the deterioration for amphibians was equivalent to 662 amphibian species each moving one Red List category closer to extinction over the assessment period, the deteriorations for birds and mammals equate to 223 and 156 species, respectively, deteriorating at least one category" (Hoffmann et al. 2010, 1507).

The Red List's power lies also in its touted objectivity, transparency, and repeatability (namely, that if another expert were to conduct the assessment he or she would reach the same listing conclusion; Brooks, interview). According to Hoffmann, the biggest source of bias is when scientists want to list "their" species as threatened, "because they're worried that if it's not, they're not going to get money." The reverse also happens, with researchers who prefer that their species be listed as Least Concern "so that they can collect their species, put it in a specimen jar, and do research on it." "Our job," Hoffmann tells me, "is to be the neutral, objective, adjudicators of that process." IUCN's Standards and Petitions Subcommittee is the particular adjudicator in cases of disagreement over a Red List designation. According to Hoffmann, they are "the experts in the criteria, and what they say ... would essentially be considered gospel" (interview).

This brings me to the issue of the Red List's credibility. Barney Long is director of Species Protection and Asian Species Conservation at the World Wildlife Fund and a member of the IUCN World Commission on Protected Areas. Long tells me, "[W]hen you say this species is red listed by the IUCN

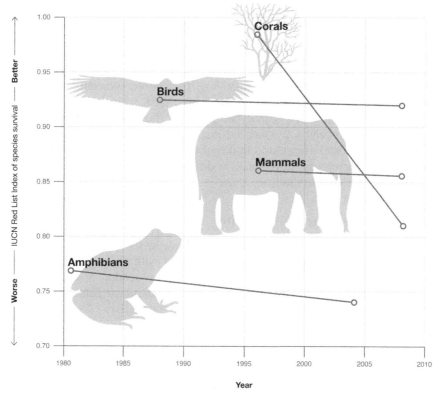

Figure 5.3 The IUCN states that, "Coral species are moving towards increased extinction risk most rapidly, while amphibians are, on average, the most threatened group." From http://www.iucnredlist.org/about/summary-statistics.
Source: The IUCN Red List of Threatened Species © IUCN.

as Critically Endangered, everyone automatically agrees and accepts that.
There's no conversation, because the experts have agreed that it is Critically
Endangered" (interview). Today, the IUCN Red List is considered one of the
most authoritative sources of information on the global conservation status of
plants and animals (Lamoreux et al. 2003). Its reach has extended into
numerous national and international regulatory systems. According to Miller,
76 countries use the IUCN methodology for their national red lists (Miller
2013, 197). Hence, "[f]rom its origins as a general interest in rare and declining wildlife, the science of threatened species assessment has blossomed into a
massive conservation theme with far-reaching influence on conservation on
the ground" (Miller 2013, 200).

But there are also adverse effects to certain listings. Brian Horne, turtle
conservation coordinator at the Wildlife Conservation Society, tells me in an
interview that collectors often "want the rare, and the unusual and different."
Hence, when turtle breeders learned that a certain turtle species was soon to

be listed under CITES' Appendix I, their prices increased dramatically. "The turtle went from being a hundred dollar turtle to [costing] one thousand dollars." Another result is that once a species is downlisted (the term used to indicate that it has become less threatened), "you become a victim of your own success ... because suddenly there's less funding sources available," which could in turn easily translate into less protection (Bennett, interview). Another example is that the price of rhino horn on Korean markets increased by more than 400 percent within two years of their uplisting from CITES Appendix II to Appendix I, which in turn coincided with a sharp increase in the poaching of black rhinos and in illegal trade in rhino horn (Rivalan 2007, 530). The listing process thus makes a difference for the lives of animals in myriad, at times counterintuitive, ways.

The economies of endangered life

"Why save endangered species?" asks a brochure by the U.S. Fish and Wildlife Service (USFWS 2005), the agency charged with enforcing the Endangered Species Act, which establishes the American version of a threatened species list. Alongside the myriad biological and emotional benefits, the brochure emphasizes an array of economic reasons, stating that: "No matter how small or obscure a species, it could one day be of direct importance to us all." A central economic benefit of saving species is for the pharmaceutical industry: "it was 'only' a fungus that gave us penicillin, and certain plants have yielded substances used in drugs to treat heart disease, cancer, and a variety of other illnesses. More than a quarter of all prescriptions written annually in the United States contain chemicals discovered in plants and animals. If these organisms had been destroyed before their unique chemistries were known, their secrets would have died with them." The "make live" of nonhuman species is thereby rendered beneficial for the "make live" of humans. In addition to the medical benefits, the brochure also details a variety of agricultural ones, finally noting that wildlife watching in the U.S. "generated 85 billion dollars in economic benefits to the nation in 2001" (2005).

Mike Parr is the Chair of the Alliance for Zero Extinction as well as the Vice President of Planning and Program Development at the American Bird Conservancy. Parr argues for the importance of lists beyond their economic value. "There's a value to it that is not economic; it's intangible, probably," he tells me in our interview, concluding: "if we don't do something about it now, people will find that hole that's left in our collective soul and be mournful of it" (interview). From Parr's perspective, acts of listing life are tied to our essential biophilic needs and desires as humans. The process of listing a species as threatened thus elevates that species from a killable to a grievable status.

The use of species as the foundational unit of threatened lists, effectively rendering them the "currency of conservation" (Lamoreux, interview), is not only ideological but also pragmatic. First, threatened species are "among the most visible and easily understood symbols of the rising tide of extinctions," making them an "emotive and politically powerful measurement of biodiversity loss" (Miller 2013, 192; see also Wilson 1992; Wilcove 2010). In other words, species are the personalization—the individuation even—of populations and ecosystems. Using the species scale thus enables conservationists to put a face onto less apparent extinction processes and losses. Additionally, species are the most common and easily quantifiable unit for assessing the state and the costs of biodiversity.

The lists' utilization of the species unit not only implies equality among species but also their comparability. The Red List, for example, is "applied to grasshoppers as well as blue whales," Lamoreux tells me. "There's something about the applicability across all groups that's just truly amazing," he adds. Yet some listed species end up being more equal than others. Lamoreux explains, for example, that, "even if you list a whole lot of dragonflies on the Red List, they're not going to suddenly get as much attention as a panda." He clarifies: "they're not all equal in the eyes of conservation funding or conservation action" (interview). James Watson is president-elect of the Society of Conservation Biology and head of Climate Change Project at the World Conservation Society. Watson points out that of 1,600 species on the Australian threatened list, only 35 percent receive government funding for conservation. "The things which get money are birds and mammals, and the things which don't get money are butterflies and plants," he tells me in an interview. The economic logic of fundable species conservation projects is thus dictated by, and entangled with, the species' level of grievability, in turn resulting in the racial differentiation between threatened species. Indeed, even the listing of a species as threatened does not promise it equal protection in relation to other listed species. Various criteria, and less formal lists, in fact determine which species are more or less worth saving.

Threatened species lists are now everywhere. National agencies routinely make choices on resource allocation among species based on these lists, typically allotting more funding to species listed in the highest threat categories (Possingham et al. 2002, 503). And although the Red List administrators insist that the list is scientific and apolitical and does not establish priorities between species, conservation biologist Arne Mooers tells me that even "the conservation community mistakenly considers probabilities of extinction as representing worth" (interview). For this reason, certain conservation scientists have been advocating for alternative or additional lists that openly justify the differentiation and prioritization between species, as I shall discuss shortly.

Conservationists show that saving endangered species is economically wise; but how much would it cost to save them—and are they worth this investment? In a 2012 article in the prestigious journal *Science*, Stuart Butchart and colleagues attempted to answer these and related questions (McCarthy et al. 2012). To assess the costs of species conservation, they sampled 211 globally threatened bird species (19 percent of all threatened bird species on the Red List), asking experts to estimate the costs for conservation actions needed to achieve the minimum improvement in status necessary to reclassify ("downlist") each species to the next lowest category of extinction risk on the Red List. Based on this assessment, the study estimated the cost of reducing the extinction risk of all globally threatened bird species by one Red List category to be approximately one billion dollars every year for the next decade. The scientists found that only 12 percent of this amount is currently funded. They further indicate that:

> Even with increased investment, careful prioritization will continue to be necessary to inform decisions about which areas to protect and which actions to undertake for species. … Our finding that species facing higher categories of extinction risk require less investment for downlisting than do those in lower categories suggests that in many cases such analyses will prioritize actions for the most-threatened species first. We also note that there is considerable global spatial variation in costs and the number of threatened species per unit area. Although the shortfalls in higher-income countries are substantial, the greatest gains per dollar will be in lower-income countries. Despite the limitations of the available data, the shortfalls we have identified clearly highlight the need to increase investment in biodiversity conservation by at least an order of magnitude, especially given the small, but growing, body of evidence linking spending and effectiveness. A particular challenge will be how to address the current mismatch between the greater resources available in richer countries and the higher potential conservation gains in financially poor, biodiversity-rich countries.
>
> (McCarthy 2012, 949)

This text exposes but a tip of the iceberg from the complexities of calculating conservation costs and funding on a global scale, illuminating some of the nuances of how conservation is affected by the disparity between poor and rich countries. The article concludes more generally that: "Resolving the ongoing conservation funding crisis is urgent; it is likely that, the longer that investments in conservation are delayed, the more the costs will grow and the greater will be the difficulty of successfully meeting the targets" (ibid.).

Clearly, the economic dimensions of species conservation are an important and highly complicated, yet surprisingly understudied, part of the biopolitical project of endangerment. Hoffmann tells me along these lines: "there are not many studies that investigate, quantitatively, the impact of listings" (interview). He notes two exceptions: in the United States, recent analyses of recovery plans based on Endangered Species Act listings suggest that there is a positive relationship between funding and trends in species status, and a study of threatened bird recovery programs in Australia for the period between 1993 and 2000 found that where funds have been dedicated to the conservation management of threatened bird taxa, they have produced positive results. "Although more threatened birds declined than increased," the Australian study noted, "many stayed stable over the study period when they might otherwise have become more threatened or gone extinct" (Garnett et al. 2003, 664).

Other lists

The last two decades have witnessed an explosion of national lists of threatened and endangered species (see, e.g., de Grammont and Cuarón 2006, 22). In 2010, at least 109 countries had produced a national red data book, national red list, or other national list of threatened species (Miller 2013, 198), and at least 25 listing systems of threatened species were used across North America (2013, 192). Of the myriad threatened species lists, Miller writes, some "are designed purely to evaluate risk of extinction, whereas others focus on ranking species to receive priority conservation attention" (2013, 194).

Yet alongside the proliferation of lists, a critique of existing listing processes has also emerged. In the words of James Watson: "The conservation field is dominated by ecologists who really like to make lists." But "conservation is also not just about *listing* something," he continues, "it is about *doing* something." "This is not a failure of the list itself," he explains, "it's the failure of the conservation community to develop other metrics beyond the list" (interview). Joseph et al. (2009) argue along these lines that existing approaches in conservation typically "ignore two crucial factors: the cost of management and the likelihood that the management will succeed" (2009, 328; see also Bottrill et al. 2011; Possingham et al. 2002; Walsh et al. 2012).

If the Red List focuses on identifying threatened species, other lists supplement this by identifying alternative targets for maintaining biodiversity. The Alliance for Zero Extinction (AZE) has identified 588 sites that serve as the single remaining location for species listed as Endangered or Critically Endangered under the IUCN Red List (AZE 2013). Of 20,934 of such species, the AZE has mapped 920 species, implying that these are the world's *most* threatened species (AZE 2013). Mike Hoffman explains that, "These are the places where, if you don't do something here, now, for this species, you're going to lose a species" (interview).

In 2013, the AZE released the results of the public poll for the winners of its "7 Wonders" campaign, which highlighted the seven *most* representative sites and species around the world (Figure 5.4). The press release described a few of the seven selected species: "A two-inch long frog so deadly that its toxin could kill ten people; a bat that is called a flying fox with males that defend a harem of up to eight females; and an enigmatic, fist-sized owl that was discovered in 1976 only not to be seen again for 26 years" (AZE 2013). "This is really a story of survival, not one of extinction," director Mike Parr was quoted saying, "but we must recognize that many of these species do still need an extra helping hand if they are to survive into the future'" (AZE 2013). The focus of the listing project is, again, on life rather than death. This is an affirmative biopolitics that promotes nonhuman survival and that resists

Figure 5.4 AZE's 7 Wonders poster. Credits clockwise from upper right: Juan Fernandez
        Firecrown by P. Hodum; Lear's Macaw by Ciro Ginez Albano; Long-
        whiskered Owlet by ECOAN; Roti Island snake-necked turtle by Anders G.J.
        Rhodin; Siberian Crane by Gunnar Pettersson; Golden poison frog by
        ProAves; Rodrigues flying fox by Vladimir Motyuka. Courtesy of Mike Parr.

extinction based on human care and founded on detailed calculations. Conservation's extensive "trust in numbers" is reflected in the narrative that
describes the selected species (2 inches, 10 people, 8 females, 26 years).

Another listing initiative that has emerged in recent years is EDGE of the
Zoological Society of London (ZSL), which focuses on Red List species that
possess a significant amount of unique evolutionary history. The EDGE idea
draws on the phylogenetic diversity (PD) concept (Faith 2013). From the ZSL
website: "We have scored the world's mammals and amphibians according to
how Evolutionarily Distinct and Globally Endangered (EDGE) they are."
"These are the world's most extraordinary threatened species," the website
notes, "yet most are unfamiliar and not currently receiving conservation
attention" (EDGE 2013).

However, biodiversity expert Arne Mooers tells me that the PD framework
could provide a more dynamic—and thus a better—list than EDGE because
of its ability to run multiple scenarios with various sets of groups. Mooers
provides the example of the kiwi bird from New Zealand to explain the differences between PD and EDGE listings. There are three kiwi species that
"aren't related to anything else on the planet," he says, which determines their
high PD score. "But even though as a group, they are fifty million years …
distantly related to everything else, amongst themselves they're surprisingly
closely related," he explains. "So if you saved any one of them, and let the
other two go extinct, … all [of] the 'kiwiness' would still be there, in that one
species" (interview). Mooers tells me, accordingly, that all three species rank
highly on the EDGE list, but that the result would be different under a PD
analysis. In his words: "you might be wasting your time trying to conserve all
three of them, when really you should conserve only one."

The "making live" and "letting die" decisions embedded in the kiwi
example demonstrate the function of lists as technologies for triage decision
making. "Like in emergency medicine, triage involves using criteria to assess
priority and make life or death decisions, not about human beings but about
the futures of entire species" (Biermann and Mansfield 2014, 266). In this
particular context, the triage was dictated by the evolutionary uniqueness of

the species. The reason for all triage decisions is limited resources; if resources were bountiful, one assumes, all valued lives would be saved. But unlike triage decisions in the human context, where higher chances of survival (rather than biological, economic, and social importance, for example) determine the decision, in the case of endangered species often the most threatened species (namely, the one with the highest risk of dying out) receives the highest conservation priority.

Epilogue: the politics of listed (and list-less) life

Traditionally, animals and plants—along with all that is considered natural or wild—have been confined to the realm of biological life: namely, to that which is killable. Conversely, humans have been privileged with political life. This chapter has described how species lists elevate listed nonhuman species from the realm of biological life into that of a political life worth saving: laws are put in place to protect life forms belonging to threatened species from being killed or harmed, databases are configured around their most recent census, costs are calculated and funding is allotted according to complex factors, and those last individuals of such species who die despite the efforts are deeply grieved. My study of threatened species lists thus provides a novel perspective on biopower that highlights both its affirmative properties and its acute relevance for understanding the management of entire nonhuman species, offering a critical examination of the species as a governable unit.

The focus of the listing project is on a species' *life* rather than on its *death*. At the same time, it is also about figuring out which species life should be privileged in this endeavor, and which can be let or made to die. But rather than a bifurcated understanding of life versus death, threatened species lists parse the life of species into much more complicated orderings according to their risk of extinction. The endangered list thus not only oscillates between life and death, or between political and biological life; it also elevates certain nonhuman species over others, effectively establishing a gradation of animal bodies that are more or less worthy of living and grieving.

This chapter has explored but a few of the myriad threatened species lists that are currently proliferating in various organizational and regulatory platforms. In particular, I have focused on the IUCN Red List for Threatened Species, the foundation of all modern threatened species lists. Despite their common origin, the various lists differ in their perspective on what is most important about life and thus on what is most worth saving, whether rarity in numbers, unique territorial configurations, evolutionary (phylogenetic) variation, or high viability rates. Even among those species who are deemed threatened, then, categories and criteria prioritize the ones who are perceived to be *the most threatened of all*: those whose lives are even more, and finally most, worth saving.

The Puerto Rican parrot is one such example. In 1973, there were only 13 Puerto Rican parrots left in the world. After four decades of intensive work and an investment of millions of tax dollars, 300 parrots have survived. During the same period, many other endangered birds became extinct. Why save the parrot rather than other endangered birds? And how much is the Puerto Rican parrot species worth or, in other words: what is this species' projected grievabililty level if it becomes extinct?

In 2011, leading Australian ecologist Corey Bradshaw and his colleagues challenged the tendency in conservation to invest in iconic and charismatic species who live on the brink of extinction, calling instead for the application of a mathematical Species' Ability to Forestall Extinction (SAFE) index that reflects the species' level of viability and its risk of extinction (Clements et al. 2011). Bradshaw's argument became highly contentious because he was quoted as suggesting that it might not be worth trying to save the kakapo (*Strigops habroptilus*), a critically endangered native New Zealand bird that has been on the brink of extinction for decades (Science Media Centre 2011). Bradshaw clarified his position: "Some species require an enormous amount of resource investment to make them even survive in the low levels that they already are at." "I am just questioning whether species like that deserve millions of dollars in investment," he concluded (Radio Live 2011). Such and many other species conservation debates are illustrative of the biopolitical logics of listing and of the complex relationship between killability, grievability, and endangerment that govern them.

Acknowledgments

I would like to thank Mike Hoffmann, Mike Parr, and Tom Brooks for their time and patience, and Kathryn Gillespie and Patricia Lopez for their insightful comments. Research for this chapter was funded by the American Council of Learned Societies' Charles A. Ryskamp Research Fellowship and by the Baldy Center for Law & Social Policy. Portions of the chapter were adapted from *Wild Life: The Institution of Nature* (Stanford, 2015) and from "En-Listing life: Red is the color of threatened species lists". In *Critical Animal Geographies*, edited by Rosemarie Collard and Kathryn Gillespie (Routledge/Earthscan, 2015).

Interviews

Bennett, Elizabeth. Vice President for Species Conservation, Wildlife Conservation Society. In person, New York City, NY, December 20, 2013.

Brooks, Tom. Head, Science and Knowledge Unit, IUCN. Telephone, January 25, 2014.

Hoffmann, Michael. Senior Scientific Officer. Species Survival Commission, IUCN. Skype, January 9, 2014; email communication, March 27, 2014.

Horne, Brian. Turtle conservation coordinator, Wildlife Conservation Society. Telephone, January 9, 2014.

Lamoreux, John. Biodiversity Analyst, National Fish and Wildlife Foundation. Telephone, January 7, 2014.

Lees, Caroline. Convener, CBSG-Australasia. Skype, May 20, 2013.

Long, Barney. Director, Species Protection and Asian Species Conservation, World Wildlife Fund. Telephone, January 9, 2014.

López-Flores, Marisel. Project leader, Puerto Rican Parrot Recovery Program, USFWS. On-site, Iguaca Aviary, PR, January 14, 2014.

Mooers, Arne. Professor of conservation biology, Simon Fraser University. Skype, January 6, 2014.

Muñiz, Edwin E. Field supervisor, Caribbean ES Field Office, USFWS. On-site, Iguaca Aviary, PR, January 14, 2014.

Olivieri, Gustavo. Coordinator, José Vivaldi Aviary, Puerto Rican Parrot Reintroduction Program. On-site, Río Abajo State Forest, January 22, 2014.

Parr, Mike. Secretary, Alliance for Zero Extinction; Vice President of Planning and Program Development, American Bird Conservancy. Skype, December 23, 2013.

Valentin, Ricardo. Coordinator, José Vivaldi Aviary, Puerto Rican Parrot Reintroduction Program. On-site, Río Abajo State Forest, PR, January 22, 2014.

Vélez, Jafet. Wildlife biologist, Iguaca Aviary, US Fish and Wildlife Service. On-site, Iguaca Aviary, PR, January 14, 2014.

Watson, James. President-elect, Society of Conservation Biology; Head, Climate Change Program, Wildlife Conservation Society, Skype, January 27, 2014.

White Jr., Thomas H. Wildlife biologist, Puerto Rican Parrot Recovery Program, USFWS. On-site, Iguaca Aviary, Puerto Rico, January 14, 2014.

References

AZE. 2013. *Alliance for Zero Extinction.* Viewed 2 November 2013. http://www.zeroextinction.org.

Biermann, Christine and Becky Mansfield. 2014. "Biodiversity, purity, and death: conservation biology as biopolitics." *Environment and Planning D: Society and Space* 32(2): 257–273.

Bottrill, Madeleine C., Jessica C. Wash, James E.M. Watson, Liana N. Joseph, Alejandro Ortega-Argueta, and Hugh P. Possingham. 2011. "Does recovery planning improve the status of threatened species?" *Biological Conservation* 144 (5): 1595–1601.

Bowker, Geoffrey C. and Susan Leigh Star. 1999. *Sorting Things Out: Classification and Its Consequences.* Cambridge: MIT Press.

Braidotti, Rosi. 2013. *The Posthuman.* Cambridge: Polity Press.

Braverman, Irus. 2014. "Governing the wild: Databases, algorithms, and population models as biopolitics." *Surveillance & Society* 12 (1): 15–37.

——2015. *Wild Life: The Institution of Nature.* Stanford: Stanford University Press.

Clements, Gopalasamy Reuben, Corey J.A. Bradshaw, Barry W. Brook, and William F. Laurance. 2011. The SAFE index: using a threshold population target to measure relative species threat. *Frontiers in Ecology and the Environment* 9 (9): 521–525.

Collazo, Jaime A., Thomas H. White, Jr., Francisco J. Vilella, and Simón A. Guerrero. 2003. "Survival of captive-reared Hispaniolan Parrots released in Parque Nacional del Este, Dominican Republic." *The Condor* 105 (2): 198–207.

EDGE. 2013. *EDGE: Evolutionarily Distinct and Globally Endangered.* Viewed 26 January 2014. http://www.edgeofexistence.org.

Faith, Daniel P. 2013. "Biodiversity and evolutionary history: useful extensions of the PD phylogenetic diversity assessment framework." *Annals of the New York Academy of Sciences* 1289: 69–89.

Foucault, Michel. 1970. *The Order of Things: An Archeology of the Human Sciences.* New York: Vintage Books.

——1990. *The History of Sexuality: An Introduction, Volume 1.* New York: Vintage Books.

——2003. *Society Must Be Defended: Lectures at the College de France, 1975–1976.* London: Allen Lane.

Friese, Carrie. 2013. *Cloning Wildlife: Zoos, Captivity, and the Future of Endangered Animals.* New York: NYU Press.

Garnett, Stephen, Gabriel Crowley, and Andrew Balmford. 2003. "The Costs and Effectiveness of Funding the Conservation of Australian Threatened Birds." *BioScience* 53 (7): 658–665.

de Grammont, Paloma C. and Alfredo D. Cuarón. 2006. "An evaluation of threatened species categorization systems used on the American continent." *Conservation Biology* 20 (1): 14–27.

Haraway, Donna. 2008. *When Species Meet.* Minneapolis: University of Minnesota Press.

Hinchliffe, Steve and Nick Bingham. 2008. "Securing life: The emerging practices of biosecurity." *Environment and Planning A* 40 (7): 1534–1551.

Hoffmann, Michael, Craig Hilton-Taylor, Ariadne Angulo, Monika Böhm, Thomas M. Brooks, and Stuart H. M. Butchart et al. 2010. "The impact of conservation on the status of the world's vertebrates." *Science* 330 (6010): 1503–1509.

IUCN. 2001a. *Summary of the Five Criteria (A-E) Used to Evaluate if a Taxon Belongs in an IUCN Red List Threatened Category (Critically Endangered, Endangered or Vulnerable).* Viewed 26 January 2014. http://www.iucnredlist.org/documents/2001CatsCrit_Summary_EN.pdf.

——2001b. *IUCN Red List Categories and Criteria Version 3.1.* Gland, Switzerland and Cambridge, United Kingdom: IUCN Species Survival Commission, IUCN.

——2013a. *Table 4a: Red List Category Summary for All Animal Classes and Orders.* Updated 21 November 2013. http://cmsdocs.s3.amazonaws.com/summarystats/2013_2_RL_Stats_Table4a.pdf (accessed December 4, 2014).

——2013b. *IUCN Red List Summary Statistics.* Viewed 26 January 2014. http://www.iucnredlist.org/about/summary-statistics.

——2013c. *IUCN Red List of Threatened Species Version 2013.2.* Viewed 26 May 2014. http://www.iucnredlist.org/search?page=1432.

Joseph, Liana N., Richard F. Maloney, and Hugh P. Possingham. 2009. "Optimal Allocation of Resources among Threatened Species: a Project Prioritization Protocol." *Conservation Biology* 23 (2): 328–338.

Lamoreux, John, H. Resit Akçakaya, Leon Bennun, Nigel J. Collar, Luigi Boitani, David Brackett, Amie Bräutigam, Thomas M. Brooks, Gustavo A. B. da Fonseca, Russell A. Mittermeier, Anthony B. Rylands, Ulf Gärdenfors, Craig Hilton-Taylor,

Georgina Mace, Bruce A. Stein, and Simon Stuart. 2003. "Value of the IUCN Red List." *TRENDS in Ecology and Evolution* 18 (5): 214–215.

Mace, Georgina M., Nigel J. Collar, Kevin J., Gaston, Craig Hilton-Taylor, H. Resit Akçakaya, Nigel Leader-Williams, E. J. Milner-Gulland, and Simon Stuart. 2008. "Quantification of extinction risk: IUCN's system for classifying threatened species." *Conservation Biology* 22 (6): 1424–1442.

McCarthy, Donal P. et al. 2012. "Financial Costs of Meeting Global Biodiversity Conservation Targets: Current Spending and Unmet Needs." *Science* 338 (6109): 946–949.

Miller, Rebecca M. 2013. "Threatened species: Classification systems and their applications." In *Encyclopedia of Biodiversity*, edited by S.A. Levin, 2nd edition, vol. 7, 191–211. Waltham, MA: Academic Press.

OED Online. 2013. Oxford: Oxford University Press.

Possingham, Hugh P., Sandy J. Andelman, Mark A. Burgman, Rodrigo A. Medellín, Larry L. Master, David A. Keither. 2002. "Limits to the use of threatened species lists." *Trends in Ecology & Evolution* 17 (11): 503–507.

Rabinow, Paul and Nikolas Rose. 2006. "Biopower today." *BioSocieties* 1 (2): 195–217.

Radio Live. 2011. "Let Kakapo Die?" 4 April. http://www.radiolive.co.nz/Let-Kakapo-die/tabid/506/articleID/19704/Default.aspx.

Rivalan, Philippe, Virginie Delmas, Elena Angulo, Leigh S. Bull, Richard J. Hall, Franck Courchamp, Alison M. Rosser, and Nigel Leader-Williams. 2007. "Can bans stimulate wildlife trade?" *Nature* 447 (31): 529–530.

Rodrigues, Ana S. L., John D. Pilgrim, John F. Lamoreux, Michael Hoffmann, and Thomas M. Brooks. 2006. "The value of the IUCN Red List for conservation." *Trends in Ecology and Evolution* 21 (2): 71–76.

Rose, Nikolas. 2001. "The politics of life itself." *Theory, Culture & Society* 18 (6): 1–30.

Rutherford, Stephanie and Paul Rutherford. 2013. "Geography and biopolitics." *Geography Compass* 7 (6): 423–434.

Sandler, Ronald L. 2012. *The Ethics of Species: An Introduction*. Cambridge: Cambridge University Press.

Science Media Centre. 2011. "DoC defends kakapo against ecological triage." 13 April. http://www.sciencemediacentre.co.nz/2011/04/13/doc-defends-kakapo-agains-ecological-triage.

Serrano, Lilibeth. 2012. "Federal and state agencies reaffirm their commitment to the recovery of the endangered Puerto Rican Parrot." USFWS. 6 August. http://www.fws.gov/caribbean/ParrotMoU2012.html.

Shukin, Nicole. 2009. *Animal Capital: Rendering Life in Biopolitical Times*. Minneapolis: University of Minnesota Press.

USFWS. 2005. "Why save endangered species." July. http://www.fws.gov/nativeamerican/pdf/why-save-endangered-species.pdf

——2012. "The economic cost of large constrictor snakes." January. http://www.fws.gov/verobeach/PythonPDF/EconImpact_LargeConstrictorSnakes.pdf.

Walsh, Jessica C., James E. M. Watson, Madeleine C. Bottrill, Liana N. Joseph, and Hugh P. Possingham. 2012. "Trends and biases in the listing and recovery planning for threatened species: an Australian case study." *Oryx* 47 (1): 134–143.

White, Jr., Thomas H., Jaime A. Collazo, Stephen J. Dinsmore, and Ivan Llerandi-Román. 2014. *Niche Restriction and Conservatism in a Neotropical Psittacine: The Case of the Puerto Rican Parrot*. Hauppauge, NY: Nova Science Publishers.

Wilcove, David S. 2010. "Endangered species management: The US experience." In *Conservation Biology For All*, edited by Navjot S. Sodhi and Paul R. Ehrlich, 220–235. New York: Oxford University Press.

Wilson, E. O. 1992. *The Diversity of Life*. Cambridge, MA: Belknap Press.

Wolfe, Cary. 2013. *Before the Law: Humans and Other Animals in a Biopolitical Frame*. Chicago: University of Chicago Press.

6 "Deep inside dogs know what they want"

Animality, affect, and killability in commercial pet foods

Jen Wrye

In 1973, Peter Singer famously popularized Richard Ryder's term, speciesism, to identify a form of discrimination based on species membership and to challenge the idea that humans' interests supersede those of other animals. Singer's work has spawned considerable analyses of pervasive animal exploitation, which broaden his critique of the brutality inherent to many animal use industries. In particular, authors have observed significant disparity in the treatment of some animals, noting that while many are killed for food, clothing, scientific research, entertainment, and so on, others are cherished, loved or honored (Torres 2007; Sorenson 2014; Francione 2000; Joy 2010). These writings highlight the deep moral ambivalence humans display toward other animals and the way categorizations are central to the ordering of some species over others. But fewer account for the role nonhuman animals play in the oppression and deaths of others (Haraway 2008). Human violence toward animals is well documented. Likewise, that some animals escape human exploitation is also noted. Yet too few have examined how animals come to exploit, or be positioned as exploiting, others outside of characterizing such relationships as a fact of nature. I consider the processes involved in normalizing violence against farmed animals on behalf of companion animals in order to reveal the hierarchy of lives and deaths and to better understand how these ambivalent orderings are embedded in processes of production and consumption. In particular, this chapter seeks to explain how pet food companies create conceptions of liveability and killability through their products. I argue that affective human–pet relationships frame the killability of farmed and 'prey' animals by cats and dogs as natural. Pet foods make farmed animals expendable through representations that hyper-animalize pet cats and dogs while simultaneously relying on our loving and anthropomorphized relationships with them. By depicting pets as family members for whom their human companions have the responsibility to care, as well as ferocious, carnivorous killers who thrive on the flesh of prey animals, pet food companies situate humans as innocent witnesses to purportedly 'natural' relations. These discourses both create and obscure economic modalities that justify the violent slaughter of millions of farmed animals, primarily for human consumption.

Animal–human relations in modernity: humans, animals and pets

Commercial pet food is the sum of both material and representational practices that both rely on and advance ideas about the separation of humans and
animals. What does this divide look like? How do we understand animals, our
connections with them, and their connections with each other? This section
considers the relationship between humans and animals more closely in order
to explore how pet foods cast animality and how discourses of animality
shape pet food. Why do some animals come to be protected and cared for
while others are not? How is this decided? Such actions are not simply about
animal bodies, per se.[1] Rather, they are about how value and worth align,
particularly along axes of power and privilege.

The ontological separation between animals and humans is a core belief
within Western society. Many rationalizations for the division find their
origins in Enlightenment beliefs surrounding the possession of physical or
cognitive abilities. Theorists identify the first scientific differentiation in the
writing of René Descartes (Baker 1993; Wolfe 2003; Ingold 1988). They
claim that Descartes viewed animals as soulless machines that act from
instinct, not thought. In *Meditations*, Descartes argues that animals are
"automatons"—physical entities that lack mental substance. He reasons that
since animals have no consciousness, and were unable to speak, think,
reason, feel pleasure, pain and even suffer, they were similar to humans only
in anatomical constitution. In other words, all animals became fundamentally different from humans.

Ideas similar to these about the animal–human divide remain common in
popular culture. Baker (1993, 78) reminds us that the human/animal dualism
remains one of a number of primary oppositions operative in Western culture.
Animals are perceived to lack that which humans possess—rationality, cognition, language, emotions, the ability to feel pain, and so on, although
these ideas have increasingly been scrutinized and even dispelled as myths
(Sorenson 2014). The physiological differences between humans and animals
are much less salient than popular culture would have us believe. Indeed, the
human/animal split as we know it cannot be attributed to biological similarity or difference because humans are more biologically similar to a
number of nonhuman animals than these distinct species are to each other.
Animals occupy varied species groups. Some are mammals while others are
insects, fish, etc. Simply, this means many animals bear little taxonomic
resemblance to other beings also called, animals. At the same time, the tacit
justification for using animals, including primates, as experimental research
subjects is that animals' reactions to such tests can provide insights into how
medicines, consumer products or other treatments will affect humans (Clark
2014). Finally, as organ and tissue demand increases beyond the capacity
provided by human donors, scientists have looked to xenotransplantation—
the transplantation of cells, tissues or organs into human beings—to fill this
demand. To date, scientists have used, on humans, tissue from mammals

including primates, dogs, cats, cattle, rabbits, rats, and pigs, as well as some bird and amphibian species![2] All of this acknowledges that animals are a lot like humans; humans, in fact, *are* animals.

Scholars have convincingly demonstrated that divisions between humans and animals are human constructions. The concept of the human demarcates the concept of the animal and vice versa. One way to understand how this occurs is to distinguish between animals and animality. This allows us to treat animals as our abject and ultimate other in spite of our close links with many of them (Philo and Wolch 1998). Here, animals can be defined as the live, material beings and animality as a trait or 'beingness.' As Wolfe puts it, there is a distinction between "the *discourse* of animality ... and the living and breathing creatures who fall outside the taxonomy of Homo sapiens" (2003, xx; *emphasis in original*). By separating animality from the bodies onto which such traits are projected, Wolfe acknowledges that much of the divide between humans and animals rests in ways of knowing rather than natural differences. His claim suggests that animals the beings, and animality the characteristic, are different. Haraway (2003) adds that Western philosophers have historically used animals to generate and legitimate the class of humans. For her, 'animality' is not necessarily tied to animal bodies, but to the discursive production of both that which is 'animal' and that which is 'human.' Ingold, however, notes that we have a tendency to employ two unique definitions of animality: we refer to it as a domain that includes humans *and* as a state or condition opposed to humanity (1988, 3–7).

The differential treatment experienced by some animals demonstrates that the animal/human split is often not the most salient classification principle. As Elder, Wolch and Emel (1998, 186) point out, "certain sorts of animals (such as apes, companion animals, dolphins, other revered species) become positioned on the human side of the metaphorical line, rendering some practices unacceptable." At the same time, Armstrong (2002) recalls that tropes of animalization have historically been crucial to colonial and imperial domination. African, Middle-Eastern, Asian, and Indigenous peoples in the Americas – in short, non-European and racialized peoples generally—have been equated with the bestial in order to justify violence toward them. In these cases, animalization operates to dehumanize populations. Such tricky processes reveal the complicated divide between the human and the animal that employs shifting dualisms and metaphors simultaneously. The referent then, is not the (biological) category of *Homo sapien*, but instead, that which is associated with the human. Some groups of people are dehumanized despite the fact that they are *Homo sapiens* while some classes of animals are humanized despite the fact they are not members of this taxonomy. The human gets defined by the animal or the bestial—its 'opposite' (Jenkins and Twine 2014). As Stanescu (2012) explains, the human and the inhuman are bound together as an inseparable dyad in which the 'human' comes to name the category of beings we work to protect. It is not actually animals, but the human interpretation of which animals mean what and when that shapes our ideas of animality. Wolfe (2003) explains this intricacy:

> One might well observe that it is crucial to pay critical attention to the discourse of animality quite irrespective of the issue of how nonhuman animals are treated. This is so, as a number of scholars have observed, because the discourse of animality has historically served as a crucial strategy in the oppression of *humans* by other humans—a strategy whose legitimacy and force depend, however, on the prior taking for granted of the traditional ontological distinction, and consequent ethical divide, between human and non human animals ... even though the *discourse* of animality and species differentiation may theoretically be applied to an other of whatever type, the consequences of that discourse ... fall over-whelmingly on nonhuman animals, in our taken-for-granted practices of using and exploiting them.
>
> (xx: *emphasis in original*)

In his view, the discourse of animality is a collection of signifiers that con-stitutes how humans understand their 'other.' This other is identified, albeit unpredictably, through language and according to solipsistic visions of the human. And as Wolfe's comments reveal, the animalization of people, that is, neglecting ontological commitments to humans as a distinct class, does not weaken 'the human.' The rhetoric of animality persists, and cultural con-structions of the animal will invariably figure as the negative term of a dual-ism when used in binary oppositions, even where multiple human or two nonhuman animal bodies are concerned.

Pet animals are said to reside on the 'human' side of the divide with the many privileges that usually entails (Haraway 2008). Rather than possessing economic utility, pets are appreciated for the love and devotion (whether real or perceived) they offer for its own sake. That many humans view pet animals as friends or companions is evident in their treatment throughout life and upon death. Many pets are indulged with a variety of specialty products intended to improve their quality of life. Individuals alter their houses, adjust their schedules, spend exorbitant amounts of money for them, and even clean up their bowel movements. People who lose their pets often experience immense sadness, grief, or even depression. They may hold funerals or bury animals in graves with markers bearing special messages (Shell 1986, 122).

These behaviors are not new to the modern period. Grier (2006; 2008) highlights the long history of affect and emotion bestowed upon pets throughout the eighteenth, nineteenth and twentieth centuries. While certain animals typically are taken as pets, as I have argued elsewhere, petness is not the exclusive domain of cats, dogs, a few rodents or birds, etc. (Wrye 2009). Pets are not categorized as such because of inherent characteristics, but through human practices and social relations. There is, after all, nothing definitively distinctive about a cow or a pig that would warrant inhumane living conditions or would even justify their consumption. Even still, many pets are certainly treated harshly or inhumanely. Yet in contrast to most other animals, such behaviors are largely judged to be socially unacceptable. The presumption is that pets are loved and adored, although they may not be loved at all. They may be treated like possessions. They may be taunted, teased, ignored, neglected, cruelly abused, given away, or 'euthanized.' Pets, much like humans, seem to exist in a state where they can be loved ones, family members, friends, companions, sources of support, objects of frustration, pests, nuisances, or victims (Shell 1986). Even under the best conditions, relations between humans and pets or companion animals are not altogether clean. Tuan (1984) argues that our affective relationships have a darker side, which forces animals to delight and serve their owners. These purported bonds between two species are necessarily based on uneven power relations and ambivalent entanglements between 'owners' and 'owned.'

In the idealized world of pet food, pets are individuals for whom humans are responsible. Pets have, according to Rollin and Rollin (2003, 107), a 'domestic' quality that attaches them in relations of protection and liability to individual humans. In contrast with other captive animals who live in proximity to humans and have been *domesticated*, pets are seen as residing with humans in the most complete sense. This is so for largely emotional, rather than economic, reasons. Farmed animals are near humans because they are financially valuable. Companion animals are near humans because closeness with them is desired. In this respect, pets differ from wild, captive, and food animals.[3] Pets' unique stories and friendships matter and are circulated among humans—told and retold to reproduce their positioning as cherished members of the home.

Farmed animals, in some instances, may live in close proximity to humans, may be treated with care or even love, and subjected to only minimal violence before their death (Pollan 2006). This is not the experience of most farmed animals, however. Animal slaughter is an enormous industry; tens of billions of animals, including pigs, cattle, chickens, sheep, turkeys, and fish, are raised and killed each year for food consumption. Most of these animals do not live on bucolic family farms. Instead, they are grown intensively in large-scale factory farms known as concentrated animal feeding operations (CAFOs). These operations are highly mechanized and designed to produce animal flesh or animal by-products, such as milk or eggs, as cheaply as possible (Kirby 2010). This requires raising tens of thousands of animals together, creating horrifying conditions and consequences.[4] For example, most animals have limited access to outdoor space, may be unable to move around, or even access adequate food or water. They are fed in order to 'fatten' them quickly, with little regard for their nutritional or biological needs, and given extensive antibiotics and other drugs to combat the illnesses that stem from living in such conditions. These animals are not treated as beings, but as meat-to-be.

While most farmed animals are deindividuated, pets' individuality is created through affective displays. Pets become subjects with valued lives and valued lives are those that are protected from violence and grieved at death. In recent works, Judith Butler investigates who counts as a morally considerable life and a grievable death (2004; 2009). In her view, grievability implicates the way others may expect to be treated (2009, 74–75). By this Butler intends to identify the mechanisms through which some lives come to matter more than others, and how acts of violence may be perpetrated against some in the name of helping or protecting others. To be sure, celebrated principles of universal human rights, which strive to confer intrinsic value to all (human) lives, are regularly and easily annulled (2004, xvii). This means that the existence and humanity of some is derealized in order to produce violence toward them. These types of activities are frequent; they occur through government policies, laws, court rulings, media representations, expert analyses, and in other ways within the popular imaginary more generally. They create and negate subjects whose value, or lack of, can be revealed through discourses and ideas related to their protection and mourning. This is especially obvious in times when loss causes grief. Grief is not only a private and personal activity, but also a political act. Expressions of grief, particularly when they occur collectively or in the public realm, show who or what is deemed worthy of sorrow. Many deaths are forgotten, ignored, or fail to elicit sorrow. In these instances, grief sorts valued and unvalued lives; grievability is political because it helps maintain exclusionary conceptions of valued life by sorting out which subjects can and cannot be grieved (Jenkins and Twine 2014).

While Butler's work focuses primarily on violence perpetrated by humans toward one another, other scholars have explored their applicability to relations with nonhuman animals (Stanescu 2012; Taylor 2008). Butler's insights about the conditions under which some individuals can be killed, or rendered killable, stand out in this field. Here grievability acts as both the response to, and the opposite of, killability. Grievable lives matter and are guarded, even if that security causes violence for others (Butler 2009, xxv–xxx). Killability means that some lives do not count fully—those bodies are already transformed into the decimated, objectified object. This is so because narratives that justify violence toward, or the death of, others mean that some lives become dead already.

Stanescu (2012) develops this insight to better understand anthropocentrism, rampant violence toward animals, and ways both can be reduced. As Taylor (2008) explains, violence is a way of life for many animals who are killed largely with impunity. This is true of the billions of animals who are not only killed for food, but have their corpses lain bare before humans in the form of packaged 'meat' (Stanescu 2012). Rather than inciting sadness, the carcasses incite hunger, and possibly delight. With the exception of those who feel sorrow for those animal deaths, animals killed for food (and other commodity products) are ignored, unseen, and unheard beyond the pieces into which they've been transformed. In the words of Derrida and Nancy (1995, 278) this process involves sizeable "noncriminal putting to death of animals" that involves efforts to "organize on a global scale the forgetting or misunderstanding of this violence." In their being, lumps of flesh represent a stark disavowal of lives. Billions of animals experience death in order for their bodies to exist as human food, and this reality is frequently obscured and/or made mundane. Stanescu (2014) points to the near unintelligibility of mourning these animals; their killability is seen as natural, inevitable, expected, and permissible. At the same time as animals experience physical violence, they are also symbolically robbed of their individuality and value. Animal death and physical violence is elided through linguistic tricks – animals, pigs and cattle, are the absent referents for the meat (e.g., 'pork' and 'beef') they are turned into (Adams 2010). Stanescu (2012) claims that the act of grieving these individuals can help to reposition and invigorate interspecies political communities that are centered on the notion of care and liberation. It can also mean affirming the political importance of grieving lives that are taken. Grief can help reveal the animals that were, perhaps violentely, disembodied and disemboweled to create meat, as well as economic value.

Shukin (2009) outlines the centrality of nature and animals to humans' lives and livelihoods, including our economic systems. She claims that the promise of neoliberal postmodernity is to move beyond production, and to create surplus value from consumption, financialization, currency, technology, etc. In these depictions, nature is a source of pleasure, rather than of physical wealth. At the same time, representations in modern society integrate nature and animals ubiquitously. Shukin contends these animal representations are hyperreal as well as inextricable to traditional capitalist production. Nature, including animal bodies, is made useable as both material objects and cultural artifacts through the simultaneous 'capitalization of nature' and 'naturalization of capital.' The overexposed, idealized, symbolic animal and the un(der)exposed, exploited, physical animal are one and the same. The former overshadows the latter by eclipsing the destruction of nonhuman lives necessary to contemporary Western consumer culture. The United Nations Food and Agriculture Organization makes clear that the human consumption of land animals has a significant ecological impact. According to Steinfeld et al. (2006, xxi–xxiii) intensive animal farming operations utilize 30 percent of the earth's land surface, including nearly 80 percent of the total land used by humans for all purposes while accounting for about 20 percent of the total terrestrial animal biomass (Steinfeld et al. 2006, xxi–xxiii). The use and exploitation of animals by humans is, no doubt, extensive. That billions of companion animals are implicated in these activities simply adds to the domination and oppression of farmed animals. The next section considers how killable, farmed animals are integrated into pet foods; how pet foods are made, and how they link with the greater human food chain.

Making commercial pet food

Pets and their food aren't typical objects of critical analysis. Mostly pet foods are invisible products that scarcely catch consumers' attention. Yet industries dedicated to living with companion animals are enormously profitable. Dogs and cats are expensive to house, feed, and otherwise care for. Expenditures include adoption, food, toys, treats, kennel or walking services, sitters, training, accessories, and health care. Holbrook and Woodside (2008) put the cost of dog or cat ownership at roughly as much as the purchase of a slightly used car (over $10,000 per animal over the course of its lifetime) which adds up collectively in the United States alone to annual outlays of close to $40 billion per year. Commercial pet food sales account for a considerable portion of the larger pet product industry's value. In 2012, sales reached an estimated $66 billion globally, a figure that has risen steadily each year driven by expanding markets in the global south as well as a move toward higher quality, premium foods within the traditional marketplaces of North America and Europe (Taylor 2012). The most popular pet food labels are also owned by some of the world's largest food and personal care corporations—Mars, Nestlé, Colgate-Palmolive, and Del Monte Foods (as well as Proctor & Gamble until they sold their stake to Mars in 2013). These brands represent an estimated 70 percent of all pet food purchases, which means they do about $45 billion in pet food business a year. Few commercial pet foods are made for or by small, independent businesses; most of these foods are produced and distributed though the same global commodity chains used to produce human foods (Nestle 2008).

The pet food industry spans several market segments from discount or generic brands to specialty and 'superpremium' foods. International corporate brands are competitive within all market segments. They dominate veterinary and supermarket sales, but have struggled somewhat in specialty pet stores where their mass appeal may negate some of the specialty qualities associated with being higher value, smaller, more specialized, etc. (Woon 2011). Their response has been to consolidate and acquire smaller, premium, independent labels.

Although there are close connections between human and pet food, in the United States, at least, pet foods are legally classified as animal feeds (Mullin 2007). This categorization means pet foods are subject to unique legal structures that impact how they are manufactured, labeled, and sold. One key legal difference in pet foods is that they are sorted principally by the moisture content of the product. Commercial pet foods take one of three forms depending on their moisture content: dry, moist or semi-moist. The first two comprise the majority of pet food sales, with dry foods making up approximately four-fifths of the market (Ockerman and Hansen 2000, 364). Moisture is operative in the industry for packaging and preservation purposes, but mainly because the nutritional quality of a food is affected by the amount of water contained in the product: the higher the amount of water, the lower nutritional density of the food. Pet foods may be classified as either "complete and balanced" or "supplemental" foods. Foods labeled 'complete and balanced' must meet the absolute nutritional needs of the species for which they are intended when fed exclusively whereas supplementary foods may complement a main diet.

Pet foods are made from any number of thousands of ingredients. Nestle and Nesheim (2010, 69–89) provide a useful typology of the ingredients used in pet foods, placing them into one of the following categories: fresh meats, fresh animal by-products, animal meals, animal by-product meals, vegetables and fruit, grains or other carbohydrate sources, binders and thickeners, vitamins and minerals, and preservatives. Fresh meats or fresh by-product ingredients include raw and unprocessed components derived from animals, including meat cuts, tissues or organs. Meals and by-product meals, by comparison, are the dried, ground products left over after animal tissue is rendered and the fats and water are removed. The primary nutritional function of both these ingredients is to fashion proteins and fats. Grains provision carbohydrates (fiber) as well as some protein and fat. Vegetables and fruits are included for their fiber and vitamin content. Fillers and binders hold the products together and preservatives keep the foods from spoiling. Vitamin and mineral additions are necessary because some ingredients may lack diverse nutritional quality or because cooking processes can remove some of the naturally occurring vitamins and minerals. The industry also adds vitamin and mineral content either for marketing purposes or to be 'certain' there are no deficiencies in the foods labeled 'complete and balanced.'

Although pet food is an animal feed, governed almost entirely outside the human food system, most ingredients used in pet food are derivatives of the human food chain. Pet foods are considered an outlet for converting human food waste into another commodity (Nestle 2008). Therefore, derivative foods are the secondary products obtained during the manufacture of a principal commodity. Derivatives are often normatively less valued, but generally not less valuable economically, and frequently in the case of food, nutritionally. Many of the ingredients used to make pet foods are "inedible" because they do not meet human food standards for an array of reasons (Hill 2003, 92).[5]

Pet foods typically include a lot of animal-derived or by-product substances including "everything produced by or from an animal, except dressed meat" (Ockerman and Hansen 2000, 4). This offal may include, but is not limited to, internal organs, cavities, skin, hair, blood, fat, feet, hooves, feathers, heads, shells, fur, glands, intestines, muscle, fat or connective tissue, bones, some meat cuts of poor aesthetic quality, and so on. In the animal food industry, the non-'meat' parts of the animal are relegated secondary even though their sales are critical to the 'primary' industry. Typically, only about 40–50 percent of a steer's body is turned into human food (Hamilton et al. 2006). To suggest pet food or other animal feed is secondary misses the point that animal feed actually makes meat-based food chains possible because meat would be exorbitantly priced without them. As Walker explains, "a portion of the profit returned to the animal production and processing industries depends on the utilization of the by-products or co-products ancillary to the production of meat, milk, and eggs for human food production" (2000, 2). These invisible uses are lucrative aspects of production.

Animal products are derived through the process of rendering. This involves heating animal carcasses in order to remove water and separate fat from proteinaceous tissue (Hamilton et al. 2006, 82). Rendering converts bodies that are difficult to utilize into commercially viable products such as food, candles, soaps, etc. The main yields are solid, protein-rich material called greaves or meat and bone meal, and 'liquid' fats like tallow or lard.[6] While fats are used in pet foods, meat and bone meal is one key ingredient used widely in the feed industry. Neither is used in human foods because commercially rendered materials are not recognized as safe for human consumption.

The pet food industry is often seen as a meat-based industry. That characterization is a misconception no doubt caused by the millions of dollars in advertising designed to stress the meat content of pet foods. Yet cereals and other plants remain essential to producing dry pet foods because this manufacturing process requires the use of cereals or other carbohydrate-rich vegetables. Dry pet foods are created through extrusion, which is widely used for making breakfast cereals, pastas, crackers, and many other snack foods (Pet Food Institute 2006). Extrusion uses high heat and air and water pressure to cook finely ground ingredient mixes, including cereal grain, potato flour, as well as meat meals, into more consistent dry food bites (Case et al. 2010, 187–8; Cowell et al. 2000).[7] The process begins when an ingredient mix is 'preconditioned,' which allows water to attach to food molecules and expand or puff them. The mix is then pushed through the extruder, which completes the cooking. Inside the cylinder, a large screw (or two) mix, knead, and proof the food as the ingredients are propelled through. The combination of (steam) heat, speed, air, pressure, and friction allows the product to cook and rise continuously. The mix is pushed into its final shapes through a die at the end of the machine, and the kibbles cut into pieces. The resulting pieces are spongy and soft. Thus, to complete the product, the kibbles are transferred to a dryer where additional moisture is removed. They are then cooled and 'enrobed' with antioxidants, more vitamins and minerals, animal fats, and other flavor enhancers.

Compared with other dry food manufacturing techniques, extrusion allows pet food companies to include more animal-based materials in their products. As obligate carnivores, cats require some animal products in their diets to thrive. Dogs are opportunistic omnivores, so they have little or no *need* for animal flesh, although this matter is hotly contested (Nestle and Nesheim 2011). Either way, both species seem to respond favorably to eating animal flesh, so Bisplinghoff puts the proportion of protein utilization in canine and feline animals at roughly 40 percent (2006, 26). But extrusion is also advantageous because it is immensely economical. It allows for the inclusion of a wide array of ingredients, effectively making it possible to include just about any ingredient in the food product. Extrusion produces consistent products that are adaptive to formulation variations, quick to make, and easily scaled. They stay together well, have a long shelf life, produce uniform kibbles that are visually appealing, and above all, produce less dense foods. Greater concentrations of air or water can be added to extruded foods, which can reduce manufacturing costs (Ockerman and Hansen 2000, 364–5). Overall, extruded pet foods seemingly allow a large-scale, global industry to meet the nutritional needs of companion animals in a cost-effective way. Therefore, extrusion and the use of grain materials makes it possible to feed farmed animals to pets. In other words, so-called ancillary ingredients and industries play an essential role in creating killable lives.

There has been significant and notable contestation over whether companion animals' needs are appropriately met by commercial pet foods. Martin (2008; 2001) and Fox, Hodgkins and Smart (2009) have been among the most vocal opponents of commercial pet foods. They claim the food industry has far too much regulatory autonomy, which has resulted in shoddily made products that use inferior and biologically inappropriate ingredients, including grains, animal meals, and by-products. For Martin and Fox et al., all foods derived from rendering are nutritionally dangerous and they advocate home-cooked or raw food feeding. In their view, the events of the 2007 pet food recall perfectly reflect key failings of this poorly managed industry.[8] The pet food recall was, at the time, the largest in the history of any consumer product in Canada or the United States. Beginning Friday, March 16, 2007, and lasting several months, a company few had heard of, Menu Foods, recalled thousands of food packages made under different brand names. The problem, according to the company and the FDA, was that the foods caused renal problems or failure in cats and dogs. It would take months to identify the underlying cause, which was revealed to be contamination with melamine, an unapproved chemical addition designed to surreptitiously improve the nutritional appearance of the foods. It affected hundreds of brands from dozens of different companies at many price points, and totaled tens of millions of pet food containers in Canada and the United States (Gillis and Kingston 2007). One of the most shocking aspects of this event is that authorities lacked the regulatory power to mandate the recall; in spite of the knowledge that the foods were life threatening to animals, the recall was voluntary!

Marion Nestle's detailed analyses of the pet food industry demonstrate that this sector has certainly deserved many of the criticisms leveled against it (Nestle 2008; Nestle and Nesheim 2010). The 2007 pet food recall is one of a long list of major recalls involving contamination of melamine, but also mycotoxin, salmonella, or *ecoli*. The number and severity of these incidents suggests the industry suffers significant problems. Nestle identifies unnecessarily long supply chains, confusing labeling and manufacturing specifications, some poor ingredient sourcing activities and too lax government regulation as four core issues that should be addressed. However, Nestle and Nesheim (2010) do not characterize the commercial pet food business as flawed or dangerous at its core. They advise some important changes in line with their critiques of the industry's shortcomings, particularly in ingredient acquisition, but maintain that both rendered and grain ingredients can be safe and nutritious ingredients. In short, their work attempts to help consumers understand commercial pet foods, and pet feeding more broadly, within a sea of public moral panic and the industry's self-congratulatory marketing. Although Nestle's work scrutinizes the industry, scant attention has been paid to the industry's marketing techniques, and specifically the roles that animals come to play in creating stories about pet foods. Both animalized pets and the dead, killable animals are salient markets of nutritional appropriateness in the pet food industry.

Representations of animals in commercial pet foods

Marketing is as fundamental to the commercial pet food industry as it is to other businesses. In an environment where thousands of new products appear annually, businesses must capture and maintain as many customers as possible. People's purchasing motivations are varied and multifaceted. They represent a mixture of individual taste (both reasoned and spontaneous), normative pressure, and broader socio-political circumstances. Advertising works to tap into those motivations while affirming, reinforcing and transforming both individual and cultural beliefs and values (Retzinger 2008, 150). It allows companies to configure their brands and products to align with consumers' tastes. As Williamson (1978) puts it, advertising shifts focus from the properties and constitution of an object toward what that object means for humans. Purchasing decisions are "triggered by the cumulative impressions formed by advertising, promotion and prior use of the product" (Cato 1985, 28).

In the pet food business, companies must use exceptional strategies to draw customers because human purchasers do not have a direct sensory relationship with the foods, and pets are mostly unable to verbalize preference or dissatisfaction with their foods beyond rejecting them altogether. The tactics pet food companies use to sell their merchandise reveals a great deal about how they create nutritional narratives. Since they are selling food, these companies must create 'nutritional realities' by other appeals (Elliott 2008). Consumers may solicit recommendations from breeders, veterinarians, store clerks, friends or salespeople. They may listen to the marketing and sales pitches carefully orchestrated by pet food companies, which Wortinger (2008) claims have a significant impact on people's ideas of pet nutrition. Consumers may also rely on their own knowledge, research and expertise. But undoubtedly pet food marketing plays a significant part in shaping individuals' decisions.

Pet food companies position themselves as pet authorities by creating what Mullin (2007) calls powerful 'origin stories' that help legitimate consumer choices. This is an important feature of their promotional activities since animal health and nutrition is made to seem obscure and complicated. Pet food companies implore human guardians to feed their pets 'properly,' by which they mean according to the standards set out by the industry. Nutrition information on pet foods is transformed into a numeric system only marginally related to the one used by human food companies. As with human foods, companies overload human consumers with extensive and highly technical health and food information. They sell a range of products designed to aid in the dietary maintenance of different physical conditions: formulations exist for oral care, hairball control, sensitive stomachs, weight control, both hairball *and* weight control, and so on, as well as for different ages and breeds or sizes of animals. Each of these signals the necessity to abandon any effort at trying to care for one's animals' health needs independently. The quantified, nutritionalized food system replaces simple animal feeding with convoluted systems where pet food companies are positioned as authorities proffering health advice to wary and weary consumers (Scrinis 2013; Pollan 2006).

Companies also regularly feature scientific tropes in their advertising. Hill's brand foods motto, 'superior and clinically proven nutrition for lifelong health,' is bolded and highlighted on the product packages, which are augmented with an additional 'seal' that claims their Science Diet line is the #1 choice of veterinarians worldwide. Outlining how scientists study foods and their constituent components makes clear that 'truths' uncovered about foods, nutrients and the needs of animals' bodies are subsequently integrated into their products. In these narratives, pet food makers are mere witnesses to nutritional (as well as behavioral) knowledge acquisition. Eukanuba characterizes this well on their website (*www.eukanuba.com*): "nature and nutrition have reached an understanding."

Companies tend to augment their nutritional expertise with additional specialization; they provide consumers with advice about food and diet as well other areas of pet-keeping such as adoption, care, health, and behavior. In these instances, their associations with recognized third-party organizations, including humane and rescue groups, animal medicine experts, kennel clubs and breed fanciers' groups, animal shelters, or veterinary associations, highlight pet food companies as leaders in the pet industry and civic-minded community partners. As Dixon, Sindall and Banwell (2004, 124) contend, affiliations and third-party endorsements from respectable organizations offer a great deal of credibility in the food environment and legitimize food claims. But more than that, they provide responsibilized pet caretakers with a single source of 'credible' information.

Promoting the health and well being of pets has brought greater attention to the nutritional quality of their foods. However, caring for dogs and cats raises questions about the costs for other animals. While pet foods – those that include greater concentrations of meat and high quality vegetable matter – may improve pets' health, they also create violent conditions of existence for farmed animals. In other words, pet foods are heavily indebted to both the idea and physicality of animal flesh as a 'natural' food source for many companion dogs and cats. There are many ways this is achieved.

Within the pet food industry, images of nature proliferate. Most companies engage in a form of what might be called agricultural and nature pornography, which include snapshots of naked agrarian splendor that titillate while suppressing potential questions or concerns about the food's quality or ingredient composition. As suggested by Johnston and Bauman (2010), pet foods deal in a language of authenticity on the websites and packages. Products are depicted as simple and unadulterated. Common names like 'By Nature,' 'Pure Essentials,' 'Nature Organics,' 'Nature's Best,' 'California Farms,' or 'Harmony Naturals' summon ideas of pure diets directly from the land or sea. At the same time, 'prime' cuts of meat, whole vegetables and fruits are displayed prominently and designed to conjure up visions of bucolic farm fresh foods. The brand line from Canadian company Orijen pet food, which sells products that are "bursting with cage-free poultry, nest-laid eggs, wild-caught fish, free-range red meats, and ranch-raised lamb" sums up the trend nicely: 'nourish as nature intended.' What nature purportedly intends is to sacrifice some animals for the hunger of others. This is a mythical construction designed to assuage fears about the content of the pet foods by suggesting that pets are predatory animals eating according to the 'natural order.'

It is unsurprising that pet food companies represent their products as natural and wholesome. Most human food manufacturers downplay the amount that their foods are processed. But these depictions extend to their construction of pet animals. Nature motifs implicate pets as animalized animals with a taste for animal flesh. Products discursively illustrate a preference for meat, although the pet foods typically include as much or more grain and carbohydrate material in formulations. They do so by making connections between domesticated animals and their wild, carnivorous ancestors. For example, the 'Before Grain' line of pet foods simply scrawls the letters 'B.G.' across its packages. For this line, grains represent the adulteration characteristic of modernity while the meat, and only the meat, is exactly what the animal needs. Blue Buffalo calls its Wilderness line a "natural, evolutionary" diet. Likewise, 'Taste of the Wild' brand pet food builds on the motifs of carnivores hunting. There are several dog and cat formulations, each of which depicts some connection between domestic cats and dogs and other wild animal relatives. The 'High Prairie Canine Formula' dog food package shows snarling coyotes on the 'Great Plains' stalking bison. On the 'Wetlands Canine Formula' package, wolves chase fleeing ducks on the shore of a mountain lake. The 'Pacific Stream Canine Formula' bag depicts a pack of wolves encircling a grizzly bear deep in the mountain woods in seeming competition for nature's resources. For cats, the 'Rocky Mountain Feline Formula' shows a cougar looking over a cliff ledge stalking a deer frolicking by a waterfall while the 'Canyon River Feline Formula' depicts a mountain lion on a river's edge catching fish. In this product line, the wolves, coyotes, and big cats do not merely get food, but hunt them competitively and ferociously.

Eukanuba's recently discontinued 'Naturally Wild' line of foods use picturesque environments to signal product constitution. One of the food formulations pictures the 'prey' ingredient, two deer walking in a wooded clearing, while a focused hound looks on. We learn that the food is "premium dog food inspired by the wilderness." Consumers are further told that the dead bodies of the consumed animals inspire their food formulations; turkey is used as a "tribute to dogs' nutritional heritage," venison is considered a quality ingredient because "the gorgeous yet rugged landscape of New Zealand yields fit and healthy wildlife that dogs lived off of for millennia" and that, "the food chain of ages past" inspired a salmon-based food because "the arduous journey salmon make to their spawning ground results in a lean source of protein that nourished dogs for thousands of years." Visitors to their website learned that "deep inside, dogs know what they want." They want to hunt, to kill, and to sate their hunger and unleash the animal repressed within.

The characterizations of pets as never truly tame and still linked with their undomesticated relations make good marketing. They also reveal a deep contradiction in our experience with animals and a fabricated history of how our relationships with them have developed. These products trade on notions of nature and ancestry for credibility by replacing the reality of pet food construction, which involves multiple layers of processing and heavy plant-based material reliance, with a hyperbolic nature. Pets become species with primal, instinctual needs to eat killable, already dead bodies. These portrayals completely erase the reality of how their nutritional needs are met today. The supposed turkeys of the Great Plains that are always moving have very little to do with the fowl raised in intensive factory farming conditions, which rarely permit them to move. The jumping fish from fresh lakes and rivers are trolled fish, caught at rates unsuitable for regeneration or raised in environmentally destructive landlocked aquaculture tanks rife with high levels of disease, bacteria, treated with rounds of antibiotics, growth hormones, etc. The factory farm operations that make meat and its by-products so widely available come to be replaced with a cartoonish nature that simply reifies the animal hierarchy and turns farmed animals into wild prey animals meeting their destiny.

Dogs and cats are transformed into bloodthirsty carnivores that cannot help themselves. It is immaterial that dogs are opportunistic omnivores, that cats and dogs are distant relatives of cougars or wolves, split from their wild 'ancestors' tens of thousands of years ago to become thoroughly domesticated species, or that there are positively no circumstances in nature in which a 15 pound cat or 40 pound dog can stalk and kill a 200 pound deer. Naturally cats and dogs will consume insects, small birds, rodents, or perhaps other mammals. They will also eat many sorts of plant foods, particularly when they are provided conveniently.

Manufactured pet foods gain credibility, as well as highly desirable premium prices, by positioning domestic breeds of cats and dogs as close relatives to wild animals. Invoking evolution as a dietary rationale collapses thousands of years of domestication, under an array of global circumstances, into an easy account that neglects humans' extensive animal breeding activities. These representations of commercial pet foods as naturally satiating our semi-wild pet animals simply instantiate a baseless origin story that normalizes existing relations between different animals. It facilitates the erasure of farmed animals while rendering their 'happy meat' replacements inevitably dead (Stanescu 2014). Naturalized advertising strategies make farmed animals further killable by decontextualizing their existence and replacing them with hunted animals. This conceals both the conditions of human food production and the farmed animals that sustain it, turning humans into innocent bystanders of nature.

Perhaps such representations have traction because it is rewarding to see in our companion animals something more than the projection of human feelings and attributes. Perhaps these foods impress upon people the need to feed animals in a way that respects their biology; that being a cherished member of the family means meals ought to suit their distinctive nutritional needs. They are, just as we are, animals with unique nutritional needs. Maybe animalized pet foods help us to celebrate the animalness of pets that is often lost or repressed in modern pet-keeping practices. Yet this animalization is wrapped into care and responsibility toward pets. Pets may be beasts, but they're also individual family members with their own tastes or desires. Longstanding advertisements, stories, articles and other documents that likely do not need elaboration here tout the closeness of humans and their 'best friends.' These ironically anthropomorphize pets, bestowing them with human-like qualities that necessitate satisfying their unique tastes and desire for individual nurturance. These beasts are lovable, grievable, and they must be fed. Their sustenance comes not from grievable animal lives cut short, but from already dead masses intended, even born, to be consumed (Stanescu 2012). Pet foods adopt a legitimizing logic that ignores, unsees and unhears as if the only traces of the consumed beings' existence are the parts of their bodies rendered into food: flesh transformed into meat. The lives of these animals simply are not lives, or are not lives that count, or are not grievable lives. Much as they feed humans, the animals turned into meat and meat by-product in pet food are dead uncounted objects celebrated for feeding our beloved and cherished pets. In pet foods, dogs and cats are actively turned into carnivores that simply cannot help themselves. Pet foods supposedly provide pets with exactly what they need. In spite of its package, pet food obscures the violence of breeding, raising, and killing of animals for food that is necessary for its creation. Our love for pets, as well as the foods fed to them, are central to making killable and ungrievable the lives and deaths of farmed animals.

Conclusion

In this chapter, I explained how the pet food industry depicts the differing values of animals. Using the framework provided by Judith Butler concerning the epistemological implications of constructing subjectivities, I have explained how pet dogs and cats are constructed as cherished and grievable while both farmed and wild animals are treated as expendable and necessarily dead. This is possible because of the loving relationships people enjoy with their pets, but also because companies depict these same pets as hyperanimalized – their human-like qualities suspended to feed a hunger for meats. In pet food industry discourse, these ravenous carnivores need significant animal flesh to thrive, and humans' loving relationships with pet animals demand we provide it to them. Such representations hide conditions of farmed animal rearing, which rely on animal suffering, and exonerate humans and human food producers from responsibility in creating these conditions. Certainly pet foods only use a portion of animals within the meat, dairy, and egg industries. But these quantities will rise as the numbers of pets increase worldwide and as human shoppers demand improved food quality. When considering violence and death, pet food is not an obvious object of critique. Yet this work has outlined how even seemingly trivial aspects of our culture can play a role in creating and rationalizing brutality and extant state of affairs for some beings. The pet food industry enrolls cats and dogs in our global industrial meat economy, valorizing the consumption of their flesh.

References

Adams, Carol J. 2010. *The sexual politics of meat: A feminist-vegetarian critical theory.* New York: Continuum.

Armstrong, Philip. 2002. "The postcolonial animal." *Society & Animals*, (4): 413–419.

Baker, Steve. 1993. *Picturing the beast: Animals, identity, and representation.* Manchester: Manchester University Press.

Bisplinghoff, Fred D. 2006. "A history of North American rendering." In *Essential Rendering—All about the Animal By-products Industry*, edited by David L. Meeker, 17–30. Alexandria, VA: National Renderers Association.

Butler, Judith. 2009. *Frames of war: When is life grievable?.* London: Verso.

——2004. *Precarious life: The powers of mourning and violence.* London: Verso.

Case, Linda P., Leighann Daristotle, Michael G. Hayek, and Melody Foess Raasch. 2010. *Canine and Feline Nutrition: A resource for companion animal professionals.* London: Elsevier Health Sciences.

Cato, Mac. 1985. "Give that product … personality! Selling by design." *Canadian Packaging*, 35 (4): 28–30.

Clark, Jonathan L. 2014. "Labourers or lab tools? Rethinking the role of lab animals in clinical trials." In *The rise of critical animal studies: From the margins to the centre*, edited by Nik Taylor and Richard Twine, 139–164. London: Routledge.

Cowell, C. S., N. P. Stout, M. F. Brinkmann, E. A. Moser, and S. W. Crane. 2000. "Making commercial pet foods." In *Small animal clinical nutrition*, 4th edition, edited by Michael S. Hand and Lon D. Lewis, 127–146. Topeka, KS: Mark Morris Institute.

Derrida, Jacques, and Jean-Luc Nancy. 1995. "'Eating Well' or the Calculation of the Subject." *In Points: Interviews, 1974–1994*, edited by Elisabeth Weber and Peggy Kamuf, 255–257. Stanford: Stanford University Press.

Dixon, Jane, Colin Sindall, and Cathy Banwell. 2004. "Exploring the intersectoral partnerships guiding Australia's dietary advice." *Health promotion international*, 19(1): 5–13.

Elder, Glen, Jennifer Wolch, and Jody Emel. 1998. "Race, place, and the bounds of humanity." *Society and Animals*, 6(2): 183–202.

Elliott, Charlene. 2008. "Consuming the other: Packaged representations of foreignness in President's choice." In *Edible ideologies: Representing food and meaning*, edited by Kathleen LeBesco and Peter Naccarato, 179–197. Albany: State University of New York Press.

Fox, Michael W., Elizabeth Hodgkins, and Marion E. Smart. 2009. *Not fit for a dog!: The truth about manufactured cat and dog food.* Fresno, CA: Quill Driver Books.

Francione, Gary. 2010. *Introduction to animal rights: Your child or the dog?* Philadelphia, PA: Temple University Press.

Gillis, Charlie and Anne Kingston. 2000. "The great pet food scandal: How one supplier caused a huge crisis, and why it's just the tip of the iceberg." *Maclean's Magazine*, April 30.

Grier, Katherine C. 2009. "Provisioning man's best friend: The early years of the American pet food industry, 1870–1942." In *Food chains: From farmyard to shopping cart*, edited by Warren James Belasco and Roger Horowitz, 126–141. Philadelphia, PA: University of Pennsylvania Press.

——2006. *Pets in America: A history.* Chapel Hill: University of North Carolina Press.

Hamilton, C.R., David Kirstein, and Richard Breitmeyer. 2006. "The rendering industry's biosecurity contribution to public health and animal health." In *Essential Rendering: All About the Animal By-Products Industry*, edited by David L. Meeker, 71–93. Alexandria, VA: National Renderers Association.

Haraway, Donna. 2008. *When species meet.* Minneapolis, MN: University of Minnesota Press.

——2003. *The companion species manifesto: Dogs, people, and significant otherness.* Vol. 1. Chicago: Prickly Paradigm Press, 2003.

Hill, Dale. 2003. "Specialty ingredients: Considerations and use." In *Petfood technology*, edited by Jennifer L. Kvamme and Timothy D. Phillips, 85–100. Mt. Morris, IL: Watt Publishers.

Holbrook, Morris B. and Arch G. Woodside. 2008. "Animal companions, consumption experiences, and the marketing of pets: Transcending boundaries in the animal–human distinction." *Journal of Business Research*, 61 (5): 377–381.

Ingold, Tim. 1994. "The animal in the study of humanity." In *What is an Animal?* Edited by Tim Ingold, 84–99. London: Unwin Hyman.

Jenkins, Stephanie and Richard Twine. 2014. "On the limits of food autonomy – rethinking choice and privacy." In *The Rise of Critical Animal Studies: From the Margins to the Centre*, edited by Nik Taylor and Richard Twine, 225-240. New York: Routledge.

Johnston, Josée, and Shyon Baumann. 2010. *Foodies: Democracy and distinction in the gourmet foodscape.* London: Routledge.

Joy, Melanie. 2010. *Why We Love Dogs, Eat Pigs, and Wear Cows: An Introduction to Carnism.* Newburyport, MA: Conari Press.

Kirby, David. 2010. *Animal Factory: The Looming Threat of Industrial Pig, Dairy, and Poultry Farms to Humans and the Environment.* New York: St. Martin's Press.

Martin, Ann. 2008. *Food pets die for: shocking facts about pet food*, 3rd edition. Berkeley, CA: New Sage Press.

——2001. *Protect your pet: More shocking facts.* Berkeley, CA: New Sage Press.

Mullin, Molly H. 2007. "Feeding the animals." In *Where the wild things are now: Domestication reconsidered*, edited by Rebecca Cassidy and Molly H. Mullin, 277–304. Oxford: Berg.

Nast, Heidi. 2006. "Critical pet studies?" *Antipode* 38(5): 894–906.

Nestle, Marion. 2008. *Pet food politics: The chihuahua in the coal mine.* Berkeley, CA: University of California Press.

——2007. *Food politics: How the food industry influences nutrition and health.* Berkeley, CA: University of California Press.

Nestle, Marion and Malden Nesheim. 2010. *Feed your pet right: The authoritative guide to feeding your dog and cat.* New York: Free Press

Ockerman, Herbert W. and Conly L. Hansen. 2000. *Animal by-product processing & utilization.* London: CRC Press.

Philo, Chris and Jennifer Wolch. 1998. "Through the geographical looking glass: Space, place, and human–animal relations." *Society and Animals,* 6(2): 103–118.

Pollan, Michael. 2006. *The Omnivore's Dilemma: A Natural History of Four Meals.* New York: Penguin.

Retzinger, Jean P. 2008. "The embodied rhetoric of 'health' from farm fields to salad bowls." In *Edible ideologies: Representing food and meaning,* edited by Kathleen LeBesco and Peter Naccarato, 149–178. Albany: State University of New York Press.

Roe, Emma. 2006. "Things becoming food and the embodied, material practices of an organic food consumer." *Sociologica Ruralis,* 46(2): 104–121.

Rollin, Bernard and Linda Rollin. 2003. "Response to 'What is a Pet?'" *Anthrozoös* 16(2): 106–110.

Scrinis, Gyorgy. 2010. *Nutritionism: The science and politics of dietary advice.* New York: Columbia University Press.

Shell, Marc. 1986. "The family pet." *Representations.* 15 (Summer): 121–153.

Shukin, Nicole. 2009. *Animal capital: Rendering life in biopolitical times.* Minneapolis, MN: University of Minnesota Press.

Sorenson, John, ed. 2014. *Critical Animal Studies: Thinking the unthinkable.* Toronto: Canadian Scholars' Press.

Stanescu, James. 2012. "Species trouble: Judith Butler, mourning, and the precarious lives of animals." *Hypatia,* 27(3): 567–582.

Stanescu, Vasile. 2014. "Crocodile tears, compassionate carnivores, and the marketing of 'happy meat.'" In *Critical animal studies: Thinking the unthinkable,* edited by John Sorenson, 216–233. Toronto: Canadian Scholars' Press.

Steinfeld, H., P. Gerber, T. Wassenaar, V. Castel, M. Rosales, and C. de Haan. 2006. "Livestock's Long Shadow: Environmental Issues and Options." *Renewable Resources Journal* 24(4): 15–17.

Taylor, Chloë. 2008. "The precarious lives of animals." *Philosophy Today,* 52(1): 60–72.

Taylor, Jessica. 2012. "Market breakdown: A global petfood update by region." *Petfood Industry* 56(7): 32–35.

Torres, Bob. 2007. *Making a killing: The political economy of animal rights.* Oakland, CA: AK Press.

Tuan, Yi-Fu. 1984. *Dominance and Affection.* New Haven, CT: Yale University Press.

Walker, Paul. 2000. "Food residuals: Waste product, by-product, or coproduct," In, *Food waste to animal feed,* edited by Michael L. Westendorf, 17–30. Ames, IA: Iowa State University Press.

Williamson, Judith. 1978. *Decoding Advertisements: Ideology and Meaning in Advertising.* London: Boyars.

Wolfe, Cary, ed. 2003. *Zoontologies: The question of the animal.* Minneapolis, MN: University of Minnesota Press.

Woon, Emily. 2011. "Private Label Performance in Global Markets." *Petfood Industry* 53(2): 30–34.

Wortinger, Ann. 2008. "Educating clients about commercial diets." *Veterinary Technician* 29(9): 534.

Wrye, Jen. 2009. "Beyond pets: Exploring relational perspectives of petness." *Canadian Journal of Sociology* 34(4): 1033–1064.

Notes

1 Biological/species disposition (animal size, ferocity, food or habitation needs, etc.) cannot be completely discounted from such processes.

2 See the journal of the International Xenotransplation Association, *Xenotransplanation* (Wiley & Sons Publishing).

3 This is true when animals are in place and under control. Conversely, animals that act outside the appropriate realm—who attack, bite or otherwise act as animals, or live outside of their designated domestic conditions as feral animals, are re-labeled as wild or even "dangerous."

4 There are also significant environmental consequences to CAFOs. According to Steinfeld et al. (2006), CAFOs cause extensive environmental damage by polluting ecosystems with fecal and biological waste contaminated with toxins, generating high greenhouse gas emissions, and even putting pressure on wild and forested regions where agricultural expansion is desired.

5 Edibility is a complicated concept that involves physiological, biological, cultural, psychological, economic, ideological, legal, and chemical processes simultaneously. No agreed upon definition of edibility can be identified within or between most disciplines. What has been widely acknowledged is that humans seem to construct the categories of edibility and food according to a changing host of stated and unstated rules (Douglas 1999; Roe 2006). At a physiological level, edibility relates to whether or not particular organic or inorganic items are safe and suitable for consumption and whether there is a nutritional benefit to the food. Social scientists focus on discerning the conditions under which individual items or whole food categories come to be consumed or not. Often perfectly safe and highly nutritious foods are not consumed for cultural, aesthetic, or ideological reasons.

6 Tallow and other animal fat materials become liquid under heat, but solidify at room temperature. Tallow is fat derived from cattle and lard is derived from pigs.

7 Extrusion does not absolutely require grain use, although the pet foods are usually more consistent with their use. Because extrusion involves the breakdown of starch (a polysaccharide), other starch sources, including potatoes, will suffice.

8 For a thorough overview of the recall, see Nestle (2007).

7 Archives of death

Lynching photography, animalization, biopolitics, and the lynching of William James

Jack Taylor

Back in those days, to kill a Negro wasn't nothing. It was like killing a chicken or a snake. The whites would say, 'Niggers jest [*sic*] supposed to die, ain't no damn good anyway – so jest go on an' kill 'em.
Black Mississippi Resident, Without Sanctuary

We Southern people don't care to equal ourselves with animals.
A White Florida Resident, Without Sanctuary

A 1909 article in the *New York Times*, titled "Cairo Mob Lynches Men of Two Races" reported:

> A negro who had murdered a white girl, and a white man accused of wife murder, were lynched here to-night. The mob is in possession of the city, although the troops are being hurried here, and other lynchings are feared. It is reported that a second negro has been captured, and is being brought into the city to be lynched.
>
> The mob was started on its course by the capture of Will James, alias 'The Frog,' one of the negro murderers of Miss Anna Pelley. After an attempt by Sherriff Frank Davis to save him, James was caught by a mob of Cairo men in the woods near Belknap, Ill., about 5 o'clock this afternoon, and brought into the city on the Big Four train arriving here at 7:45. He was taken to the most prominent square in the city and strung up. The rope broke and the man was riddled with bullets. The body was then dragged by the rope for a mile to the scene of the crime and burned in the presence of at least 10,000 rejoicing persons. Many women were in the crowd, and some helped to hang the negro and drag the body.
>
> (1909, 1)

The newspaper account continues with a description of how Will James was tracked down, shot, and burned:

> When the negro was found word was sent along the line to the scattered mob, which now numbered about 1,000 men, to board a Big Four train

at Belknap. This order was obeyed and a [*sic*] train was jammed when it reached Cairo.

At Tenth Street the mob stopped the train, took the negro off, and marched him through the leading streets of the city to the public arch at Eighth and Commercial Streets. The crowd had swelled by this time to nearly 10,000. Women joined in the procession and applauded, and some cheered ...

Then some grasped the rope and the march to the scene of the crime was taken up. The body was dragged through the streets all about the city amid most joyful demonstrations on every hand.

When the alley where the crime was committed was reached a big fire was built and the body was burned. A woman applied the torch.

(1909, 2)

William James was a young African American male charged with the crime of raping and strangling Ann Pelly, a twenty-four-year-old white woman. He worked at the local Cairo Ice and Coal Company where he shoveled coal and lifted blocks of ice. Sherriff Davis attempted to save William James by boarding him on a train out of Cairo and subsequently hiding with James and his deputy in the woods. Eventually James was taken from Sherriff Davis to be lynched at the center of the city after the sheriff was subdued by mob violence (Dray 2002, 173). That the sheriff could not prevent the mob from lynching William James is indicative of the power of lynching as a vigilante form of extra-legal violence as is the fact that Sherriff Davis did not arrest any of the people who participated in the lynching although there was photographic evidence of who committed this crime. The lynching and the subsequent photographs functioned as visual reminders to discipline blacks and also as objects of nostalgia for the perpetrators who acted out such violence. Today, all that is left is the newspaper story and photographs, before and after the lynching, of William James.

This chapter concerns itself with the animalization, that is, the dehumanization, of African Americans as an ideological tool to mistreat blacks and deny them the most basic human rights so as to make black bodies killable, and their deaths ungrievable. I argue it is precisely the animalization of blacks that places them below and thus outside of the law, and allowed whites to kill them with impunity. The animalization of African Americans has a long history that was ultimately legitimized by the anthropological sciences and which had important political implications in post-slavery United States. Post-slavery United States was a time of heightened rhetoric of black animality, and a time when tensions intensified between black and white wage laborers as blacks joined the waged labor force. I argue that lynching is a biopolitical and necropolitical tactic of political subjugation that helped construct the white community through the death of blacks. Thus, lynching and lynching photography possess an exchange value that constructs American identity buttressed by white supremacist ideology.

To advance this claim, I draw on Roberto Esposito (2011) in order to argue that community itself is founded on violence. With regard to lynching photographs we see community founded on the negation of the black Other which is apparent in the practice of lynching and is represented in lynching photographs, a lead I take from Shawn Michelle Smith (2004, 127–134). As Jacqueline Goldsby notes, the death of blacks paved "the way for America's turn to modernism" (2006, 279). Modernity as a political, economic, and social project is inscribed within the image as the camera and photographs are markers of the modern moment. A constitutive feature of modernity is the increase in lynchings in the post-slavery United States where former slaves were no longer commodities to be bought and sold, and thus black life became less valuable from a purely economic perspective. The transition from black slave labor to wage labor increased the racial and economic tensions between black and white workers. From an economic standpoint, white laborers felt threatened by the increased economic and social gains of blacks, producing anxiety that expressed itself in lynchings.

To draw this out, I discuss lynchings as a site where we can read the spectacle of death, of punishment, as constituting a feature of the modern biopolitical moment. Although Foucault argues that a politics in the name of, and over, life and death emerged and solidified in the modern moment, biopolitical moments occurred before the onset of modernity. Slavery, in particular, as a racialized mode of political subjugation that controlled all aspects of black life in an effort to increase the health of the white population, is a prime example of biopolitics. I will provide a relatively brief historical overview tracing how African Americans were animalized in the nineteenth- and twentieth-century United States as a political tactic designed to justify their oppression. From there I will move to a discussion of the lynching of William James and the subsequent photographic representations of this particular lynching spectacle. I read the phenomenon of lynching from the standpoint of American modernity, bio and necropolitics (the politics of death),[1] and the formation and immunization of the white community from the putative threat of blackness. I utilize Jacques Ranciere's (2007) notion of the "naked image" to argue that lynching photographs do the work of witnessing and testifying. Lynching photographs are also "tear images" in Georges Didi-Hubermann's (2008) sense of the term, referring to images that allow the viewer to make contact with the Real and to imagine what otherwise might remain unimaginable. Photographs are in service to the imaginary and allow the unimaginable, the unthinkable, and unspoken utterances of history, to be seen. I close this chapter with a discussion of lynching photography that has become a permanent exhibition at the National Center for Civil and Humans Rights in Atlanta that opened in June 2014—a full fifty years after the passage of the Civil Rights Act of 1964.

Confronting the lynching photo

Historically, lynching locates its roots in the Revolutionary War when Loyalists to the British Crown were tarred-and-feathered. Outside of the southern states, victims of lynching were predominately white, usually Catholics, new immigrants, union organizers, Mexicans, and Germans (Rice 2003, 4). After 1890, most lynching victims were black. Lynchings occurred primarily as a means of political and economic control. Blacks were often lynched to maintain the economic system of slavery although many slaveholders would not kill what was valuable property (Rice 2003, 4). Ida B. Wells rightfully points out that although the primary reason given for lynching is the rape of a white woman, she provides evidence to show that this assumption is fallacious as less than one-fourth of lynching victims were charged with raping or assaulting a white woman (Wells 1997, 82–88). More often than not blacks were lynched for being "uppity"—that is to say, for making economic and political advancement—or for no reason at all (Wells 1997, 82–88). Lynching reached a high point in the post-slavery United States. In 1897, for example, the news reported two or three lynchings every week, totaling 123 blacks killed (Dray 2002, x). In total, about 4,800 lynchings have been documented from 1882 to 1981 (Apel 2004, 23). Today, lynching photos depicting the spectacle of the lynching party survive, reminding us of a past that bears remembering.

When looking at lynching photographs the viewer is confronted with images that make the very act of looking a moral concern. The viewer encounters a tragic and traumatic past and directly participates in the objectification of dead black bodies killed at the hands of racist mobs. As Dora Apel writes in *Imagery of Lynching*, the viewer is challenged by "the responsibility of historical witnessing" that places him or her in a difficult position of being a voyeur consuming horrific acts of pain inscribed on black bodies and a responsible witness trying to make sense of what lynching photographs represent and what can be learned from viewing them (2004, 7). The relationship between the viewer and the visual grammar of the lynch photograph is indeed a moral issue that has not gone unremarked by social critics. Michael Eric Dyson, for example, thinks commercializing and commodifying the historical legacy of black suffering is morally suspect: "To commercialize the suffering of black people is to do the ultimate disservice to blacks" (Cited in Apel 2004, 12). Dyson further asserts, "To make coffee-table books out of that kind of pain is highly problematic'" (Cited in Apel 2004, 12). Dyson is referencing a book collection of lynch photographs, *Without Sanctuary: Lynching Photography in America*. The book itself contains nearly one-hundred lynching photographs and retails for about $20.00 and is therefore a prime example of how the murder of blacks at the hands of persons unknown has become a commodity to be bought and sold. What is alarming to Dyson is the fact that *Without Sanctuary* may very well be cashing in on the pain and suffering of black bodies, much like photographers at lynching parties who sold postcards of the event.

The commodification of the black body in pain is certainly morally murky territory when faced with the politics of representation. Dyson's concern about the exploitation of the black body as a site of suffering, pain, and death is not too far removed from the general problematics photography critics have with the practice of photography. Walter Benjamin in his address, "The Author as Producer," given at the Institute for the Study of Fascism in Paris in 1934 argues that photography has succeeded in turning poverty itself into "an object of enjoyment" and "human misery" into an object of enjoyable consumption for the masses who are being sedated by photographic images (1982, 24–25).[2] Victor Burgin continues this line of thinking in "Looking at Photographs" by arguing, "The structure of representation – point-of-view and frame—is intimately implicated in the reproduction of ideology (the 'frame of mind' of our 'points-of-view')" (1982, 146). Burgin doubles down on this claim and argues, "But excess production is generally on the side of ideology, and it is precisely in its apparent ingenuousness that the ideological power of photography is rooted—our conviction that we are free to choose what we make of a photograph hides the complicity to which we are recruited in the very act of *looking*" (1982, 148, emphasis in original). And in the spirit of Benjamin, Susan Sontag argues that photographic images function as anesthetics: "But our ability to stomach this rising grotesqueness in images (moving and still) and in print has a stiff price. In the long run, it works out not as a liberation but as a subtraction from the self: a pseudo-familiarity with the horrible reinforces alienation, making one less able to react in real life" (1977, 41). Photographs, in this framing, normalize violence and thus function as a means to suppress political mobilization and liberation.

The concerns of these postmodern critics are certainly not without virtue and are similar to Michael Eric Dyson's unease about lynching photographs as they too are concerned with the ideological and ethical traps governing images in a society structured by capitalism. What must be challenged, however, is the essentialist notion of photography as always-already in the service of (re)producing capitalist ideology and that viewers are not free to choose what they make of an image. If we resist the broad claim that the meaning taken from images only reinforces the ideological structures of capitalism and view images as objects with agency as W.T. Mitchell (2005) calls for in *What do Pictures want?*, we can interrogate photographs in general, and lynch photographs in particular, beyond the reproduction of capitalist and racist ideology. This is precisely what Judith Butler calls for when she argues that images of atrocity and suffering are important as they are channels through which we can know and grieve certain bodies (2004, 146).[3] Such an approach allows for a reading of photographs that does not strip agency from the viewer in that it side steps the notion that capitalist structures solely determine what the viewers see and the meaning they extract from photographs. Viewers are no longer passive observers continuously becoming more alienated from the terrible every time they gaze at an image of atrocity, and images are not always-already simply static carriers of capitalist ideology.

That is to say, we can investigate and read particular images in terms of the ideology that *produced* them and the historical, political, and social moment they reflect, contain, signify, and at times challenge. Viewing lynching photographs this way allows for an understanding of the ideology that produced them and not solely the ideology the photographs (re)produce. From this perspective photographs begin to break down the very ideology they are thought to support. One way of reading lynching photographs is in terms of how they expose the deadly logic embedded in capitalism and its close friend racism.

Leon F. Litwack details the connection between history, memory, and national identity in an introductory essay to *Without Sanctuary* from which I take my cue:

> Even as these scenes recede into that past, they should continue to tax our sense of who we are and who we have been. *Without Sanctuary* is a grim reminder that a part of the American past we would prefer for various reasons to forget we need very much to remember. It is part of our history, part of heritage. The lynching and terrorism carried out in the name of racial supremacy cannot be put to rest, if only because the issues they raise about the fragility of freedom and the pervasiveness of racism in American society are still very much with us.
>
> (2010, 34–35)

Photographic images are points of access into our historically produced political, economic, and social reality. Lynching photographs, then, can be understood as intertextual engagements with the social world and other forms of discourse so as to extract meaning from them in regards to how social, economic, and political modes of governance allowed for black bodies to be killed openly and with impunity. The photographic image comes to be understood in terms of a dialectic between the image and the social reality that produced it and the image that provides a unique and singular perception of that social and political landscape. Photographs illuminate social reality, not simply mask it in a veil of ideology. To put it in Derridean language, photographs function as a supplement to our social world and aid perception – they are prosthetics to memory and disclose an instant that "has taken place only *once*" and has now been archived (2010, 3).

Susie Linfield argues that images should not be viewed as static objects removed from reality, but as phenomena in need of being read through what is outside their frames: "[W]e can *use* the photographs' ambiguities as a starting point of discovery: by connecting these photographs to the world outside their frame, they begin to live and breathe more fully" (2010, 29). I want to breathe life into the lynching photographs of William James by focusing on the intellectual and social context and the racist political and economic conditions that produced them. Such an approach allows us to understand lynching photographs dialectically and further affords us the capacity to come to terms with the political practice of lynching as an instrument of biopolitical subjection. Lynching photographs, in their particularity, expose instants of the past and express objective political and social conditions still lingering in the historical imaginary of the United States.

Spectacle of punishment

Lynching photographs disclose a spectacle in both Debord's and Foucault's senses of the term. Debord argues that the spectacle is "far better viewed as a *weltanschauung* that has been actualized, translated into the material realm – a world view transformed into an objective force" (2005, 13). The spectacle of lynching photography can be understood as nothing short of an articulation of society's relationship with itself and the biopolitical tactics mobilized to preserve the status of whiteness on the American landscape through the denigration of blackness. Michel Foucault details in *Discipline and Punish: The Birth of the Prison* how the means of punishment changed from the eighteenth to the nineteenth century with a crucial component being the demise of the spectacle of punishment. This brought forth an era of discipline and punishment that laid the groundwork for a politics in the name of, and over, life—that is to say, for biopolitics—as the dominant organizing principle of power relations. Foucault argues, "By the end of the eighteenth and the beginning of the nineteenth century, the gloomy festival of punishment was dying out, though here and there it flickered momentarily into life" (1995, 8). Foucault's study is Eurocentric and as such his historical tunnel vision did not allow him to work the U.S. landscape and the forms of punishment that marked it into his historical optics, particularly in regards to how the festival of punishment was executed against blacks. Lynching photographs leave empirical and archival evidence that the spectacle of punishment still "flickered" in the United States. The lynching of blacks in the United States follows the punitive techniques Foucault describes in his *Discipline and Punish*:

> Furthermore, torture forms part of a ritual. It is an element in the liturgy of punishment and meets two demands. It must mark the victim: it is intended, either by the scar it leaves on the body, or by the spectacle that accompanies it … public torture and execution must be spectacular, it must be seen by all almost as its triumph. The very excess of the violence employed is one of the elements of its glory: the fact that the guilty man should moan and cry out under blows is not a shameful side-effect, it is the very ceremonial of justice being expressed in all its force. Hence no doubt those tortures that take place even after death: corpses burnt, ashes thrown to the winds, bodies dragged on hurdles and exhibited at the roadside. Justice pursues the body beyond all possible pain.
>
> (1995, 34)

Although Foucault is discussing state sanctioned public executions in the seventeenth and eighteenth centuries, there are some overlaps between state sanctioned rituals of torture and extralegal lynchings. Lynchings, like the state sanctioned public executions Foucault addresses, were spectacular and communal events (Raiford 2011, 39). There were times when bodies were tortured after death and corpses were often burned. Body parts were often hung on lampposts or other fixtures to serve as visual reminders, to discipline and instill fear in other blacks, as was the case with the lynching of William James. Anti-lynching activist Ida B. Wells, in writing about the lynching of Henry Smith in Paris, Texas on February 1, 1893 notes the inadequacies of words to detail how Smith was tortured, maimed, and burned in front of a cheering crowd of 10,000 who became more feverish with each sigh of pain let out by Smith (1997, 95). Lynchings, then, are representative of political tactics Foucault charted in the eighteenth century, but are also bio and necropolitical modes of governance in that they pivot on the production of death in an effort to increase the life of the white community through the death of blacks. Recall what Foucault says about the primary function of racism as a means to create a division in regards to who must live and who must die: "What in fact is racism? It is primarily a way of introducing a break into the domain of life that is under power's control: the break between what must live and what must die ... That is the first function of racism: to fragment, to create caesuras within the biological continuum addressed by biopower" (2003, 254–55). Creating a break within the races is precisely what the anthropological sciences did by animalizing and Othering black life.

Anthropology, animalization, and biopolitics

The animalization of blacks is an important move that held political and social ramifications due to the zoo-ethno-politics embedded within anthropological discourse that began to gain full force in the mid-nineteenth and early twentieth centuries. Many scientists supported a polygenesis approach to the origins of humanity and argued that blacks and whites were not part of the same human species, placing blacks outside of the political sphere. Jacques Derrida suggests that the animal (and therefore the human deemed animal), like the sovereign, exists *outside* of the law—that is to say, the sovereign exists above the law while the animal exists below the law: "For the current representations, to which we are referring for a start, sovereign and beast seem to have in common their being-outside-the-law ... [being-outside-of-the-law can also] situate the place where the law does not appear, or is not respected, or gets violated" (2011, 17). The connection between animality and the law figures into the ideological and the biopolitical registers vis-à-vis lynched black bodies.

The animalization of blacks as formulated and hardened by the anthropological sciences works to sustain and disseminate a lethal ideology that renders black life as less valuable than white life and extinguishable in the face of the law of which they are outside (below). The animalization of black life is nothing short of the dehumanization of black life so as to create a racial hierarchy. This holds particularly true in post-slavery United States, particularly following the 1896 *Plessy v. Ferguson* ruling which determined that blacks were not 'persons' protected by the constitution of the United States and the famous 1857 *Dred Scot v. Sanford* decision, which dictated that blacks were not citizens to be protected under the constitution as "they [blacks] had no rights which the white man was bound to respect" (Bell 2000, 41). Such language inscribed in the law is remarkably similar to the figure of *Homo Sacer* who has the capacity to be killed, but not sacrificed, who has been reduced to mere *zoē*, to pure life, as opposed to *bios*, or political life (Agamben 1998, 8).

The animalization of blacks negates black personhood and by extension negates black humanity by introducing a radical break in the biological continuum of human. "This *dispositif* of the person" writes Esposito, "in other words, is that which at the same time superimposes and juxtaposes humanity on human beings and animality of human beings; or that distinguishes the part of humanity that is truly human from another that is bestial, that is enslaved to the first" (2010, 128). The negation of one's personhood allows for biopolitical mobilization through the channels of racism. As Foucault argues in *Society Must be Defended*, racism mobilizes biopower in its most lethal form by dictating who must be protected and who must die so as to support white supremacy and putatively create a "healthy" white community (2003, 255). It is precisely this ideological and political basis grounded in the animalization of blacks that allowed for the continued lynching of blacks throughout the course of the modern era.

The animalization of African Americans was largely informed by the anthropological and ethnological sciences in the nineteenth century. These newly emerging fields of intellectual inquiry sought to distinguish, hierarchize, and categorize 'types of humankind.' As slavery began to wane due to increased abolitionist agitation, anthropologists responded with a lethal 'science' to counter what they saw as a barrage of ideology that upset the established racial order of things. Anthropological sciences began to hypothesize that blacks were a separate species thus further negating black humanity. Texts like *Types of Mankind* (Nott et al. 1854), although operating and masquerading as 'objective science,' supported and generated knowledge claims working to animalize blacks. The authors of *Types of Mankind* sought to draw a close proximity between nonhuman primates and people of African descent: "And what is not a little remarkable, is the fact that the black orang occurs upon that continent which is inhabited by the black human race, while the brown orang inhabits those parts of Asia over which the chocolate-colored Maylays have been developed" (Nott et al. 1854, 75). While not a direct association of orangs and individuals of the 'black human race,' it does demonstrate how nineteenth century anthropological sciences labored to make the connection between blacks and animals. The imagery within the text is perhaps more revealing of how the nineteenth century anthropological sciences worked to animalize blacks. Indeed, one figure (Figure 179) shows an image of a 'type' of Negro with exaggerated features. The commentary reads: "Fig. 179 ... may be considered caricatured, although one need not travel far to procure, in daguerreotype, features fully as animal ... " (1854, 260).

This animalization of blacks found its way into everyday, common language as well. The inscription on a lynching postcard depicting the lynching of an unidentified African American male in Georgia in 1902 reads, "Warning [:] The answer of the Anglo-Saxon race to black brutes who would attack the womanhood of the South" (Allen et al. 2000, plate 60). It is precisely the animalization of black bodies that allows the State and the general public to transform this ideology into the *practice* of lynching allowing for the destruction of black bodies with impunity. It is no surprise, given the legal measures passed at this time coupled with the increase in scientific proclamation and everyday rhetoric claiming that blacks are animals, that the lynching of African Americans reached a high point between 1882 and 1930, during which time an African American man, woman, or child was killed once a week on average (Rice 2003, 4).

In another popularly read 'study,' "Race Traits and Tendencies of the American Negro," statistician Frederick L. Hoffman notes that blacks are not of the same human status as their white counterparts and were better off subjected to the conditions of slavery:

> Nothing is more clearly shown from this investigation than that the southern black man at the time of emancipation was healthy in body and cheerful in mind. He neither suffered inordinately from disease nor from impaired bodily vigor. His industrial capacities as a laborer were not of a low order, nor was the condition of servitude such as to produce in him morbid conditions favorable to mental disease, suicide, or intemperance ... Unless a change takes place, a change that will strike at the fundamental errors that underlie the conduct of the higher races towards the lower, gradual extinction is only a question of time.
>
> (1896, 311–329)

Hoffman produced this report for Prudential Insurance to argue against selling life insurance to African Americans in post-slavery United States. Hoffman waxes nostalgic for a time when society had 'order,' a time when society reflected the 'will of God' and nature through the institution of slavery, when black lives had a quantifiable value, as opposed to those same black bodies that had become devalued and corrupted in an economy structured on wage labor. Hoffman's anxiety reflects the threat of increased tension between black and white workers, a tension that contributed to the persecution of black bodies in the new economy. His commentary is evidence of a crucial point I am trying to illustrate concerning the ideology that blacks were discursively constructed as a threat to themselves and to the overall health of the republic after emancipation in their turn to wage labor, as it is exactly this threat from which the social body tried to immunize itself through the act of lynching.

Community and violence

Those involved in lynchings were not only destroying black bodies, but also constructing a further entrenched conception of white community and subjectivity. In lynching photographs the corpse of the dead black body is central to the formation of white community and whiteness itself. As Shawn Michelle Smith argues: "These photographs produce whiteness through an absolute disavowal of blackness. The black corpse remains bound and circumscribed by white supremacy in these images displayed front and center, the corpse functions as the negated other that frames, supports, and defines a white supremacist community" (2004, 127). Whiteness is constructed out of the dead black Other, which is circulated through the medium of lynching photography. That most lynching photographs show a group of whites surrounding a dead black body demonstrates the centrality of negating blackness so as to produce white community grounded in white supremacist ideology (Smith 2004, 127).

The writer Ralph Ellison honed in on the phenomenon of lynching as a means to construct white American identity in his 1940 short story "A Party Down at the Square." The story is narrated from the point of view of an unnamed, young white boy who experiences his first lynching with his Uncle Ed. Ellison places the lynching at a common site of ritual violence, the courthouse, and thereby suggests that lynchings at the hands of white mobs have a close proximity to, and are supported by, U.S. 'democratic' institutions such as the judicial system.[4] Ellison's short story depicts how American identity is constructed by the execution of an African American. When the narrator arrives the lynched black man's pants are now on fire, initiating a crucial step in the lynching ritual. A conversation occurs between the lynch victim and Jed, a white man who will run for sheriff next year, which again demonstrates how blacks exist outside of the space of the deliberative democracy: "'What you say there, nigger?' And it came back through the flames in his nigger voice: 'Will one a you gentlemen please cut my throat?' he said. 'Will somebody please cut my throat like a Christian?' And Jed hollered back. 'Sorry, but ain't no Christians around tonight. Ain't no Jew-boys neither. We're just one hundred percent Americans'" (Ellison 1998, 8). That this scene can be read as a critique of American democracy is highlighted through the fact that the lynch victim initially cannot be heard. And when his request is finally heard, his request is denied. Like lynching photographs themselves this story demonstrates how U.S. identity and community are founded in the disdain and rejection of blackness itself and that the democratic ideals are not extended to blacks.

"Party Down at the Square" highlights Ellison's idea concerning the fantasy of ridding the U.S. of blacks. Moreover, it also highlights how blacks are deemed not fully American, as they exist outside of the democratic sphere – an apt dramatization of Agamben's notion of bare life. Jed constructs his identity on the basis of national belonging—"We're just one hundred percent Americans"—not on racial identity, though the two are linked: his whiteness *is* his Americanness. Blacks in this instance can be understood as making up the 'constitutive outside' against which Americanness is defined racially.[5] Ellison understood blacks to be outside yet fundamental to, that is *within*, the American project: "One of the ways that has been used to simplify the answer has been to seize upon the presence of black Americans and use them as a marker, a symbol of limits, a metaphor for the 'outsider'" (2003, 587). At the conclusion of the short story Ellison suggests that lynchings further function as a means for whites to identify along racial lines instead of economic lines so as to fragment the working class. This is enunciated when the narrator notes "a white [share]cropper said it didn't do no good to kill niggers 'cause things don't get no better. He looked hungry as hell. Most of the croppers look hungry" (1998, 11).

Ellison's short story can be utilized to interrogate lynching photographs as markers of the limitations of the American project and its failure to live up to democratic ideals. Lynching photographs also demonstrate the fantasy of ridding blacks from the American landscape while simultaneously affirming blackness as central to—though outside of—American identity and commu- nity. What Smith and Ellison demonstrate in regards to the construction of white community through the lynching of blacks has crucial implications for a biopolitical reading of lynching.

Lynchings function as a mode of biopolitical governance as they were used as a means to protect against the putative threat of blackness that disrupted the white community at a time of increased rhetoric of black criminality. Robert Esposito (2011) notes that the construction of community requires violence and the logic of immunity corresponds with this moment. He argues, "Far from being limited to the role performed by the law of immunizing the community from the violence that threatens it, violence actually comes to characterize the immunitary procedures themselves: instead of being elimi- nated, violence is incorporated into the apparatus it is intended to repress – once again, violently" (2011, 9–10). The immunitization of community and the protection of (some) life is hinged to the death of others. Community is disclosed and produced through the death of William James and constitutes a portion of the exchange value of lynching.

The language of immunity found its way into the everyday language of those who participated in lynchings. As one Mississippi resident put it, "'A white man ain't agoin' to be able to live in this country if we let niggers start getting biggity'" (qtd. in Allen et al. 2000, 27). "Biggity" here is code for black economic and political advancement that whites thought would dis- place their privileged position in the United States. And a Memphis resident in 1909 used surprisingly biopolitical language of immunity when he said "We whites have learnt to protect ourselves against the negro, just as we do against the yellow fever and the malaria—the work of noxious insects" (Allen et al. 2000, 34). The putative threat of black violence is a threat to the health of the white community and will be treated like a virus; introducing violence will cure the virus. As Esposito argues in regards to the founding of community in general, and as the Mississippi and Memphis residents expressed, the immunization of the black other is necessary for the preservation of the white U.S. republic. The death of some blacks, so it was thought, would increase the health of the republic in general and the white community in particular. The immunitary process founded on violence is disclosed in the photographic image and allows for an intertextual interplay between the photographic image, and social, economic, and political reality.

The lynching of William James was a ritualistic immunitary practice allowing biopolitics to function as a mode of governance. As the newspaper report at the beginning of this chapter details, the community used violence to stop the threat of violence. This lynching can be further interrogated as ritual by analyzing another crucial component of lynching parties—celebration—as it is the celebratory aspects of lynching that partially give lynchings their communal basis. In the account of the lynching of Will James "[w]omen joined in the procession and applauded and some cheered" (*New York Times* 1909, 1). Thirteen years later Countee Cullen honed in on this phenomenon in his 1922 poem in *Kelly's Magazine* titled "Christ Recrucified" in an effort to not only draw parallels to the sacrifice of Jesus, but to expose lynchings as an articulation of vigilante justice, and ritualistic and celebratory moments:

> But lest the sameness of the cross should tire
> They kill him now with famished tongues of fire,
> And while he burns, good men, and women, too,
> Shout, battling for his black and brittle bones.
>
> (2003, 222)

This poetic formulation by Cullen indexes points I have been highlighting in that "Christ Recrucified" refers to celebratory moments of lynching and the religious undertones residing therein, but also points to how the lynched black body was dismembered and consumed by 'respectable' members of society so as to form community.

Reading the lynching photography of William James

That Ida B. Wells notes the insignificance of words to convey the horrors of lynching scenes makes photographic representations of lynching important cultural artifacts as they achieve what words cannot express. The image on the right in Figure 7.1 of Will's half-burnt head on a pole discloses a trace of historical reality and shows how lynch photographs are naked images intent on witnessing, intent on testifying and giving voice to an otherwise silent past. In *The Future of the Image* Ranciere develops and defines three types of

Figure 7.1 Composite Photograph of Will James Before and After his Lynching, 1909. Cairo, Illinois.

Figure 7.2 The Lynching of Will James.   November 11, 1909, Cairo, Illinois. From *Without Sanctuary: Lynching Photography in America.*

images that reside in contemporary museums and art galleries: the naked image, ostensive image, and metamorphic image. He defines the naked image thus:

> the image that does not constitute art, because what it shows us excludes the prestige of dissemblance and the rhetoric of exegeses. Thus, a recent exhibition entitled *Memoires des camps* devoted one of its sections to photographs taken during the discovery of the Nazi camps. The photographs were often signed by famous names ... but the idea that brought them together was the trace of history, of testimony to a reality that is generally accepted not to tolerate any other form of presentation.
>
> (Ranciere 2007, 22–23)

I am committed to the argument that lynching photos are 'naked' images in Ranciere's sense of the term in that they are excluded from the realm of art and function as pure testimony and witnessing—they are pieces of visual testimony captured from reality, sites where past atrocities can be reckoned with, and spaces where political modes of governance are revealed. They are flashes, revelations of the truth presented to the spectator and they express past historical injustices revealed through a trace of history now presented, copied, and archived in the photograph.

Racialized violence is witnessed in this image. The pole itself divides the image in half. The composition of the image is instructive in terms of the meaning it conveys. The elevation of the head and the fact that the pole is placed at the center and the front of the image is indicative of the centrality of the dead black other to the formation of white community. "Half burnt head of James" is etched into image. It is as if the head itself replaced a flag or some other symbol used to provide a sense of solidarity or unity amongst the community.

The poet and educator Esther Popel gave poetic expression to the centrality of the dead black body as constitutive of American identity by juxtaposing lines from the "Pledge of Allegiance" with detailed descriptions of lynchings. A portion of the poem reads:

> '*I pledge allegiance to the flag-*
> They dragged him naked/Through the streets [...]
> '*Of the United States of America*'-
> One Mile they dragged him
> Like a sack of meal,
> A rope around his neck[...]
> '*And to the Republic for which it stands*'[...]
> Of men, and boys, and women with their babes,
> Brought out to see the bloody spectacle.
>
> (2003, 283)

Esther's poem demonstrates a key point in regards to the centrality of lynching to formation of the United States of America while simultaneously honing in on lynchings as communal events used to solidify the community through the deadly exclusion of blacks. The placement of Will James' head on a pole demonstrates that James remains outside of the white community, but foundational to its formation. This is further highlighted by the fact that his charred remains were placed in the communal space of Candee Park in Cairo, Illinois. In the background to the left of the pole is a suburban house, which if read through James' charred remains indicates what is preserved, namely white community, by the lynching and burning of Will James. This is evidenced by the fact that the victim's head was attached to the top of a post to serve not only as a totem to keep other African Americans in line through a visual reminder that signifies the little regard for black life on the U.S. landscape, but also served as a means to solidify the community by putting on display the work they had done to produce the dead black other through the extralegal murder of Will James.

The second image of Will James further reveals lynching's close relationship with modernity.[6] The image shows a crowd of thousands in downtown Cairo, Illinois in the commercial district gathered together by modern means to (mass) consume and participate in the lynching. The space was lit by electricity so the spectators can view the lynching at Hustler's arch. That the lynching took place in the middle of a commercial district in front of thousands of people discloses lynching's close affiliation with American consumer culture that was on the rise at this particular time, which perhaps represents a struggle over the modern urban city due to recent black migration and relatively recent emancipation, which heightened the racial tension amongst black and white workers as whites viewed themselves in economic competition with blacks. This is signified by the lynching's closeness to businesses such as saloons and a circular sign that reads 'Dowling Pressing co. Both Phones' attached to a pole reading 'Pressing Club.' One postcard has engraved into its image the "Spot Where Will James, Body was Riddled with Bullets, After Being Lynched Nov 11th 09 At Cairo ILL" (Allen et al. 2000, plate 50). The image shows three well-dressed men in top hats standing on the site where James was killed and a woman and two men are standing closely behind the men and another woman is coming out of the building. All but one directs their gaze at the camera. A dialectical understanding of the two images reveals that only modern phenomena can protect modernity by resorting to both archaic (the spectacle of punishment, for example) and modern practices (technology to make the spectacle happen and the photograph to document and archive the event).

In the image below, eight youths surround the site where Will James was burned, and where his ashes remain, seemingly unafraid of permanently attaching themselves to his death. One of the youths wields a stick, which was probably used to sift the ashes in search of pieces of flesh, bone, and teeth that are now valuable commodities, as parts of lynched black bodies were often sold as mementos. Orlando Patterson notes that the perpetrators of

Figure 7.3 The charred remains of Will James, 1909. Cairo, Illinois. From *Without Sanctuary: Lynching Photography in America.*

violence might keep parts of the victim (1998, 195).[7] In this instance the community shared the mementos from the victim. Only one of the kids directs his gaze at the camera, perhaps suggesting he cannot come to terms with the act, but we can only speculate. All the others appear to hover over the ashes in a contemplative fashion. In the ashes there are cans that may have once contained flammable liquid to cook Will James' body, or perhaps are empty containers of alcohol that contributed to the festive spectacle killing and served as means to further negate James' body. Behind the youths there appear to be adults. The juxtaposition of the youths with the adults surrounding the ashes, points to the idea that this act was an initiation into manhood and a promotion of white male masculinity. Following Hazel Carby, Shawn Michelle Smith argues that white males participated in lynching as a means to promote white masculinity and to control the black male body during post-emancipation America (2004, 115).

Returning to the composite photograph above, the dual images show Will James before and after his death. On the left hand side, there is a standard portrait photograph of Will James on gelatin silver print. James looks straight at the camera with an empty look on his face. His clothes are somewhat worn, perhaps signifying James' class status as a shop clerk. Beneath the portrait of Will James the text reads "Will James (alias) Froggie." The portrait is from 1907—two years prior to his lynching. A black border separating the portrait of Will James from his burnt head placed atop a pole frames the image. The black gap marks the two years that have passed between his portrait and his lynching and burning. The gap, however, may be read as a means to provide distance between the two images. However, the pictorial grammar of the first image leads, despite the gap, to the second image. The first image is reminiscent of a criminal mug shot, which if understood in relation to the second image, implies that Will James has always been guilty and in need of punishment. The black gap can be read as the time that has elapsed and the violence that was necessary to produce the second image in the composite photograph, to which the spectator does not have access. James' lynching and burning is left to the imagination of the spectator of the post-card, who can construct the event as they please. The image on the right hand side shows the after effects of such violence as most lynch photographs do as there are only a few lynch photographs where the person is still alive. That the gap in the post-card does not show the actual violence itself, but the end result of such violence works to fetishize violence by way of not representing the violence – that is, the labor—that went into the production of Will James' burnt head (Goldsby 2006, 279).

But the fetishization of violence absent in the image does not make the image itself a "fetish image" as Dyson may have thought. As Didi-Hubermann rightfully argues in his defense of analyzing four photographs from Auschwitz – an impossible and fetishizing task according to his critics – images of atrocities are not fetish-images where the spectator becomes a voyeur. They are tear-images "from which a fragment of the real escapes" in that images of atrocity do not veil the catastrophic, but in fact disclose it by revealing a slice of the horrific, the otherwise unimaginable (2008, 113). The images, then, are archival documents that "aim" at the truth and allow for not voyeurism, but the capacity to imagine the otherwise unimaginable (2008, 113). Lynching images are pieces, fragments of the real that function as a form of testimony and a way of historical remembrance and recollection (2008, 93).

Like Ranciere's naked image and Didi-Huberman's tear-image, lynch photos show what they do not show in that they do not merely index a horrific event in its singularity, but also point to the lynched bodies that were not captured by the photographic medium and perhaps the potential lynchings to come. Ranciere further details the naked image thus, "the 'naked' image intent solely on witnessing. For witnessing always aims beyond what it presents. Images of the camps testify not only to the tortured bodies they do show us, but also to what they do not show: the disappeared bodies, obviously, but above all the very process of annihilation" (2007, 26).

Following the logic advanced by Ranciere, then, lynch photographs contain a surplus value or surplus content by pointing to events beyond what is represented in the image: they represent an absence. The image, then, is caught within a dialectical matrix of presence and absence. It is the 'realness' of the 'tear-image' that is the lynch photograph that ignites the surplus content not fully contained "in" the image and points to other lynchings and acts of violence. By making present and disclosing pieces of the real, the lynch photograph negates the spectator's doubt concerning the violence perpetrated against African Americans and further discloses an era in American history that has largely been forgotten – the images force the viewer to not forget and brings to the surface a historical moment that has been repressed in America's collective consciousness. All attempts to deny the history of violence become senseless as spectators can now begin to *visualize* this history of violence and *imagine* other similar atrocities. The photographs, then, work as an aid to memory, while simultaneously testifying and archiving past atrocities. Lynching photography allows for a repetition of a past event that enables the spectator to witness and archive the referent into their memory and reconstitute their perception of the world. This is precisely what the lynching photographs allow for at the National Center for Civil and Human Rights.

Conclusion

Lynching photographs haunt the American imaginary and yet, the historical legacy of lynching is something we still must come to terms with. A collection of lynching photographs and postcards collected by James Allen are now part of the permanent collection at Atlanta's new Center for Civil and Human Rights. A recent trip I took to the center functions as the perfect metaphor in regards to the legacy of lynching and in regards to some of the points I have been trying to make throughout the chapter in terms of historical memory and the biopolitical consequences of lynching. After walking through the museum, I became somewhat disappointed that the collection of photographs was not in fact present as I was told. I quickly asked someone about the collection of photographs and they seemed somewhat surprised by my inquiry. I was told there is in fact a lynching photograph present in the museum and that it is at the very beginning of the exhibition – on the ceiling. The placement of the photograph is revealing in regards to the historical legacy of lynching and lynching photographs. The curator who placed this photograph on the ceiling seems to be all too aware of how such tragic events have been repressed in our collective historical imaginary. But the placement hovers above representations of Jim Crow segregation with the wall to left reading "White" and the wall to right reading "Colored" as if to suggest lynchings and the threat of death are partially what made Jim Crow possible. This photograph asks the viewer to not forget and to understand the biopolitical logic of such practices. This is what I have attempted to do throughout the course of this chapter.

References

Agamben, Giorgio. 1998. *Homo Sacer: Sovereign Power and Bare Life*. Edited by Werner Hamacher and David E. Wellbery, translated by Daniel Heller-Roazen. Stanford: Stanford University Press.

Allen, James, Hilton Als, John Lewis, and Leon F. Litwack. 2000. *Without Sanctuary: Lynching Photography in America*. Santa Fe: Twin Palms Publisher.

Apel, Dora. 2004. *Imagery of Lynching: Black Men, White Women, and the Mob.* New Jersey: Rutgers University Press.

Bell, Derrick. 2000. *Race, Racism, and American Law.* New York: Aspen Law & Business.

Benjamin, Walter. 1982 "The Author as Producer." In *Thinking Photography*, edited by Victor Burgin, 15–31. London: Macmillan Press.

Burgin, Victor. 1982. "Looking at Photographs." In *Thinking Photography*, edited by Victor Burgin, 142–53. London: Macmillan Press.

Butler, Judith. 2004. *Precarious Life: The Powers of Mourning and Violence.* London: Verso.

——2009. *Frames of War: When is Life Grievable?* London: Verso.

Cullen, Countee. 2003. "Christ Recrucified." In *Witnessing Lynching: American Writers Respond*, edited by Anne P. Rice, 220–222. New Brunswick: Rutgers University Press.

Debord, Guy. 2005. *The Society of the Spectacle.* Trans. Donald Nicholson-Smith. New York: Zone Books.

Derrida, Jacques. 2011. *The Beast & the Sovereign.* Edited by Michel Lisse, Marie-Louise Mallet and Ginette Michaud, translated by Geoffrey Bennington. Chicago: University of Chicago Press.

——. 2010. *Copy, Archive, Signature: A Conversation on Photography.* Edited by Gerhard Richter, translated by Jeff Fort. Stanford: Stanford University Press.

Didi-Huberman, Georges. 2008. *Images in Spite of All: Four Photographs from Auschwitz.* Translated by Shane B. Lillis. Chicago & London: The University of Chicago Press.

Dray, Phillip. 2002. *At the Hands of Persons Unknown: The Lynching of Black America.* New York: The Modern Library.

Ellison, Ralph. 2003. "What America Would be Like Without Blacks." In *The Collected Essays of Ralph Ellison*, edited by John F. Callahan, 581–88. New York: Random House.

——1998. "A Party Down at The Square." *Flying Home.* New York: Vintage Book, 3–11.

Esposito, Roberto. 2011. *Immunitas: The Protection and Negation of Life.* Translated by Zakiya Hanafi. Cambridge: Polity Press.

——2010. "For a Philosophy of the Impersonal." *The New Centennial Review* 10 (2): 121–34.

——2008. *Bios: Biopolitics and Philosophy.* Translated by Timothy Campbell. Minneapolis: University of Minnesota Press.

Foucault, Michel. 2003. *Society Must Be Defended: Lectures at the College de France, 1975 - 1976.* Edited by Arnold I. Davidson, translated by David Macey. New York: Picador.

——1995. *Discipline and Punish: The Birth of the Prison.* Translated by Alan Sheridan. New York: Vintage Books.

Graves, Joseph L. 2005. *The Emperor's New Clothes: Biological Theories at the Millennium.* 2nd ed. New Jersey: Rutgers University Press.

Goldsby, Jacqueline. 2006. *A Spectacular Secret: Lynching in American Life and Literature.* Chicago & London: The University of Chicago Press.

Hoffman, Frederick L. 1896. "The Race Traits and Tendencies of the American Negro." *Publications of the American Economic Association* 11 (1/3): 1–329.

Laclau, Ernesto. 2007. *Emancipation(s).* London: Verso.

Linfield, Susie. 2010. *The Cruel Radiance: Photography and Political Violence.* Chicago & London: The University of Chicago Press.

Litwack, Leon F. 2000. "Hellhounds." In *Without Sanctuary: Lynching Photography in America,* edited by James Allen, 8–37. Santa Fe, N.M.: Twin Palms.

Mbembe, Achille. 2003. "Necropolitics." Translated by Libby Meintjes. *Public Culture,* 15 (1): 11–40.

Mitchell, W.J.T. 2005. *What Do Pictures Want? The Lives and Loves of Images.* Chicago: University of Chicago Press.

New York Times. 1909. "Cairo Mob Lynches Men of Two Races; Women in the Crowds That Take Vengeance on Negro and White Murderers. Other Victims Sought Negro Captured After Sheriff Flies with Him – Gov. Deneen Orders Troops to the City." *The New York Times,* November 12. http://query.nytimes.com/gst/abstract.html?res=9B01E4D6123EE733A25751C1A9679D946897D6CF# (accessed October 21, 2014).

Nott, Josiah Clark, George R. Gliddon, Samuel George Morton, Louis Agassiz, William Usher, and Henry S. Patterson. 1854. *Types of Mankind: or, Ethnological Researches:*based upon the ancient monuments, paintings, sculptures, and crania of races, and upon their natural, geographical, philological and biblical history, illustrated by selections from the inedited papers of Samuel George Morton and by additional contributions from L. Agassiz, W. Usher, and H.S. Patterson. Philadelphia: J.B. Lippincott, Grambo.

Patterson, Orlando. 1998. *Rituals of Blood: Consequences of Slavery in Two American Centuries.* New York: Basic Book.

Popel, Esther. 2003. "Flag Salute." In *Witnessing Lynching: American Writers Respond,* edited by Anne P. Rice, 282–83. New Brunswick: Rutgers University Press.

Raiford, Leigh. 2011. *Imprisoned in a Lumious Glare: Photography and the African American Freedom Struggle.* Durham: The University of North Carolina Press.

Ranciere, Jacques. 2007. *The Future of the Image.* Translated by Gregory Elliot. London: Verso.

Rice, Anne P. 2003. "Introduction: The Contest Over Memory." In *Witnessing Lynching: American Writers Respond,* edited by Anne P. Rice, 1–24. New Brunswick: Rutgers University Press.

Smith, Shawn Michelle. 2004. *Photography on The Color Line: W.E.B. Du Bois, Race, and Visual Culture.* Durham: Duke University Press.

Sontag, Susan. 1977. *On Photography.* New York: Picador, 1977.

Thomas, William J. 2005. *What do Pictures Want? The Lives and Loves of Images.* Chicago & London: The University of Chicago Press.

Wells, Ida B. 1997. *Southern Horrors and Other Writings: The Antilynching Campaign of Ida B. Wells, 1892–1900.* Edited by Jacqueline J. Royster. Boston: Bedford St. Martins.

Notes

1 Here I have in mind Achille Mbembe's (2003) notion of necropolitics.
2 For a detailed and wonderful discussion of the critiques of photography see Susie Linfield's *The Cruel Radiance: Photography and Political Violence* (2010, 3–31).
3 To be sure, for Butler, images possess the dual function of having the capacity to both humanize and dehumanize, to make some lives grieveable and others ungrievable.

4 A courthouse was the site of the 1920 lynching of Lige Daniels in Center, Texas where a spectator can be seen watching the event from a window in the photograph capturing a group of whites proudly standing below Daniel's hanging corpse without fear of prosecution.

5 Here I read Ellison from the vantage point of Ernesto Laclau's Derridian formulation of the constitutive outside. Laclau argues, "The system is what is required for the differential identities to be constituted, but the only thing – exclusion – which can constitute the system and thus make possible those identities, is also what subverts them. (In deconstructive terms: the conditions of possibility of the system are also its conditions of impossibility)" (2007, 53).

6 For a detailed discussion of lynching and its relationship to modernity see Leigh Raiford's *Imprisoned in A Luminous Glare: Photography and the African American Freedom Struggle*, 37–40.

7 James Allen writes that a studio photographer, Lawrence Beitler, printed thousands of copies of the photograph of Thomas Shipp and Abram Smith lynching "for ten days and nights" selling them for fifty cents a copy (2010, 178).

8 Remains to be seen

Photographing "road kill" and *The Roadside Memorial Project*

L.A. Watson

How does theory become practice? And how can art function as activism? As an interdisciplinary artist, many people are surprised to learn that the foundation of my visual arts practice is rooted in research. A majority of my time is spent thinking about how to connect both aesthetic and conceptual concerns in an artistic praxis that goes beyond the white walls of the gallery and out into the world in order to *do* something. The ways in which art has the ability to merge with activism in order to not only critique but also *intervene* in the social and political landscape is something that I am very much interested in. How can abstract processes of art-making have a practical and positive impact on the world? After I moved from an urban environment to a rural one, I was increasingly confronted by the deceased bodies of animals who had been killed on our winding one- and two-lane roads; this has always been a sight that has saddened and disturbed me, and so began the process of thinking about these animals who are not so affectionately termed "road kill."

In this chapter, I'll be discussing some of the research that has led up to and inspired *The Roadside Memorial Project*, a site-specific art installation on the rural road that leads to my house. First, I'll be using Judith Butler's question, "What makes for a grievable life?" (2004, 20) as a starting point to consider the ways in which non-human animals killed on the road are framed as "ungrievable lives" in contemporary sociopolitical discourse. Then I'll turn my attention to the visual, photographic frame and focus on the work of contemporary artists who have chosen to document the bodily remains of animals killed on the road, in order to question the photographs' potential to awaken an ethical responsiveness in the viewer. Particular attention is paid to photography's historical associations with death and challenging the anthropocentrism found throughout traditional photographic theory—how can photography, which has historically been viewed as "an art of the Person" (Barthes 1980, 79), begin to address non-human animals not only as a subject matter but also as subjectivities that matter? Finally, I will conclude by presenting my own work, which utilizes photography as an aesthetic and conceptual tool to document *The Roadside Memorial Project*—a sculptural installation of reflective road signs that constitutes a public site of mourning for animals killed on the road, as well as a new kind of warning sign to alert human drivers.

Vulnerable lives

> [We] all live with this particular vulnerability, a vulnerability to the other that is part of bodily life, a vulnerability to a sudden address from elsewhere that we cannot preempt.
>
> (Butler 2004, 29).

The phenomenon of "road kill" has been around since the advent of automobile transportation. Unsurprisingly, the rate at which non-human animals have been killed on the road has steadily increased in conjunction with the proliferation of cars as a primary mode of human travel. Today, the sight of a dead or dying animal on or off to the side of the road is a common one in both urban and rural environments and on roadways large and small. A staggering number of animals—*an estimated one million*—are killed *each day*—in motor vehicle collisions in *the United States alone* (Soron 2011, 58) and these numbers are continuing to grow. According to the organization Animal Road Crossing (ARC), "Collisions between wildlife and vehicles have increased by 50 per cent in the past 15 years" and "cost Americans $8 billion every year" (ARC 2014).

The accidental nature of "road kill," coupled with the sheer numbers of animals killed and encountered on a daily basis, has worked to normalize the phenomenon, and this has contributed to a fatalistic atmosphere of disengagement with these animals and the politics of their deaths. According to Dennis Soron, "The very banality of this everyday violence reinforces the tendency in commodity culture to regard animal bodies as things whose routine destruction inspires morbid curiosity, but never empathy or concern" (2011, 59).

Human disregard for non-human animals killed on the road is elucidated in numerous consumer products, such as flattened stuffed animal toys, "Twitch the Raccoon," and "Smudge the Squirrel," and prank toys like "Liquid Roadkill," which helps consumers "recreate the special odor of road kill" in a place of their choosing.[1] These goods often capitalize on what Mike Michael calls a "cartoonified" (2004, 285) aesthetic, one that mocks the real, lived experiences of animals by poking fun at their deaths through "comically protruding tongues, crossed and bulging eyes, buck teeth, expressions of dazed shock, and other stereotypical signs of imbecility" (Soron 2011, 63). These visual tropes seek to signify the silliness and/or stupidity of the animal, and constitute a "blame the victim" mentality in order to defer the blame from humans to non-human animals. Human culpability in the death of the animal is further distanced by the deceiving and inadequate terminology of "road kill" itself—it is the vivified road and not the person driving down this road that has risen to act as an agent of death. Other euphemisms that describe the animal's deceased body as "flat meat," "highway pizza," or "pavement pancakes" elucidate how the animal's corpse is rendered palatable both literally and symbolically.[2] Terms such as these also draw attention to the ways in which non-human animals are made "killable" (Haraway 2008, 80) and therefore "ungrievable" (Butler 2009, 31) by being labeled as an edible object. In other words, the construction of other animals as edible works to further rationalize and justify their deaths.

While it is impossible to know whether, or to what degree, human-animals mourn the death of other animals who have been killed on the road, it is clear that non-human animals are not recognized in mainstream sociopolitical discourse as subjects of a life, who can and should be grieved.[3] Rather, they are visually and discursively framed as lives who do not matter. In the book *Frames of War*, Judith Butler (2009) investigates our "epistemological capacity to apprehend a life" (ibid., 3) by analyzing the "normative conditions for the production of the subject" (ibid., 4) that "frame" or actively construct our perception of reality (ibid., xiii) and allow us to distinguish "whose lives count" (ibid., xx). Butler's notion of a "precarious life" is one that we all share as embodied beings, whose lives are dependent on one another and are always vulnerable to injury, violence, and death from the start (2009, 30–31). Although Butler's analysis is primarily concerned with the vulnerability and precarity of marginalized human lives (immigrant workers, non-US nationals, women, prisoners of war, etc.), she does admit that precariousness is "a condition that links human and non-human animals" (2009, 13) and that precarity cannot be understood in relation to one's own life alone, but must be understood in relation to "the precariousness of the Other" (2004, 134). Butler's non-anthropocentric notion of precarity emphasizes embodied connections that extend beyond what we call "the human," and this opens up new pathways for considering ourselves in relation to *other* animals' lives whose shared "finitude" (2009, 30) echoes our own. Unfortunately, according to Butler, our capacity to understand our shared condition as vulnerable bodies in the world does not create an egalitarian state of existence, but instead produces "specific exploitation of targeted populations, of lives that are not quite lives, cast as 'destructible' and 'ungrievable.' Such populations are 'lose-able,' or can be forfeited, precisely because they are framed as being already lost or forfeited: they are cast as threats to human life as we know it rather than as living populations in need of protection" (2009, 31).

All of this can be said to describe the situation of wildlife populations that make up the majority of animals killed on the road; many species are considered nuisances and are therefore not only framed as "lose-able" (2009, 31) but also actively destroyed by sports hunters and state wildlife agencies when their populations increase beyond "carrying capacity."[4] The same can be said of *predatory* animals who are targeted for destruction when they threaten the life of human beings or other animals who are considered the financially viable private property of human beings such as "*live*stock." On the road, big "game" animals constitute a mortal and economic threat to human drivers—the

National Highway Traffic Safety Administration estimates that there are close to one million collisions with deer each year, which kill two hundred Americans and result in $1 billion of damage (Rice 2011). In order to help combat human fatalities and vehicular damage, wildlife warning signs featuring large-bodied animals are erected to warn drivers to the possibility of their presence; yet signs warning of smaller wildlife—who pose a much lesser threat to human life or property—such as turtles, squirrels, raccoons, or possums, are overwhelmingly absent on our nation's highway road signs. While wildlife warning signs have been shown to reduce collisions with animals, and can function to protect *both* human and non-human animal lives, their primary purpose remains to protect human lives above all Others (as evidenced by the disparity between signs for large-bodied vs. small-bodied wildlife).[5] In this way, the wildlife warning sign, as a highly visible, public marker, creates a particular kind of frame that works to establish "whose lives can be marked as lives, and whose deaths will count as deaths" (Butler 2004, xx–xxi). Unfortunately, the visual economy of the wildlife warning sign disregards the diversity of species who are vulnerable to destruction from "a sudden address from elsewhere" (Butler 2004, 29). Therefore, warning signs can be seen as visible markers that reflect a human-centered economy, which disregards the precarity of non-human animal's lives, whose bodies are overwhelmingly more vulnerable to destruction when struck by an automobile.

Meanwhile, the complexity surrounding the social and material forces that converge to create the phenomenon of "road kill" seems invisible and impenetrable, and as such the fate of animals is overlooked in favor of human or non-human animal issues that seem intentionally caused or "solvable." The animal is hit, and we run—not only from our own culpability in the matter as individuals, but also from seeking to address the ways in which this violence and these deaths are systemically built into our own systems of survival.[6] The animal, these issues, and our shared vulnerability as sentient beings living in the world are continually passed by and overlooked—seen as an unfortunate by-product of industrialized living. But are there other ways that we can apprehend the phenomenon of "road kill"? Ways of seeing that help us reimagine our relationship with animals killed on the road and reframe the phenomenon of "road kill"?

Remains to be seen

Although the bodies of animals killed on the road are witnessed on an almost daily basis, one rarely, if ever, stops to slow down and have a look—it is a sight that is generally avoided, or is seen only partially and momentarily as one speeds by. What then, if anything, can be gleaned from a kind of sustained looking (one that seems especially absent in the case of animals killed on the road)? In an attempt to reframe the phenomenon of "road kill," and reorient the human gaze (or lack thereof) upon that of the non-human animal, a number of contemporary artists have used photography as a tool to document (and forever freeze) their own encounters with animals killed on the road. These up-close, individuated encounters seek to confront the realities of "road kill" by situating the human body alongside and with that of the non-human animal's remains in order to transcend the remote and fleeting views one would normally have through a car. A surprising number of artists document the decomposing bodies of animals as they encounter them, without moving or manipulating the body in any way.[7] These straight, untouched, documentary-style photographs incorporate the framing techniques of landscape photography as well as those of forensic science in order to accumulate a seemingly endless catalog of "road kill" images. Almost all of these images are accompanied by text titles that state the geographic location where the animal was found, as well as the date and type of species killed.[8] Not surprisingly, many of these images are hard to look at and could be considered "shock art" by some, who may see the bloodied and disemboweled bodies of animals as sheer spectacle or, worse, a glorification of the violence portrayed. And while these are understandable positions to take, which are rooted in an ethics of photography (a concept that I will be returning to), photographs such as these can be seen as early precursors to the recent road kill observation systems that have sprung up in three states (California, Maine, and Idaho) since 2009 (Wildlife Crossing, n.d.; Idaho Fish and Game 2014). These state-run systems rely on data collected by volunteers in the community; anyone who comes across "road kill" can help identify the type of wildlife killed, where and when the body was located, and other pertinent information, such as traffic or road conditions that may have contributed to the animal's death (Wildlife Crossing, n.d.). Photography plays an important role, as users are encouraged to submit a photograph of the animal as well. This accumulated data is being used to determine geographical "hotspots," where particular animal deaths frequently occur, and to quantify these deaths in order to "estimate [the] benefits of different remedial actions" (ibid.). Road kill observation systems are undoubtedly a step in the right direction, and something that every state should adopt in order to better understand and respond to the ecological impacts that roadways are having on local fauna. And while this is a promising start, it does not mean that future remedial actions won't continue to privilege projects that focus on alleviating the impacts of certain larger species—who threaten human life or property— over and above the needs of smaller species. As mentioned earlier, the economic impact of collisions with larger animals is costly. The most commonly reported collisions in the United States are with white-tailed deer, which cost the average driver $3,000 or more in repairs and total over $1 billion annually (Taylor 2013; Rice 2011). It is not surprising then, that statistics such as these are calculated into remedial actions for wildlife that address first and foremost the concerns of human drivers. When a highway overpass for deer was built over Interstate 80, near the Utah–Nevada border last year, Michael Murphy from the Nevada Department of Transportation said that "the decision to build the 2.75 million dollar structure was based on a cost-benefit analysis that looked at human fatalities and damage done to cars" (Taylor 2013). While cost-benefit analyses such as these are helpful in determining geographical "hotspots" for collisions with large-bodied wildlife and are persuasive in enacting mitigation measures that can greatly reduce these collisions, they are unable to alleviate impacts with smaller wildlife whose deaths fall outside of these equations.

The ecological diversity of life affected by the phenomenon of "road kill" has only recently entered our cultural consciousness as a topic worthy of research and concern; yet this is something that has been documented for decades in the work of artists: Bob Braine, Stephen Paternite, Clive Landen, and Joy Hunsberger. The images produced by these artists certainly draw our attention toward the vulnerability of non-human animal bodies and the precarious nature of their lives, but they do not necessarily allow us to mourn the loss of the animal, or call attention to the animal's life as one that can and should be grieved.

Artists such as Brian D. Collier, Emma Kisiel, Meagan Jenigen, and Jamie Garrison seek to address this problem by appropriating the visual language of human roadside memorials, in order to create and install memorials or shrines for animals killed on the road.[9] In all of these works, artificial flowers that typically decorate gravesite displays for humans are thoughtfully arranged near the animal's remains. Placed out in the public sphere, where the animal has died, and where these deaths continue to occur, these memorials confront drivers and passersby, draw attention to the death of the animal, and act as a public site of mourning. In the work of both Brian D. Collier and Meagan Jenigen, visual representations of the animal prior to death and fully formed are placed near the deceased animal's body in order to highlight the individual subjectivity of the animal and give a face to that which is physically eroding and socially effaced. Other iconography associated with human sites of mourning, such as white crosses and candles, appears along with flowers in the work of Jamie Garrison and Meagan Jenigen. All of these sites seek to test the limits of the cultural frames that constitute what lives can be considered a loss, and silently ask us to consider, "What makes for a grievable life?" Finally, I want to consider the work of two artists who not only document the bodies of animals killed on the road but also complicate our relationship to "road kill" by directing the gaze of the viewer in very particular ways.

Roadkill (After Life)

In Claudia Terstappen's series, *Roadkill (After Life)*, the deceased bodies of animals who have been killed on Australia's roads are depicted in large-scale photographs that overshadow gallery viewers who seem almost small in comparison.[10] The animal's presence in these images is inescapable—not simply because of his or her size, which rivals that of a human body in certain images, but also because the body of the animal is the only thing that exists within the frame of the photograph. The background contents that one would normally see (i.e., the road and landscape where the body was found) have all been digitally removed to call attention to the animal's body, which has been centered in the frame and now rests on a continuous dark plane. The resulting images are surprisingly and somewhat disturbingly beautiful when compared with the majority of "road kill" photographs. The blood, guts, and gore that are typically found in this genre of photography are completely absent, with the exception of one image: that of a blotched blue-tongued lizard whose bloody lip has been pulled away from his or her body—yet even this does not register as repulsive. In all of these images the body of the animal is highly aestheticized—it is easy to linger on the patterns, textures, and colors of the animal's fur, feathers, and flesh. The careful placement and clean treatment of the animal's body exude a quiet peacefulness that is reminiscent of the way deceased human bodies were posed so they could be memorialized in the popular practice of nineteenth-century postmortem photography. In a written statement about the work, Terstappen says that she "sought to create a death mask—as used for identification during the 18th and 19th centuries—to permanently record the characteristic and distortions of the animals, like a true portrait" (Terstappen 2010).[11] It is clear that Terstappen is interested in highlighting the individual subjectivity of the animals she photographs by creating memorial portraits that function in a similar way to those of human portraits of the deceased, which she says, "makes the deceased [into] a non-interchangeable character and brings them back to life by showing us their face" (ibid.). The images in *Roadkill (After Life)* eschew the violence inherent in a majority of "road kill" photographs that are documentary in nature; their aesthetic allure offers viewers an opportunity to stay with these images, and quietly contemplate their own relationship to these animals and their deaths, which is something that is not likely to occur with overtly grotesque imagery. Viewers are encouraged to connect with the animal, not just as a subject *matter* but as a subject who matters, yet at the same time, the subjectivity of the animal is threatened, if not completely overturned, when seen in the context of a private gallery as a highly aestheticized object. The terrible acts of violence that destroyed these bodies are contextually distant within the confines of the gallery, which always threatens to aestheticize death and to turn the animal "into *only* an image" (Azoulay 2008, 126). Perhaps this is why Terstappen has allowed these images to circulate beyond the gallery's walls and out onto the street so that they can be seen in the context of where these deaths occur. Several images in the series have been printed as billboard signs, so that automobile drivers rather than gallery goers can view them. In a striking image taken at night, a group of three billboards depicting a lizard, a cockatoo, and a crushed turtle are shown lit up and next to a busy road, and a fourth billboard, placed prior to these images, features only text, which asks motorists to "remember me" (Terstappen 2010). When these images are sequestered in the space of a gallery, death is de-realized and viewers are more easily removed from their own complicity in the act—this is a death that *has happened* and *was caused by someone else*, "out there" on the road. When drivers become viewers, who are asked to "remember me," they are made complicit in the act of driving and the iterable nature of these deaths becomes palatable—*I might cause a death, here, at any moment.*

Norfolk Roadkill, Mainly

Steve Baker's photographic series *Norfolk Roadkill, Mainly* documents the corpses of animals that have been killed in the rural terrain of Norfolk, England. Each photograph is shot in a landscape-style format, in natural light with the camera pointed directly down at the animal's remains (McHugh 2011, 7). The animal's body is not manipulated in any way or moved, and the resulting image is never retouched or cropped (ibid.).[12] Each image is captioned with the date and location of when and where the animal was found. In this respect, Baker's working method is akin to a number of other artists who document and catalog "road kill"; however, Baker does not make a point to list the type of species found in his title's descriptions, which he says could "invite viewers to indulge their likely sympathies for some species over others" (ibid., 9). This is an interesting observation because the "type" of animal that has been killed is not always apparent as the material nature of the animal's body shifts, depending on its state of decay, from recognizable features full of flesh, fur, and feathers to bare and undistinguishable traces. When thinking about viewers' potential engagement with the work, Baker knew he wanted to move beyond straightforward documentation, saying, "It didn't seem to me that simply presenting individual captioned roadkill images would be enough. It wasn't that they couldn't have been presented like that in an art context; it just didn't seem sufficiently interesting or engaged" (ibid., 1).

Further engagement came in the ultimate form of a "stacked diptych," whereby the photograph of the animal's corpse is situated directly above or sometimes below another image that appears to be completely arbitrary (ibid., 2). In one image, the flattened body of a rabbit rests above a worn-away bas-relief of a lion and is titled *Woodbastwick Road, 24/6/09*; in another image, the headless body of a bird on bare blacktop sits above a photograph of a flowering tree against a bright blue sky and is titled *Church Lane, Spixworth, 9/8/09* (ibid., 1–14). Concrete surfaces, medieval buildings, and a modern traffic sign overtaken by ivy also make appearances in these juxtapositions, and while some visual correlations can be made between the remains of the animal and its visual counterpart in relation to similar textures or shapes, for the most part the pairing of the animal's body with its corresponding image seems jarring and out of place. The only similarity between the animal's body and that of the image, according to Baker, is their "geographic proximity" (Baker 2013, 190). Pairing the animal's body with unrelated imagery was an intentional decision in order to discourage "obvious" readings of the work, that if left alone, might seem "gratuitously gory, sensationalist, and exploitative, or else as didactic, moralizing, and sentimental" (ibid., 192).

In some, but not all of these images, Baker makes his presence as the photographer known within the frame of the photograph—his bicycle's metal body, pedal, wheel, or shadow offers a distraction from the animal's body and disrupts conventional techniques of aesthetic framing. Baker's presence directs viewers not only to the outside of the frame toward human-created technology—to the camera, bicycle, and car—all of which have contributed to creating the scene that lies before us, but also to the act of photographic framing itself. According to Butler, "To call the frame into question is to show that the frame never quite contained the scene it was meant to limn, that something was already outside, which made the very sense of the inside possible, recognizable" (2009, 9). By inserting himself into the frame of the photograph, Baker acknowledges himself not only as a witness but also as an active participant in the construction of the frame. And while the non-neutral subject position of the photographer always has a certain authority in crafting who or what is shown in the photograph, Butler is quick to point out that "[t]he frame never quite determine[s] precisely what it is we see, think, recognize, and apprehend. Something exceeds the frame that troubles our sense of reality; in other words, something occurs that does not conform to our established understanding of things" (2009, 9).

Through the form of a stacked diptych, viewers oscillate between the inside and outside of both frames and bodies. Images of eviscerated animals threaten to contaminate the disjointed images that "exceed the frame" above or below them. These images, which do not "conform to our established understanding of things" (ibid., 9), compete for our attention like a scenic landscape or unusual architecture might.[13] In this way, looking at Baker's work feels very much like driving. Death and violence are glimpsed, but one quickly redirects oneself to some other, more pleasant sight/site, only to incur this violence again and again. Questions of ethics, "if they even [figure] at all," according to Baker, "[seem] to look after themselves" (2013, 192). So what are we as viewers encouraged to do when looking at a series of work such as this? Baker is insistent that the series "aims to distance itself from anything like 'moral edification' and to frustrate readings that seek to recuperate it for such purposes" (ibid., 194), and in this regard it seems that he is successful. One can't help but feel trapped in this work—there are only two directions in which the gaze can go, and even when our eyes are averted from the dismembered body of the animal, it does not remain latent; instead it seeps into and stains everything around it. The inability to escape the death that lies before us and to understand it creates a sense of helplessness that corresponds to the seemingly unsolvable phenomenon of "road kill."

Photographing "road kill"

All of the artists that I have discussed so far have responded to the phenomenon of "road kill" by photographing the deceased bodies of animals killed on the road for a variety of personal reasons, which I am unable to fully elaborate on or completely convey. However, I wanted to begin to explore the scope and variety of works that have engaged "road kill" as a subject matter through the lens of photography not only as a means of thinking alongside these artists in relation to my own artistic practice, but also to begin to think about the ethics of photographic framing in relation to non-human animals as the subjects of photographs. In *The Civil Contract of Photography*, Ariella Azoulay explores the ethics of photographic framing and its relationship to a photographed person whose "citizen status is flawed, or even nonexistent (as in the case of refugees, the poor, migrant workers, etc.)" (2008, 118). According to Azoulay, there is always a "measure of violence" involved when photographing persons, "even when the situation is one of full and explicit consent between the participant parties" (ibid., 99) because the photographed person is always vulnerable and the "threat of violation always hangs over the photographic act" (ibid., 119). In order to explore the photograph's potential for violation, Azoulay begins to describe a photograph that depicts the dead body of a migrant worker taken by Miki Kratsman, titled *Migrant Worker, Tel Aviv, 1998*(ibid., 120). She states,

> The body lying on the ground is silent; it is utterly exposed to the photographer who has arrived with his camera and calmly set himself in front of it, using the time at his disposal to compose a dramatic frame. Should the photographer not have taken this picture of the exposed body, abandoned without anyone bothering to cover it, or was it his duty to take the picture, to draw our attention to the length of time that elapsed between the disaster's occurrence and someone going to the trouble of honoring the dead by covering it, as is customary?
>
> (ibid., 119)

Can the same questions not be posed in relation to photographing the deceased bodies of animals killed on the road? Unburied and unmourned, the deceased body of the animal remains "utterly exposed to the photographer" (ibid., 119), but what are the political ramifications for images such as these?[14] Does a sustained looking at death through photography help us to reimagine our relationship to non-human animals and empathize with them through a photographic framing that deems these deaths (and therefore these lives) as worthy of our attention? Or are we sustaining death by looking at a death sustained? In other words, does a kind of forced looking at these images lead to a paralyzing state of disengagement, one that in many ways continues to reinscribe the very violence that has been directed toward these now deceased non-human animal bodies? These may be unanswerable questions;

however, the questions that are raised when considering representations of human pain, suffering, and death should apply no less to non-human animals. And either way, the differential status accorded to non-human animals who exist outside of the law demands new ways of looking at foundational photographic texts, taking into account the literature that continues to emerge from the field of human–animal studies.

Yet the camera's lens seems like an appropriate tool to help "capture" the remains of the animal, given the photograph's historical associations with death. Death, according to the philosopher Roland Barthes, is an ever-present component in the photograph that "does not necessarily say *what is no longer*, but only and for certain *what has been*" (Barthes 1980, 85). While a photograph may not necessarily show "what is no longer" in the case of a still living subject, for instance, the photographed remains of an animal depict both *what is no longer* as well as *that which has been*.[15] The photographic image haunts viewers in an almost hallucinatory way by testifying to both past and future events all at once—the *"this will be"* and the *"this has been"* (ibid., 96) of the subject or event that has been trapped in time. Death is apprehended in all photographs regardless of the life stage at which the subject is captured, according to Barthes:

> In Photography, the presence of the thing (at a certain past moment) is never metaphoric; and in the case of animated beings, their life as well, except in the case of photographing corpses; and even so: if the photograph then becomes horrible, it is because it certifies, so to speak, that the corpse is alive, as *corpse*: it is the living image of a dead thing.
>
> (ibid., 78–79)

The photograph of a corpse is horrifying, according to Barthes, because its deadness is forever brought to life and sustained through the photographic image. In this way, when viewing the "living image of a dead thing," regardless of whether it is a human or non-human animal, we are confronted with the undeniable fact of a death that-has-been, while simultaneously being redirected, as it were, to a necessary and previous state of aliveness. The moment where life ends and death begins is captured in the photograph, according to Susan Sontag, who writes in *On Photography*, "Photographs state the innocence, the vulnerability of lives heading toward their own destruction, and this link between photography and death haunts all photographs of people" (1977, 64). I would like to argue that the link between photography and death haunts all photographs of non-human animals as well. Acting as an evidentiary object, the photograph makes the death before us (in this case an animal killed on the road) real. The reality of this death seems to prod us toward the moment of death itself, into contemplating the particularities surrounding the cause of death and the previous state of aliveness that must have preceded it. The state of looking at a life in reverse, projecting from a death back into a life, is a similar process (albeit backwards) to that of Sontag's, and it is one that is worth considering in relation to images of the deceased.

Another important question to consider when thinking about the ways in which non-human animal bodies are framed and formed within the field of photography is that of metaphor. According to Barthes, the presence of the body or thing before us, whether it is alive or dead, is never metaphoric (1980, 78). This point is an interesting one to consider when thinking about the ways in which non-human animals are frequently depicted as metaphors, such that the real, lived experiences of non-human animals—what they, in and of themselves, might be, feel, and experience—are taken from them in order to help better understand and structure the thoughts and feelings of human animals.[16] Therefore, is it possible to perceive of the animal as always present and never metaphoric in the sense that Barthes proposes?

Barthes seems to indicate that the photograph testifies to the fact that the thing we see before us is real, has existed as such, and is captured as it has been. But while all bodies may be equally real, are they necessarily seen as such? Butler suggests that all images necessarily perform an act of framing, a way of making real in the world, where some bodies are made real (and therefore grievable) while others are not (left ungrievable) (2009, 77). How, then, are we to presume that we are being confronted by the animal itself, as it "has been" within *any* image, even those that are free from digital manipulations, those that are supposedly more truthful and documentary in nature? There is, of course, no doubt that the animal pictured certainly *has existed*— the image emanating from the photographic paper tells us as much—but how much of our perception of and ethical responsiveness toward the deceased animal depicted in the photograph is shaped by external discourse that lies outside the photographic frame? In other words, I'm thinking alongside Butler, who asks how "our cultural frames for thinking the human set[s] limits on the kinds of losses we can avow as loss?" (2004, 32).

If the category of "the animal" is already determined to reside outside of and against that of "the human," then our perception of what we see within the frame of the photograph is already directed by a particular set of beliefs that depend upon certain socially constructed norms. These norms typically regard non-human animals, especially wild animals, not as individuals but rather as representative of an entire species—a species that is then subsumed under the categorical title of "animal," which is defined against and devalued in relation to "human" animals. Given this, does the death of the animal apprehended through the photographic image even constitute a proper death as such? Life as such?

Whether dead or alive, the visage of a human subject automatically connotes his or her own personhood, according to Barthes: "Photography, moreover, began, historically, as an art of the Person: of identity, of civil status, of what we might call, in all senses of the term, the body's *formality*" (1980, 79). We are able to recognize persons depicted in photographs as individuals with particular identities based upon the civil status of personhood, a definition that has widened over time and has been defined in relation to and against the status of non-human animals. Butler states, "Wherever there is the human, there is the inhuman: when we now proclaim as human some group of beings who have previously not been considered to be, in fact, human, we admit that the claim to "humanness" is a shifting prerogative" (2009, 76). The cultural construct of "the human" has never been stagnant, although pseudoscientific studies in physiognomy throughout the ages have attempted to prove the "inferiority" of particular populations of people by anatomically comparing them to non-human animals, or that which was assuredly *not* human, in order to impose a hierarchy of persons and further codify and constrain the concept of the human.[17] Not only was the anatomical structure of the face important in drawing distinctions between "higher" and "lower" races and classes of people, a great deal of importance was also placed upon the way in which human and non-human animal eyes operated and the "superior" ways in which human-animals were able to see (and therefore comprehend) the world around them (Lee 2006). The ways in which vision became intertwined with the ability (or supposed inability in the case of animals) to reason are evidenced by a thought process akin to that of the twentieth-century philosopher Georges Bataille, who posits this about non-human animals: "There was no landscape in a world where the eyes that opened did not apprehend what they looked at, where indeed, in our terms the eyes did not see" (Broglio 2011, xvi).

Bataille's conceptual framework elucidates the ways in which non-human animals who were alive occupied a conceptual space so vacant as to be considered dead. Today, thankfully concepts such as these have been discredited, and many animals are recognized for their extraordinary vision, as well as their problem-solving skills.

However, a politics of vision that preferences the human-animal's ability to see is something that continues to be enforced by the human-created technology of the automobile, which alters not only the sensory perceptions of drivers but also those of non-human animals.

For human drivers, the automobile functions not only as a physical barrier that helps shield drivers from physical injury and harm, but also as a psychological barrier that insulates the driver from certain sights/sites that are seen and felt inside the machinery of the car. A majority of collisions that kill wildlife occur in the low light of dusk and throughout the night when human visibility is compromised (Wildlife Collision 2004). Human technology works against non-human animal biology, as the artificial light of headlights emanating from vehicles disorients nocturnal animals, whose eyes have adapted to see best in low-level light. The fast-approaching and stunningly bright light of oncoming drivers creates the well-known "deer-in-headlights" effect, which literally blinds and paralyzes animals, who can no longer see to escape. Moreover, if the animal does manage to escape, it will take them 10–40 minutes on average to fully regain their normal night vision (Beier 2006, 33).

In many ways, the interaction between human-drivers and nocturnal wildlife forcibly asserts a hierarchy of vision, whereby the superior night vision of the non-human animal is sacrificed to the inferior night vision of the human driver. Interestingly, roads have actually been made safer for human drivers thanks to reflective technology inspired by non-human animal biology. Common within the eyes of many vertebrate mammals is a thin layer of tissue called the tapetum lucidum, which enhances the vision of nocturnal animals by reflecting light back to the retina (DCNR 2007–2008). The tapetum lucidum, which translates in Latin to "bright tapestry," is the eyeshine we see reflected in nocturnal animals' eyes (ibid.). A number of commercial products for road safety have been inspired by the tapetum lucidum; the earliest patent was used in the "Catseye" brand reflectors we see embedded in the pavement of roads, inspired, of course, by the shape and retro-reflectivity of cat's eyes (Reflecting Roadstuds 2014). Advancements in retro-reflective technology have led to a number of products for safer roads, such as reflective traffic signs, paint, and high-visibility safety clothing.

The Roadside Memorial Project

If the human-created technology of the automobile impedes the vision of nocturnal animals who have directly inspired the creation of products for safer roads (safer for humans, that is), how can this be reflected in the work that I produce? How can the one-sided gaze of human headlights be returned? And if road signs are visible markers that reflect a human-centered economy, which values some but not all lives, how can both the memorial and the sign be reimagined as one and the same?

These were some of the questions I was asking myself when I began thinking about how I would personally respond to the deaths of animals killed on the road. I knew I wanted to create a public site of mourning that would (like the roadside memorial artists discussed earlier) question the "ungrievable" status of animals killed on the road. However, I wasn't necessarily interested in making a memorial that would be situated alongside a specific animal per se. It was important for me to figure out how to create a dialogue about the death of animals killed on the road that avoided literal depictions of these deaths. Instead of creating a memorial for individual animals that would be placed next to the animal in disparate geographic locations (dependent on where the animal had died), I thought it could be interesting to think about creating a series of memorials that would accumulate in a specific location, like the bodies of animals over time—a series of memorials that would publicly mark the past, present, and future deaths of animals killed on the road. This would be something that drivers could not ignore—that they would be forced to move through—and would create a durational experience that would slowly build and eventually overwhelm the geography of the road and haunt the human driver. As mentioned earlier, I had been thinking about the visual economy of wildlife warning signs, and the differential allocation of signs depicting large mammals that are viewed as a threat to human life. What would an egalitarian representation of road signs that reflects the true diversity of animals killed on the road look like? When I discovered that the retro-reflective technology of the road sign was inspired by the eyeshine of nocturnal animals, and that a majority of wildlife are killed in low-level light, creating a series of reflective road signs that could also function as a memorial for animals killed on the road seemed to make sense.

And so *The Roadside Memorial Project* began. I started by tracing the silhouettes of animals commonly killed on Kentucky's roads onto wooden boards that were then cut out on a scroll saw. I ordered the retro-reflective material used on street signs and adhered this to the front of each board. I decided to use white reflective material, not only because it is the most highly reflective color, but also because it subtly references the iconography of human roadside memorial crosses and denotes innocence, sacrifice, spirits, and ghostly specters. Unlike standard road signs, each sign was made with a reflective front and back, so that drivers could see the signs no matter which direction they were coming from. In order to decide on a location for the installation, I spent several months "getting to know" the geography of my local roads and noting the incidence of animals killed. I ended up narrowing my focus to a dangerous curve that comes just before our property, which has been notorious for automobile collisions and wildlife fatalities over the years. I placed the first batch of signs (a total of seventeen) on the sides of the road around this curve and up a hill where drivers tend to accelerate in speed.[18] Unlike standard road signs, these signs were positioned so that they sat low on the ground and they were staggered—some of them sat on the very edge of the road, while others were placed further back. Positioning the signs in this way was a purposeful decision in order to shift the gaze of the driver from looking up, toward signs that are situated at the height of a human body, to looking down, toward signs that are situated at the height of the non-human animal's body and toward the edges of the road, where wildlife is most likely to appear.

Over the next few months, I documented the installation when it came to life at night and was "turned on" by the headlights of passing drivers that illuminated it. I wasn't prepared for how extremely bright these signs would be, and none of the photographs or video that were taken was able to capture the phenomenological experience of being there.[19] I also wasn't prepared for the reaction of drivers—I was extremely surprised by how many people slowed down—some drivers reduced their speeds dramatically and others stopped. Of course, this wasn't always the case, but many drivers did and this was an unexpected and pleasing outcome of the project, as I had learned through my research that the number one way to reduce wildlife mortality is to reduce driver speed. What was originally envisioned as an alternative means to memorialize animals killed on the road was slowly becoming something much more. The format of a reflective road sign was allowing me not only to critique the phenomenon of "road kill" but also to actively intervene and possibly even reduce the number of animals killed.

Figure 8.1 L.A. Watson, *The Roadside Memorial Project*, 2013. Detail of a memorial/ sign before dark.

Figure 8.2 L.A. Watson, *The Roadside Memorial Project*, 2013.

When I began photographing the installation and drivers' interaction with it, my original intention was just that—to document the work. This project was never meant to be seen in a gallery. But as I spent more time with the photographs, I began to realize they created an affective experience that was entirely their own. As vehicles drove past the installation, the artificial light

Figure 8.3 L.A. Watson, *The Roadside Memorial Project*, 2013.

Figure 8.4 L.A. Watson, *The Roadside Memorial Project: Possum*, 2013.

emanating from them not only illuminated the memorial signs but also became indelibly recorded in the photographic frame itself. Headlights and taillights registered as lasers of light streaking through the night—an evidentiary trace of the destructive speed and blinding light of the human-created technology of the automobile. I realized the interplay of light in the photograph between the ghostly reflections of the roadside memorials and the traces of light left by the automobile visually conveyed many of the things

Figure 8.5 L.A. Watson, *The Roadside Memorial Project: Chipmunk*, 2013.

Figure 8.6 L.A. Watson, *The Roadside Memorial Project: Raccoon*, 2013.

Figure 8.7 L.A. Watson, *The Roadside Memorial Project: Fox*, 2013.

that I had been thinking about: the precarious nature of non-human animal lives who are exponentially more vulnerable to "a sudden address from elsewhere" and the animal as a spirit or specter whose life can and should be mourned. I finally came to see the physical installation and the photographic documentation of the installation as two separate but related bodies of work whose audience and affective impact change depending upon the work that is seen. Because light was a fundamental material and conceptual component in both the physical installation and photographic documentation of *The Roadside Memorial Project*, I decided to print the photographs as large transparencies that were illuminated in light-boxes and shown in a dimly lit room.

In the end, *The Roadside Memorial Project* was a small gesture, a way for me to come to terms with a phenomenon that has always saddened me and to formulate a personal and political response to it. While slowing the speed of some drivers was an unintended and welcome consequence of the project, one that could potentially save lives, the format of the road sign is limited and partial, for it can engage only human drivers. Therefore, continued thought must be given to creative solutions that account for the sensory perceptions not only of human travelers but also of non-human travelers.[20] Like the work of other artists discussed earlier, *The Roadside Memorial Project* does not attempt to "solve" the phenomenon of "road kill," but seeks to create an expanded dialogue about other-than-human animals whose remains are all around us, yet remain to be seen as an urgent sociopolitical issue. Through different tactics of photographic framing, viewers are asked to confront the phenomenon of "road kill," a subject that is, according to Helen Molesworth, "as important as endangered species, for in death, in the transformation of one element of a system, the system itself becomes exposed" (1996, 179). Human complicity in the deaths of other animals on the road is evidenced in the frame of the photograph, which forces us to acknowledge the ways in which the automobile—as the primary form of human *mobility*—is intrinsically tied to the *immobilization* of non-human animal bodies. How we use this information to incite concrete political action on behalf of *all* animals killed on the road has less to do with our ability to *see* the death that lies before us, and has more to do with our ability to *feel* the magnitude of it. Photographic frames that mourn the death of the animal may not allow every viewer to feel the full magnitude of these losses, but they are profoundly important because they publically expose and visibly challenge a hierarchy of death. Frames that ask, "What makes for a grievable life?" (Butler 2004, 20) unsettle the boundaries between the human and the non-human animal and seek to establish relational ties that galvanize an ethical responsiveness. When ungrievable lives become grievable, losses that were tolerable become intolerable and deaths that seemed inevitable become preventable.

> In eastern Oregon, along U.S. 20, black-tailed jackrabbits lie like welts of sod—three, four, then a fifth. By the bridge over Jordan Creek, just shy of the Idaho border in the drainage of the Owyhee River, a crumpled adolescent porcupine leers up almost maniacally over its blood-flecked teeth. I carry each one away from the tarmac into a cover of grass or brush out of decency, I think. And worry. Who are these animals, their lights gone out? What journeys have fallen apart here?
>
> (Lopez and Eschner 1998, 1)

References

ARC. 2014. "Why Are Animals Dying on Our Roads?" http://arc-solutions.org/new-thinking (accessed December 1, 2014).

——2012. "Study Launched to Determine Effects of Wildlife Warning Reflectors." http://arc-solutions.org/article/study-launched-to-determine-effects-of-wildlife-warning-reflectors-on-wildlife-vehicle-collisions (accessed December 1, 2014).

Azoulay, Ariella. 2008. *The Civil Contract of Photography*. New York: Zone Books.

Baker, Steve. 2013. *Artist Animal*. Minneapolis: University of Minnesota Press.

Barthes, Roland. 1980. *Camera Lucida: Reflections on Photography*. New York: Hill and Wang.

Beier, Paul. 2006. "Effects of Artificial Night Lighting on Terrestrial Mammals." In *Ecological Consequences of Artificial Night Lighting*, edited by Catherine Rich and Travis Longcore, 19–42. Washington, DC: Island Press.

Broglio, Ron. 2011. *Surface Encounters: Thinking with Animals and Art*. Minneapolis: University of Minnesota Press.

Butler, Judith. 2009. *Frames of War: When Is Life Grievable?* London: Verso.

——2004. *Precarious Life: The Powers of Mourning and Violence*. London: Verso.

DCNR. 2007-2008. "Eyeshine Highlight's Wildlife's Nocturnal Habits." Commonwealth of Pennsylvania. www.dcnr.state.pa.us/wrcp/wildnotes/winter0708/eyeshine-pg20108.html (accessed September 2).

Fincham, Ben. 2006. "Bicycle Messengers and the Road to Freedom." In *Against Automobility*, edited by Steffen Böhm, Campbell Jones, Chris Land, and Matthew Paterson, 208–222. Malden: Blackwell.

Haraway, Donna J. 2008. *When Species Meet*. Minneapolis: University of Minnesota Press.

Idaho Fish and Game. 2014. "Roadkill & Wildlife Salvage." https://fishandgame.idaho.gov/species/roadkill (accessed September 6).

Lee, Paula. 2006. "Taming the Two-Eyed Beast: Doubtful Visions in the 17th-Century French Academies." Paper presented at the conference Beyond Mimesis and Nominalism: Representations in Art and Science, London, June 22–23. http://philsci-archive.pitt.edu/2799 (accessed December 1, 2014).

Lin, Doris. n.d. "What is Cultural Carrying Capacity?" http://animalrights.about.com/od/wildlife/g/What-Is-Cultural-Carrying-Capacity.htm (accessed June 15).

Lopez, Barry H. and Robin Eschner. 1998. *Apologia*. Athens: University of Georgia Press.

McHugh, Susan. 2011. "Stains, Drains, and Automobiles: A Conversation with Steve Baker about *Norfolk Roadkill, Mainly*." *Art & Research* 4 (1): 1–14. www.artandresearch.org.uk/v4n1/baker.php (accessed December 1, 2014).

Michael, Mike. 2004. "Roadkill: Between Humans, Nonhuman Animals, and Technologies." *Society and Animals* 12 (4): 277–298.

Molesworth, Helen. 1996. "This Car Stops for Road Kill." In *Concrete Jungle*, edited by Mark Dion and Alexis Rockman, 177–180. Bookstore Distribution.

Reflecting Roadstuds. 2014. "Percy Shaw O.B.E. 15th April 1890 to 1st September 1976." www.percyshawcatseyes.com/history (accessed August 14).

Rice, Doyle. 2011. "Deer-Car Collisions Increase This Time of Year." *USA TODAY*. http://usatoday30.usatoday.com/news/nation/story/2011-10-31/deer-car-accidents-rise/51019604/1 (accessed December 1, 2014).

Soron, Dennis. 2011. "Road Kill: Commodity Fetishism and Structural Violence." In *Critical Theory and Animal Liberation*, edited by John Sanbonmatsu, 55–69. Plymouth: Rowman & Littlefield.

Sontag, Susan. 1977. *On Photography*. New York: Farrar, Straus and Giroux.

Taylor, Elaine. 2013. "New Highway Crossing for Deer Near Wendover." Utah Public Radio. http://upr.org/post/new-highway-crossing-deer-near-wendover (accessed December 1, 2014).

Terstappen, Claudia. 2010. "Roadkill (After Life)." http://www.claudiaterstappen.com/roadkill (accessed May 13).

Wildlife Collision Prevention Program. 2004. "When Do Collisions with Wildlife Occur?" www.wildlifecollisions.ca/when.htm (accessed June 5).

Wildlife Crossing. n.d. "Wildlife Observation Reporting." www.wildlifecrossing.net (accessed September 6).

Notes

1 For "road kill" stuffed animal toys, see www.roadkilltoys.com; for "Liquid Road-kill" see www.selfdefenseproducts.com/special-ingredients-liquid-roadkill-p-17443. html (accessed December 1, 2014).

2 For phrases see http://advocacy.britannica.com/blog/advocacy/2013/10/eliminating-roadkill (accessed December 1, 2014).

3 Ethnographic studies are needed to collect data such as this.

4 The biological "carrying capacity" of a population is the maximum number of an individual species that can survive in a particular environment indefinitely without negatively affecting other species in that habitat. Population management is inherently problematic in that non-human animal populations are controlled first and foremost by and for the benefit of human populations. This is evidenced by state wildlife agencies that view non-human animals as a resource for recreational hunting and are funded by the sales of hunting licenses. Because of this, populations are determined by a "cultural carrying capacity," or the number of non-human animals that can be tolerated by humans—rather than their actual biological carrying capacity (Lin n.d.).

5 A study led by Rob Found and a team of scientists from the University of Alberta published in September 2011 reported that when warning signs are placed specifically in a targeted location where deer are known to cross, they can reduce collisions by 34 percent (Rice 2011).

6 The continued survival of humanity is now problematically bound up with and dependent upon the continued survival of automobility itself. Ben Fincham notes, "The tyranny of the motor-car is that there is an expectation that you should be prepared to drive, whether you like it or not. A frequent cry from drivers, when asked if they would give up their car, is that they would but they 'have to have it for work'" (Fincham 2006, 221).

7 I am continuing to compile a list of artists who document the bodies of "road kill" in their work, which is far from exhaustive. For the purposes of this discussion I am focusing on the work of these artists: Bob Braine, Stephen Paternite (www. spaternite.com), Clive Landen, and Joy Hunsberger (www.joyh.com) (all accessed December 1, 2014).

8 Joy Hunsberger takes a somewhat different approach and gives each animal that she photographs a name. The bloodied body of a dead squirrel reads, "Jeff 7/11/ 2000-Sellersville, PA." Many of her photographs also forgo a forensic framing of the animal's body (taken from directly above), and instead pay particular attention to the animal's face (zoomed in, taken at eye level), akin to the framing techniques of portrait photographers.

9 Brian D. Collier, http://briandcollier.net/html/roadkill/shrine-landing.htm; Emma Kisiel, http://emmakisiel.com/project/at-rest; Meagan Jenigen, www.thelostfur.com/ roadkill-memorials; Jamie Garrison, http://untitledcereal.com/artists/jamie-garrison (all accessed December 1, 2014).

10 www.claudiaterstappen.com/roadkill (accessed December 1, 2014).

11 A death mask is a plaster or wax cast made of a person's face after he or she has died.

12 The resulting images are matter-of-fact and evidentiary akin to forensic crime-scene photography.

13 The haphazardness of the corresponding images also recalls the accidental nature of "road kill".

14 The "Migrant Worker" image elucidates the paradox of the photograph, which works to both humanize and dehumanize the subject pictured. Azoulay states, "Photography, at times, is the only civic refuge at the disposal of those robbed of citizenship" (2008, 121). And while the photograph may incite outrage, empathy,

and possibly political action on behalf of human beings who have been the victims of violence, how does this change when the violated body is a non-human animal who has never been legally recognized as a citizen or a subject?

15 This is the case for both human and non-human animals.

16 An example of this would be when the term "road kill" is used to describe human loss or defeat, as in "economic road kill" See www.zerohedge.com/contributed/economic-roadkill (accessed December 1, 2014).

17 See the anatomical drawings of seventeenth-century French artist Charles Le Brun.

18 I am planning on expanding *The Roadside Memorial Project.*

19 The original, full-color photographs of *The Roadside Memorial Project* can be found on my website: www.lawatsonart.com (accessed December 1, 2014).

20 The effectiveness of warning reflectors that seek to alert wildlife to oncoming traffic is still unknown. A three-year study is currently underway by the Wyoming Department of Transportation and Conservation Research Center of Teton Science Schools to determine if wildlife warning reflectors will help reduce wildlife collisions (ARC 2012).

9 Love, death, food, and other ghost stories

The hauntings of intimacy and violence in contemporary Peru[1]

María Elena García

Amaneció, y me encontré con que emprendiste un largo viaje/Mi corazón se te escapó del equipaje y se quedó/ Fué pa llenarme de recuerdos. (Morning came, and I found you had left on a long trip/My heart escaped from you/It stayed to fill me with memories).

Fonseca, *El Arroyito*

Recordar: Del latín *re-cordis,* volver a pasar por el corazón. (Recordar: To remember, from the Latin *re-cordis*, to pass back through the heart.)

Eduardo Galeano, *El Libro de los Abrazos*

Poet chose to die in our home, in my arms, when he and I were alone, with no one to intervene. Poet and I had been together for 17 years and he resented any intrusion into our intertwined lives. He was willful. Tough. Loving. Before the final decline that led to his death, he insisted on meowing loudly before jumping onto our bed and settling in for the night, his cheek firmly pressed against mine. I sometimes had trouble breathing through his thick fur, but his warmth, his smell, his breath quickly became necessary for me. Sleep would simply not come without this. Without him. The morning after his death I woke to find him next to me. Cold. I remembered and the pain was the most intense I had yet felt in my 40 years of life.

A year later, sitting in my grandmother's house in Lima, Peru one drizzly September day in 2012, I was still mourning Poet's death. That day I was struck by the juxtaposition of two front-page newspaper stories. One was about the twentieth anniversary of the capture of Abimael Guzmán, leader of *Sendero Luminoso* (or the Shining Path), a bloody Maoist army that introduced itself to Lima by hanging dead dogs from lampposts in 1980. The other story was about *Mistura*, a culinary festival that celebrates the new cosmopolitan, multicultural, and economically dynamic Peru. Informed by my grief, I saw these two narratives as part of the same story. Some readers may find it hard to understand, or even problematic, to link the violent deaths of so many humans in Peru with the death of my cat, in our home, and in my arms. But it was precisely this gulf between these different kinds of deaths that my grief helped me to bridge. Combined with my familiarity with the broad and growing literature in critical animal studies, the experience of loss and mourning helped me to re-think the connections between notions of the "good life" with the complex political economies of dispossession, internal colonialism, and development.

Narratives of post-war prosperity in Peru are always already stories of confrontations with the bloody ghosts from our histories of violence. In this essay I argue that these histories must be understood, felt, and explored as multispecies and multicultural "hauntings" in the sense used by Avery Gordon to think about the marginalizations, gaps, and silences in the historical record. "What are the alternative stories we ought to and can write about the relationships among power, knowledge, and experience" (Gordon 2008, 23)? Reckoning with ghosts is important for a critical understanding of both Peruvian food festivals *and* histories of political violence that made spectacles out of the killing of both humans and non-humans. I connect these national multispecies narratives with my own experience of losing and remembering Poet, to show how inter-species intimacy is so often co-constitutive of massive suffering that comes with industrialized food production.

My exploration of these multispecies hauntings is framed and inspired by Native scholar Dian Million (Athabascan) and her work on "felt theory." Million reminds us that "stories … contain the affective legacy of our experiences. They are a felt knowledge that accumulates and becomes a force that empowers stories that are otherwise separate to become a focus, a potential for movement" (Million 2014, 32). The work I do in this essay to move through stories of violence, to unearth and acknowledge ghosts, to uncover painful memories, to *see* that which so many of us refuse to see, also resonates deeply with Gordon's work on haunting. For Gordon, haunting evokes those moments when you lose your bearings, "when the over-and-done-with comes alive, when what's been in your blind spot comes into view. Haunting raises specters, and it alters the experience of being in time, the way we separate the past, the present, and the future" (Gordon 2008, xvi). Significantly, while ghosts for Gordon primarily represent different kinds of loss ("sometimes of life, sometimes of a path not taken"), they can also represent "from a certain vantage point … a future possibility, a hope" (Gordon 2008, 63–64). This ghostly journey of loss leading to hope, of a past that yields to futuricity, provides a theoretical path that links temporality and affect with the politics of loss and projects of healing.

Sendero's ghosts

> Sendero Luminoso no es recuerdo sino una presencia … . (Sendero Luminoso is not a memory, but a presence.)
>
> Machuca, "Herencia Peligrosa"

Writing about Sendero is difficult for me. Although my parents, my sister, and I left the country four years before Peru descended into what many have called "the time of fear" (Poole and Renique 1992), my family, like most Peruvians, was deeply affected by the years of political violence. The history of Sendero Luminoso and the political conflict that (according to the Peruvian Truth and Reconciliation Commission) lasted 20 years (1980–2000) is complicated. There are many competing narratives about this conflict,[2] but it is safe to say that the war between the Peruvian state and Sendero Luminoso—a ruthless Maoist-inspired army—is among the darkest periods of our history.[3] It is estimated that between 1980 and 2000, close to 70,000 Peruvians died; 6,000 disappeared; 600,000 were forcibly displaced; 500 villages razed; and at least 22,000 people were detained under "anti-terrorist" legislation. Of those killed, a disproportionate number—75 percent—were Indigenous casualties (Comisión de la Verdad y Reconciliación 2004).[4]

I struggle to find the words to describe how those years felt. We were living in Mexico City in 1980, when Sendero sent its first message to Peru and the world: they hung dead dogs from lampposts in the city of Lima (and all over the country) with signs around their necks that read "Deng Xiaoping, son of

Figure 9.1 The hanging of dead dogs was one of the first public acts of Sendero Luminoso. Photograph by Carlos Bendezú. Permission for use from Caretas photographic archive.

a bitch." This was in reference to market-friendly reforms in China that in the eyes of Sendero's leaders marked a betrayal of Mao's legacy.[5]

The placards hanging on the necks of dogs seemed to connect this shadowy organization more directly with China than with Peru, though one could certainly find commonalities in the histories of uneven development in both countries. While Peruvians were disturbed by the sight of hanging dogs, most dismissed Sendero as a fringe group, insane, creepy, and perhaps irrelevant. I will return to the bodies of those dogs, and to the other non-human victims of Sendero, soon. But for the moment, I want to return to Avery Gordon and her ghosts. She writes:

> To look for lessons about haunting when there are thousands of ghosts; when entire societies become haunted by terrible deeds that are system- atically occurring and are simultaneously denied ... when the whole situation cries out for clearly distinguishing between truth and lies, between what is known and what is unknown, between the real and the unthinkable and yet that is what is precisely impossible; when people you know or love are there one minute and gone the next; when familiar words and things transmute into the most sinister of weapons and meanings; ... when the whole of life has become so enmeshed in the traffic of the dead and the living dead ... To broach, much less settle on, a firm understanding of this social reality can make you feel like you are carrying the weight of the world on your shoulders.
>
> (Gordon 2008, 63–64)

Gordon's words resonate deeply with me. I was only nine years old when dozens (hundreds?) of dogs were killed and hung during a damp Lima night.[6] And at that time I did not know about this—nor did I know about the increasing instances of kidnapping, disappearance, rape, and torture; the kill- ing of men, women, and children; the burning of entire villages; the terror and rage and fear permeating Peru, particularly in the Peruvian highlands and lowlands. Like many Peruvians who did not live close to the Andean heart of the war, I did not know until much later that Indigenous Peruvians were the primary victims of violence from both Sendero and the Peruvian military.

Over the next several years, we returned to Peru every summer to visit our extended family. We began to feel the way Peruvian society, and our family, were experiencing this conflict; we learned how to navigate the specter of violence. Frequent blackouts meant having flashlights, radios, and water at hand. The possibility of car bombs meant we should never sit too close to glass windows. Curfew opened up spaces for card games and popcorn and reading by candlelight.

I don't think about these years often. But I do vividly remember the moment when my father announced, in the summer of 1985, that we would not be returning to Peru until the violence ended. We would not be returning to the arms of my grandmother, to laughter with my cousins, to the smells and sounds and sights of the city I continued to think of as home. That same year, our family moved from Mexico City to the United States. I experienced that move as a radical disruption. A disruption of life, of identity. And I blamed this on Sendero. I suddenly needed to know more. As I read the little information available at the time, as I tried to have a stronger grasp on what was happening in my country, what my family was living through, I began to feel, as Gordon notes in the quote above, like I was carrying the weight of the world on my shoulders. No one around me understood or cared. My parents' reply to my questions was always the same: Peru is living through terrorism. Sendero is a terrorist organization. Human rights activists who accuse the government of abuse are apologists for terrorism. And I should not be wasting my time reading propaganda or trying to understand something I had no business thinking about. End of discussion.

What do you do when people around you do not want see the ghosts; when they don't want to acknowledge that "the whole of life has become … enmeshed in the traffic of the dead and the living dead" (Gordon 2008, 64). As I went on to college, I became obsessed with what I now think of as Sendero's ghosts. But as I deepened my understanding of this conflict, as I learned about the disproportionate impact of this violence on Indigenous men, women, and children, and as I learned about the brutality of government forces in particular, I was haunted by other ghosts. "The ghost … has a real presence and demands its due, your attention. Haunting and the appearance of specters or ghosts is one way … we are notified that what's been concealed is very much alive and present, interfering precisely with those always incomplete forms of containment and repression ceaselessly directed toward us" (Gordon 2008, xvi). What had been concealed by my family, by the Peruvian government, by so many others, was nothing less than the legacies of colonial violence and the ways in which they lived on in the very fabric and structure of Peruvian society.

Colonial legacies in Peru are still evident, particularly in the deep racial divide that colors everyday life. It was racism, inequality, and societal neglect that created the necessary conditions for the emergence of Sendero. Abimael Guzmán and the other leaders of this organization offered a different vision of the future to those who had lived this marginalization. In a bloody struggle that would destroy the existing system, they would be the "initiators" of a new world, one born of blood and fire, but one in which they would no longer be forgotten and humiliated. Peruvian racial geographies divide the country into "backward" peasant highlands and Native lowlands, and a "modern" coast. Because the conflict began in the highland department of Ayacucho, one of the poorest regions of the country, Limeños were slow to worry about Sendero. As long as only "Indians" were being brutalized, this violence was not seen as impacting Peruvians (read: real citizens). This view permeated through the military response, which led many counter-terrorist forces to torture and kill Quechua peasants simply because they were unable to communicate in Spanish. Testimonies of marines and other military actors reveal that simply speaking in an Indigenous language was read by counter-insurgency forces as meaning these Native men, women, or children could be hiding something; they were not "real citizens" (Comisión de la Verdad y Reconciliación 2004). And from the perspective of coastal, urban Lima, these were not grievable bodies. Limeños only began paying attention once violence arrived in the city of Lima. When blackouts became an almost nightly affair and car bombs became routine; when urban, "modern," *citizens* were being killed, Peruvians in Lima woke up. By then it was too late.

Re-membering Peru

> These images of pain challenge the logic of time to achieve an always intriguing permanence. They are ... an expansion of time, a past that imposes itself upon our present, so that it calls out and awakens us.
> Salomón Lerner, president of Peruvian Truth and Reconciliation Commission

It is understandable that many Peruvians do not want to remember this part of our history. Sendero's ghosts, many say, should be eliminated, or at least ignored. For my parents, to bring forth these ghosts and memories is akin to the violence of that past. But as so many have eloquently described, this "past" violence is alive and well in the present (Kaneko 2008; Milton 2014; Taylor 2003). It is experienced in the now; manifested in the present in a multitude of ways. And it is called forth, challenged, complicated, and lived. It is this contemporary experience of the past that ghosts allow us to see; what they call attention to. As Gordon notes: "What's distinctive about haunting is that it is an animated state in which a repressed or unresolved social violence is making itself known, sometimes very directly, sometimes more obliquely" (2008, xvi).

The Peruvian Truth and Reconciliation Commission (*Comisión de la Verdad y Reconciliación* in Spanish, hereafter 'CVR') was tasked with making sense of the years of internal war and authoritarianism. One of its innovations, building on the South African experience, was a series of public and even televised *audiencias* that would broadcast the testimonies of those who had experienced the violence and terror most intimately. The hope was that public witnessing would provide an opportunity for national remembering. An extension of this project was a striking photographic exhibit that was titled *Yuyanapaq*, the Quechua word meaning "for remembering." During the inauguration of Yuyanapaq in Lima, Salomón Lerner, president of the CVR, spoke to the "tricks of time" that are all the more evident in times of haunting. Speaking directly about the painful images included in the photographic exhibition, Lerner stated: "these images of pain challenge the logic of time—which is to pass and vanish—to achieve an always intriguing permanence. They are, thus, an expansion of time, a past that imposes itself upon our present, so that it calls out and awakens us" (Lerner cited in Poole and Rojas-Peréz 2010).

Gordon reminds us: "Haunting raises specters, and it alters the experience of being in time, the way we separate the past, the present, and the future" (2008, xvi). I remember sitting in my dorm room in college on the day president Alberto Fujimori (1990–2000) declared a "self-coup" in April 1992 (only five months before Guzman's capture in September 1992). Having learned about the history of "dirty wars" in Latin America and the impact of dictatorships on civil liberties and human rights, I was well aware that this move—the militarization of the country, the escalation in the use of force by security forces, the "cleansing" of anyone deemed a terrorist (which included students, artists, writers, and any other "potential threat")—would only mean more kidnapping, more torture, more death. And yet, I remember the gut-wrenching feeling of doubt; the wondering if this might not in fact be a good thing; if this could lead to greater security; if this could mean my family would be safer, protected from the violence that had engulfed our country. I sat on my bed that morning as the phone rang. Friends called to say they had just heard. They were so sorry. How was I coping?

I never told anyone about that lingering knot inside me; that feeling of fear and hope. I was not alone. As Peruvian political scientist Martín Tanaka notes, "public support for Fujimori jumped from 53% in March 1992, to 81% after the auto-golpe [in April 1992]" (Tanaka 1998, 219). Just one year earlier human rights organizations had listed Peru as among the most dangerous countries in the world, and as the country with the highest number of disappearances.[7] But even as I understand *why* so many of my compatriots may have supported a dictatorship (at least at first), just the thought of my mixed feelings, of that moment of doubt, still fills me with shame and guilt. How could I possibly support actions that would lead to someone's torture or death? As I think back to this moment I am reminded of Patricio Guzmán's powerful film, *Chile, Obstinate Memory*. This film explores the reactions of young Chileans after viewing Guzman's previously banned documentary, *The Battle of Chile*, an earlier film about the bloody events of September 11, 1973 that inaugurated decades of dictatorship in Chile. In a poignant scene, a young man breaks down in tears thinking back to September 11, and remembering how happy he was to learn that school had been cancelled. How could we have known so little?

Seeing Yuyanapaq for the first time had a powerful impact on me. I remember asking my family if they had seen the exhibit; if they wanted to join me. And I will never forget the look on their faces. After what seemed like an interminable silence, one of my aunts asked why I would want to see those images. That was our past, she said. It was horrible, and it is better to forget and move forward. Forgetting and moving forward, to most of my family, seemed to be the only sensible thing to do, and those of us who wanted to see, to remember, to feel, were in fact holding Peru back. The most extreme expression of this ideal has been the criminalization of protest; of activism; of demands for justice. Human rights organizations and activists are accused of worrying "only about terrorists and criminals and their rights," and are thus themselves linked to (and sometimes equated with) so-called terrorists. Any criticism of government repression or military or police brutality is read as irreverent: disrespectful at best, subversive at worst (with chilling consequences).

Returning to my desire to see this exhibit, I think the fact that I live in the United States; that I had been "away" for so much of my life, helped me. It gave my family (and me) an excuse; a box in which they could put me. *I didn't know better. I wanted to understand because I had not lived through the violence.* So in the end, they simply warned me that the exhibit told a one-sided story. I wanted to know more, but they were done talking. They were moving forward.

I remember riding in the taxi to the National Museum where the exhibit is now permanently housed. I was saddened by the exchange with my family but not surprised. When I finally arrived I made my way up to the sixth floor of the museum, devoted entirely to Yuyanapaq. The elevator door opened and I walked out into a cold, damp, gray room. I saw the face of a man, a rag covering one of his eyes, a sad, faraway gaze coming from the other.

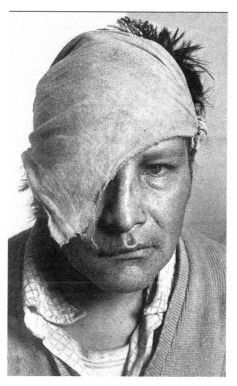

Figure 9.2 A photograph of Celestino Ccente. Photograph by Oscar Medrano. Permission for use from Caretas photographic archive.

I walked through the exhibit, following the suggested pathway, facing image after image of mutilated bodies, charred buildings, hands holding identity cards, and faces of fear, terror, and indescribable grief. There were distinct sections depicting particular periods of violence (Sendero's public executions, army counter-insurgency tactics, the creation of peasant self-defense patrols) and events (the murder of eight journalists in 1983, the bombing of a building in an upscale Lima neighborhood). I walked through a room filled with voices; testimonies read in Spanish and Quechua. And as I wound my way through the halls and rooms, as I looked carefully at each of the black and white photographs hanging, sometimes crookedly, against unclean white walls, my sadness began shifting toward anger. I was suddenly enraged. The exhibit was empty. It was neglected. It had already been forgotten. The CVR's recommendations—about reparations, about the need to address structural inequality, about dealing with the inter-generational impacts of this violence—were ignored by the government of Alejandro Toledo (2001–2006) and dismissed by president Alan García (2006–2011) as leftist propaganda.[8]

My rage was about this power to dismiss, to ignore, to erase from history. But I was also angry about the periodizing of history, and of violence, that the CVR and the exhibit perpetuated. Establishing a clear beginning (1980—Sendero's declaration of war) and end (2000—the fall of Fujimori), this official narrative (even if contested) marked this as a time of exception. This was exceptional violence. This was violence we could see in the terrorized expression of a young girl as counter-insurgency forces take her hooded father away. This was violence we could taste in the bloodied faces of torture victims; violence we could smell in charred remains of buses. But was this exceptional violence not keeping us from thinking and feeling the violence of poverty, of colonial legacies, of marginalization and despair that in many ways created the space for Sendero, and which continues even after the "end" of violence in Peru? How might we open up spaces to see and feel routinized violence, the everyday forms of brutality that we unsee? Does looking at this kind of exceptional violence invite us to avert our eyes and search for other things, anything, that will help us look away?

Haunting flesh

> I am inhabited by the ghosts of my dead and my devoured and … I cannot ignore them, nor will they be ignored.
>
> Dian Million, *There is a River in Me: Theory From Life*

Let us return to my grandmother's living room that afternoon in September 2012 when I came across two seemingly distinct stories in the paper, one about Guzmán's capture, the other celebrating the culinary festival *Mistura*. These two stories appeared on the front page of *La República*, one of the more important national newspapers in Peru. The paper's Sunday supplement also included stories about both Sendero and Mistura. Indeed, they bracketed the supplement (which started with Sendero, and ended with Mistura), almost as if to say this is where we were, but look at us now.

This layout was logical, and the logic was almost magical. In the presence of the ghosts of past violence, we were in need of incantations, counter-spells, something that would help us clear the air and keep violence at bay. Mistura serves as such an incantation, a way to dispel Sendero's ghosts. Moreover, it was a collective ritual—all were seemingly invited to this beautiful new Peru. And I can understand the urge to celebrate, to tell a story about Peru that is not about exclusion, and violence, and death. And yet, I cannot take part in that story; it comes with a price that is too high. The multicultural celebration that is Mistura is another way to avoid seeing the images of Yuyanapaq, it is a gentle and artful attempt to manage difference. As I have argued elsewhere Mistura offers up, exquisitely and powerfully, a particular aesthetics of colonialism and celebratory framing of the nation that obscures a dark side of marginalization and violence against Indigenous and non-human bodies (García 2013). Mistura is not a benign incantation, but rather another kind of witchery, beautifully described by Leslie Marmon Silko as something that works to "see how much can be lost, how much can be forgotten," to "destroy the feeling people have for each other" (Silko 2006, 213). In the fog of pleasure and the promise of social inclusion, the feelings of pain, fear, and disdain—those feelings that still characterize so much of Peruvian everyday life—are lost. As a largely middle- and upper-class phenomenon, Mistura offers what Slavoj Žižek (2009) calls a pure experience of "cultural capitalism"—the opportunity to feel the simultaneous joys of consumerism and social justice, relieving oneself from looking more deeply into the violence of capitalism and its exclusions.

What I want to focus on here is the violence that is not seen; the violence that is in fact marked as beauty, as hope and promise. When I saw the familiar images of Guzmán's capture, I felt the usual pang associated (for me) with Sendero. But turning the pages, seeing images of the culinary festival I was hoping to participate in that year, was a powerful disruption to my thinking about violence. Throughout the week, newspapers and other media outlets proclaimed the glory of Mistura, and suddenly, I could not help but see representations of this festival as spectacles of violence, of death. There is one page in particular, which appeared in *El Comercio*, the Peruvian paper of record, inviting readers to participate in "an evening at Mistura," that has stayed with me. It is a page with photographs of burning flesh: pigs, lambs, calves, chickens, cow's hearts, all over open flames or being fileted. Part of the page reads: "At night, Mistura is another. A different charm overpowers this gastronomic fair when the lights are turned on and the cold leads us through a path of sizzling coal, in search of succulent bites and comforting drinks" (Contreras 2012). There is something about the darkness, the fire, the charred flesh.

In her work on cinema, embodiment, and the senses, Laura Marks writes about what she calls "haptic visuality," or "the way vision itself can be tactile,

as though one were touching a film [or photograph] with one's eyes … "
(Marks 2000, xi). Sitting in my grandmother's house at that moment, looking
at these juxtaposed images of human and non-human death, of violence we
clearly identify as brutality, and violence that is routinized, made invisible by
our own complicity, I understood Marks' idea of haptic visuality. I could
touch—and smell, and hear—those bloodied, burning bodies, roasting on
skewers and waiting to be devoured. This was a visceral response to seeing; an
affective engagement with images that pushed me to remember who those
charred bodies had been. It may have been grief (my cat Poet's absence was
still palpably painful) that allowed me to see; to remember.

Eduardo Galeano reminds us that to remember is "to pass back through
the heart" (Galeano 1992, 11). My heart, still in mourning, was wounded and
perhaps more open to remembering, to seeing other beings. I learned much
from Poet, from my relationship with this willful cat. Among those many
lessons, our relationship is a constant reminder of the possibilities of inter-
species connection; a reminder that other-than-human beings have rich and
complex emotional lives; that they are individuals with unique personalities
and capabilities. Remembering Poet as I flipped through the pages of that
newspaper allowed me to feel, to remember those non-human bodies being
consumed at Mistura as not just killable, but grievable. Yet, I was all too
aware of how my own experience was an unusual one. I understand that the
visible and extraordinary economic power of the gastronomic boom in addition to the national pride that culinary celebrations have enabled and
encouraged work to obscure the violence involved from farm to table.

Grief can heighten these affective possibilities, particularly when the pain is
still raw, when the heart is still open. You see and feel during moments of
grief in ways that don't happen later. But while grief can bring a heightened
sense of connection, it is only temporary. Grief can be fleeting. In this
moment, as I write almost exactly two years after this powerful encounter
with violence, I can look at similar images of animals used for food in *Seattle
Magazine* or *Gastronomica*, and I don't feel them in the same way as I did
that afternoon at my grandmother's house. I can look at images from Mistura
2014, happening as I write, and the viscerality of that previous experience is
simply not there. The urgency slips away, like a ghost. This may be why so
many animal activists need to be reminded as to why they must act. I
remember one of my students at Sarah Lawrence College in New York who
made herself watch the graphic documentary *Earthlings* (earthlings.com),
depicting the various forms of violence to which animals are subjected by
humans, once a week so that she would not forget why she worked in animal
rescue. Similarly, anthropologist Naisargi Dave documents the work of
animal rights activists in India, quoting Maneka Gandhi saying "I only wish
there were a slaughterhouse next door. To witness that violence, to hear those
screams. … I would *never* be able to rest" (Dave 2014, 439–440).

Do we need to feel pain in order to be open to the pain of others? I am
reminded of Elaine Scarry's oft-cited observation that "to have pain is to have

certainty; to hear about pain is to have doubt" (Scarry 1985, 13). What Scarry meant about the language-destroying aspects of pain means something different to me at this moment. Now I see Scarry's two options, of having pain and hearing about pain, not as mutually exclusive experiences. Instead, I see them as suggesting dialectically another possibility: the possibility that being in pain is another way to hear and connect with the pain of others. It is in the entanglements of our pain, perhaps, that we can be most clear sighted about the suffering that runs throughout societies. This is perhaps the only way to be attuned to the kind of sickness that Silko says is "part of something larger" and whose cures can only be found "in something great and inclusive of everything" (Silko 2006, 113).

Entanglements

The juxtaposition of graphic images of political violence and of dead animal bodies at Mistura heightened my reading of this gastronomic fair as a spectacle of death and flesh; a graveyard haunted by ghosts. But I must be careful here. Exploring this juxtaposition, thinking through the violent intimacies that are part of human–animal entanglements, can be read as elevating the suffering of animals over the suffering of humans. This is especially the case in Peru, given the dominant discourse of Mistura as a space of social inclusion, and Peruvian cuisine as a "social weapon" (Santos 2012) used to combat cultural and racial exclusion. According to most Peruvians, food is transforming Peru for the better, and Mistura is the perfect example of a more tolerant, beautiful country of cultural fusion. Past critiques of the festival and Peruvian food have been received angrily, and represented as a national betrayal (García 2013). This makes Mistura (and Peruvian gastronomy more generally) a dangerous contact zone for those who in recent years have been trying to call attention to the suffering of animals, especially young men and women daring to protest against Mistura on behalf of the killing and consumption of animals.

Additionally, seeing (political) violence against humans and violence against animals as somehow comparable, placing them in the same analytic frame (in the same sentence even), can be read as enacting another kind of violence, evoking other colonial (genocidal) ghosts. Long histories of racial violence, of the animalization of Native peoples, make this a particularly powerful concern. Indigenous peoples in Peru have long been seen as "just animals." During previous fieldwork on Indigenous cultural politics in Peru, I heard many Peruvian bureaucrats say that Indigenous peoples did not feel cold or pain in the same way we did, "because they are more like their animals." Andean peoples have often been compared to alpacas and llamas (García and Lucero 2010). So, this concern is one to which we must pay particularly close attention, especially at this moment when Peru is basking in the multicultural glow of Mistura, while around it Indigenous peasants and migrants suffer from hunger, extractive industries wound glaciers and rainforests, and systemic inequality continues to marginalize the poor.

And yet, it is perhaps all the more important that in this context, and at this time, we call attention to the entanglements of human–animal violence. What happens when we refuse to see connections? Quite predictably, we miss the ways in which animality and racialization, nature and culture, have long mutually shaped each other. The same logics of classification and hierarchies of difference that govern human mastery over non-humans are at work in projects of coloniality and racism (Kim 2014). We must acknowledge this history of entanglements, and find ways to think critically and carefully about what these connections might offer us. What does thinking of violence against humans and animals in critical juxtaposition and relation, and not in terms of moral or phenomenological equivalence, do? Quite simply, this kind of thinking moves us from atomistic calculations to considerations of broader webs of life, kinds of relational ontologies that have long been a part of the worldview of Native peoples throughout the Americas.

What I call for, then, is not something new. Rather, it is to look for the many keen observers who have seen connections that go beyond the human. For example, José María Arguedas, Peru's most prominent novelist, known primarily for his important writings about cultural resilience and racial revolution, wrote powerfully about the death of the Peruvian pelican on the Peruvian coastal town of Chimbote. Arguedas describes the bodies of dying, mutilated birds on the beaches of Chimbote as a result of the pollution and toxic waste of multinational factories in that town (Arguedas 1990). Literary critic Maureen Shea argues that Arguedas anticipated contemporary work in animal and posthumanist studies, as the novel "offers a critical challenge to an anthropocentric world view and its devastating consequences to the natural world" (Shea 2010, 1). Importantly, Arguedas makes a clear link between the suffering and death of these birds, and the suffering of Indigenous peasants living in this town who "struggle for survival through desperate and creative means to overcome disease, hunger, despair and violence in the marginalized *barriadas* or slums of Chimbote, the discards of a frenetic and irresponsible industrialization" (Shea 2010, 2).

Seeing animals as both actors and victims of the political violence of past years, and of contemporary manifestations of that violence, is critical. This is not the place to list all the places where human and non-human deaths have made it into the official archive of political violence. Yet, such a list would include Indigenous peasants who in their testimonies before the CVR describe the killing of their animals as violence done to them and their families, the "burro-bombs" used in Ayacucho during the 1980s, dead dogs hanging from lampposts, and the killing of hundreds of alpacas at a US-backed agricultural station. What is perhaps more important for the purpose of this essay is that these kinds of lists are almost never created. Beyond their symbolic or iconic value, there is little recognition of animal deaths or the grief that accompanies them. Indeed, the very iconicity of some of these animal deaths perpetuated the invisibility of more routine animal and human deaths. I remember seeing images of the dead dogs and alpacas and feeling terrible pain—but does this not let us off the hook? We focus on scenes of exceptional violence, but what about the everyday violence against Native peoples, against animals, that goes unseen all the time? For many Peruvians living in the capital city of Lima, the first "seeing" of Senderista violence came in the form of dead dogs. Yet, such a sight did little to provoke concerns about "dead Indians" or the many dogs dying slow deaths in the streets of the city.

Poiesis

> The ghost is alive, so to speak. We are in relation to it and it has designs on us such that we must reckon with it graciously, attempting to offer it a hospitable memory *out of a concern for justice*. Out of a concern for justice would be the only reason one would bother.
>
> Gordon (2008)

In her beautiful essay on Native studies and "theory from life," Million writes "We are living in a time when the most vulnerable die (this includes many, many life-forms), a worldwide experience that affects our vital relations with life itself. There is a struggle against the capitalization, the commoditization of life even as it is happening" (2014, 32). And she asks "what do we know that we might act from?" (2014, 32). I knew Poet. Can I act from him? Inspired by him? With him I experienced the possibility of inter-species intimacy and connection. From him I know other-than-human animals can feel joy, terror, fear, and they suffer, both physically and emotionally. "What do we know that we might act from?" I see Million's question as a plea towards a radical relationality.

Reading Million also reminds me of the concept of poiesis, a bringing-forth or blossoming. I first encountered this idea reading anthropologist Bob Desjarlais' powerful work on the experiences of death and mourning, life and loss, among Yolmo Buddhists in Nepal and Queens, New York (Desjarlais, n.d.). Poiesis, writes Desjarlais, "implies a begetting, a fabrication and bringing forth, of some new form or actuality; something that was not present is made present" (Desjarlais n.d., 16). Desjarlais continues:

> Poiesis is found in the strivings of all peoples—and, perhaps, of all life forms more generally. Poiesis is there in the urge we have to make something of, and in, our lives, both individually and collectively. ... People fashion something out of the elements of their lives, even if those elements are bone bare, at times. We go beyond what is given to us, in one way or another. There is a creative tendency in life itself. Poiesis is found in moments of joy and suffering, and of life and death. It is inscribed in the very fact of rituals. Peoples throughout the world turn to ritual and symbolic forms in the wake of death and absence. Form comes of loss. Something is made present when something else is no longer present.
>
> (n.d., 16)

Desjarlais' words echo Gordon here when she tells us that while "haunting … registers the harm inflicted or the loss sustained by social violence," it is also "distinctive for producing a something-to-be-done" (Gordon 2008, xvi).

Inspired by these scholars, I can't help but hope for poiesis, for the bringing-forth or emergence of an expansive politics of compassion. The possibility of protest at a place like Mistura, for example, signals hope. In a political context where protest is often criminalized, where the stakes are about life and death, the emergence of "anti-speciesist" activism is nothing short of the kind of radical relationality Million is calling for. I also see signs of poiesis in a column that appeared in the same Sunday newspaper as the stories of Sendero and Mistura. In this column, a young Peruvian scholar writes about eco-feminism. The piece begins with a strategically composed set of sentences about her colleagues—well-known Peruvian academics, cultural and political critics—who laugh at the very idea of eco-feminism. Having dealt with the skeptical laughter, she then proceeds to explain the importance of eco-feminism, and implicitly, of her very presence in the pages of that paper. She then describes an eco-feminist conference in Cajamarca (a city in the North of Peru), noting, importantly, that she is not alone. Her steady, persuasive and clear words appear in one of the more important newspapers in the country. They mark the beginning, not an end (Santisteban 2012).

The word poiesis comes from the Greek poiein, "to act, to do, or to make," and is related to the words "poetics" and "poetry." It is perhaps fitting, then, that I end this meditation by returning to my Poet, and to a song about a cat. It was composed by the Peruvian musician and philosopher Jorge Millones, who is also a friend. His song is called *Siete Vidas* (Seven Lives) and it tells the story of the life and death of a rambunctious cat.

Entre los pelos, de la dulzura	Among the fur, and the sweetness
Mi casa se revienta de ternura	My house trembles with tenderness
Con un maullido de amor	With a meow of love
Creció una flor	A flower grew
Y al cantar	And with song
El tigre creció …	A tiger grew …
Cuando me quieras encontrar	When you want to find me
Busca en el cielo una señal	Look in the sky for a sign
Y las estrellas con ardor	And the burning stars
Te dibujaran, con un gran miau,	Will show, with a great meow
Donde estoy yo … [9]	Where I lie …

I read Millones' song as a song about love, intimacy, and hope. My relationship with Poet was—is—about all three. He expanded my capacity to love; he taught me that inter-species intimacy is possible, even desirable; but he also challenged me to see, to not turn away from the violent intimacies of which I am a part. And he still fills me with hope; the hope that others will encounter other beings with compassion and respect, that we might rethink our place in the world, and that of other beings in the world.

As I write these words, I can't help but think that even sympathetic readers will be skeptical about my attempt to link my loss of Poet with other losses that take place at much larger scales, either in the billions of animals consumed as food or the tens of thousands of human lives lost in the internal war in Peru. As many others have observed, we are more accustomed to a moral schizophrenia in which we care intensely about "our" animals (dogs, cats, and other companions) but we rarely stop to think about those animals killed for our food. Timothy Pachirat argues that this seeming contradiction or schizophrenic view of animal lives is better understood as a constitutive relationship. A focused care about specific bodies often allows us to not concern ourselves with more distant and systemic suffering. Worrying about exceptional violence like "dog fighting, pardoning the Thanksgiving turkey and the bacon festival piglet ... don't contradict the industrialized killing of billions, they are a part and parcel of that system, and, these things are coded by race and class" (personal communication, March 14, 2013).

And yet what I describe in this essay is very different. The loss of Poet allowed me to see and feel other losses in a new light. I struggle to articulate why. It may be because the loss of Poet did not only mean the loss of a life close to me, it meant the end of a set of relationships, the end of a pattern of emotions and embodied routines of care. In the most real way I know, it meant the end of a world. Thinking about the world-altering power of death made me reflect on the world-making and world-destroying projects I saw all around me. I can understand why so many are invested in seeing Mistura as part of a good life. My pain made me less interested in that notion of the good life and more open to the deaths that made that good life possible.

Appendix

SIETE VIDAS, by Jorge Millones

Érase un gato, que perseguía
La madeja de canciones de la vida
Y sonreía, se revolcaba
Por todos los rincones de mi casa
Con un zarpazo feliz, fundaba el sol
Y al cantar
Venía a mí.
Con siete vidas, yo te daría
Las cosas más hermosas de mis días
Bajo la luna, aprenderías
A ver el claroscuro de la vida
Un ronroneo cantor
Se oyó al volar
Y al maullar
Decía así ...
Cuando me quieras encontrar
Busca en el cielo una señal
Y las estrellas con ardor
Te dibujaran, con un gran miau, con un gran miau
Donde estoy yo
Donde estoy yo
Donde estoy yo
Este un gato, José María
Qué haremos para que se quede quieto
Entre los pelos, de la dulzura
Mi casa se revienta de ternura
Con un maullido de amor
Creció una flor
Y al cantar
El tigre creció ...
Cuando me quieras encontrar
Busca en el cielo una señal
Y las estrellas con ardor
Te dibujaran, con un gran miau, con un gran miau. Donde estoy yo

References

Alarcón, Daniel. 2006. "Lima, Peru, July 28, 1979." In *War By Candlelight: Stories*, Daniel Alarcon, ed. New York: Harper Perennial.

Arguedas, José María. 1990. *El Zorro de Arriba y el Zorro de Abajo*. Pittsburgh: University of Pittsburgh Press.

Comisión de la Verdad y Reconciliación. 2004. *Hatun Willakuy: Versión Abreviada del Informe Final de la Comisión de la Verdad y Reconciliación, Perú*. Lima.

Contreras, Catherine. 2012. "Para Una Noche Misturera." *El Comercio*, 13 de septiembre: 18.

Dave, Naisargi. 2014. "Witness: Humans, Animals, and the Politics of Becoming." *Cultural Anthropology*, 29 (3): 433–456.

Degregori, Carlos Ivan. 2012. *How Difficult It Is to Be God: Shining Path's Politics of War in Peru, 1980–1999*. Madison: University of Wisconsin Press.

Desjarlais, Robert. n.d. *Subject to Death: Life and Loss in a Buddhist World*. Unpublished manuscript.

Galeano, Eduardo. 1992. *The Book of Embraces*. New York: Norton.

García, María Elena. 2013. "The Taste of Conquest: Colonialism, Cosmopolitics, and the Dark Side of Peru's Gastronomic Boom." *Journal of Latin American and Caribbean Anthropology*, 18 (3): 505–524.

García, María Elena and José Antonio Lucero. 2010. "Exceptional Others: Politicians, Rottweilers, and Alterity in the 2006 Peruvian Elections." *Latin American and Caribbean Ethnic Studies*, 3 (3): 253–270.

Gordon, Avery. 2008. *Ghostly Matters: Haunting and the Sociological Imagination*. Minneapolis: University of Minnesota Press.

Gorriti, Gustavo. 1999. *The Shining Path: A History of the Millenarian War in Peru*. Robin Kirk, translator. Chapel Hill: The University of North Carolina Press.

Human Rights Watch. 1991. *Into the Quagmire: Human Rights and U.S. Policy in Peru*. New York: Human Rights Watch.

Kaneko, Ann, Alfredo Márquez, Natalia Iguíñiz, Claudio Jiménez Quispe, and Eduardo Tokeshi. 2008. *Against the Grain: An Artist's Survival Guide to Peru?*. [Harriman, NY]: New Day Films.

Kim, Claire. 2014. *Dangerous Crossings: Race, Species and Nature in a Multicultural Age*. Cambridge: Cambridge University Press.

Machuca, Gabriela. 2012. "Herencia Peligrosa: Sendero, 20 Años Despues." *Somos*, 8 de septiembre.

Marks, Laura. 2000. *The Skin of the Film: Intercultural Cinema, Embodiment, and the Senses*. Durham: Duke University Press.

Million, Dian. 2014. "There is a River In Me: Theory From Life." In *Theorizing Native Studies*, Audra Simpson and Andrea Smith, eds. Durham: Duke University Press.

Milton, Cynthia, editor. 2014. *Art from a Fractured Past: Memory and Truth-Telling in Post-Shining Path Peru*. Durham: Duke University Press.

Poole, Deborah and Gerardo Renique. 1992. *Time of Fear*. Washington, D.C.: Latin America Bureau.

Poole, Deborah and Isaías Rojas-Pérez. 2010. "Memories of Reconciliation: Photography and Memory in Postwar Peru." *E-misférica*, 7 (2), Winter: http://hemisphericinstitute.org/hemi/en/e-misferica-72/poolerojas (accessed December 1, 2014).

Santisteban, Rocío Silva. 2012. "Ecofeminismo." *Domingo. La Revista de La República.* September 12: 8.

Santos, Jesús M. 2012. *Peru? sabe la cocina, arma social.* Lima: Media Networks.

Scarry, Elaine. 1985. *The Body in Pain: The Making and Unmaking of the World.* Oxford and New York: Oxford University Press.

Shea, Maureen. 2010. "José María Arguedas' Sacred Link to the Animal in *El zorro de arriba y el zorro de abajo.* Paper presented at the annual meeting of the Latin American Studies Association, Toronto, October 7.

Silko, Leslie Marmon. 2006. *Ceremony.* New York: Penguin Books.

Stern, Steve. 1998. *Shining and Other Paths: War and Society in Peru, 1980–1995.* Durham: Duke University Press.

Tanaka, Martin, 1998. *Los Espejismos de la Democracia: El Colapso del Sistema de Partidos en el Peru, 1980-1995, En Perspectiva Comparada.* Lima: Instituto de Estudios Peruanos.

Taylor, Diana. 2003. *The Archive and the Repertoire: Performing Cultural Memory in the Americas.* Durham: Duke University Press.

Theidon, Kimberly. 2014. *Intimate Enemies: Violence and Reconciliation in Peru.* Philadelphia: University of Pennsylvania Press.

Žižek, Slavoj. 2009. *First As Tragedy, Then As Farce.* New York: Verso.

Notes

1 I am very grateful to Tony Lucero, Claire Kim, Tish Lopez, and Katie Gillespie for their thoughtful comments on earlier drafts of this essay. I also want to thank the Peruvian magazine *Caretas* for their permission to use the two photographs included here.

2 Among the many debates over the violence, there is controversy over the terminology used to describe the conflict between the state and various leftist forces. For the state, this was always about terrorism, not a civil war. For leaders of Sendero Luminoso, it was nothing less than the beginning of a global revolutionary struggle (see Degregori 2012, Goritti 1999, Stern 1998).

3 There were other leftist political organizations that also participated in this struggle, such as the MRTA (Tupac Amaru Revolutionary Movement). For more on Sendero Luminoso and the political violence of this time in Peru, see Degregori (2012), Gorriti (1999), Stern (1998), and Theidon (2014).

4 These figures are estimates made with the assistance of a US-based Human Rights Data Analysis Group (HRDAG), affiliated with the American Association for the Advancement of Science (AAAS). See Comisión de la Verdad y Reconciliación (2004) for more.

5 See Daniel Alarcón's (2006) powerful short story about this event.

6 As far as I know, there are no recorded estimates of the numbers of dogs killed and hung from lampposts that night. While there is at least an effort to count the number of human casualties of this conflict, as is usually the case, non-human victims are not counted or considered in the same way.

7 From 1987 to 1990, the United Nations recorded Peru as having the highest number of disappearances anywhere in the world (Human Rights Watch 1991).

8 García was also president between 1985 and 1990, and oversaw some of the worst human rights abuses during the conflict. It was in his interest to dismiss the report as he was directly implicated in the violence.

9 Excerpt from the song *Siete Vidas* (Seven Lives) by Peruvian philosopher and musician Jorge Millones. Entire song appears as an appendix at the end of this chapter.

10 Economies of death

An ethical framework and future directions

Kathryn A. Gillespie and Patricia J. Lopez

The project we have outlined in *Economies of Death* is an introduction to thinking about a multispecies ethical framework that critiques the violence of economic logics governing who lives, dies and how—and who is made grievable or not. The case studies included herein reveal various ways in which capitalism itself—as a socio-economic system—is reliant on a particular objectification that at its end is death and killing. Under capitalist logics, a differential hierarchy operates in which some bodies and lives must die so that others may live and flourish. Thus, 'economies of death' as a framework draws attention to the destructive nature of capitalism, the breaking down of living bodies for labor, commodity extraction, and the accumulation of capital. Indeed, as Foucault (1980, 58) mused in an interview, "I wonder if, before one poses the question of ideology, it wouldn't be more materialist to study first the question of the body and the effects of power on it." We are both attentive to, and critical of, these economic logics—their motivations, implications, and complex mechanisms that articulate the valuation of life and death through calculative technologies inherent to capitalism.

Our authors have examined the ways in which human and animal lives are made killable and/or grievable under national and global economic regimes of power. Reading these case studies alongside one another demands that we take seriously the ethical implications of violence against, and killing of, different kinds of bodies and it asks us to think in more deeply nuanced ways about the very nature of violence, killing, and the erasures of certain marginalized lives in a multispecies context. This book calls for taking seriously the suffering and deaths of humans and animals together and, in drawing these connections, to ask the hard questions about how violence that we may or may not readily acknowledge in human contexts also gets reproduced, normalized, and invisibilized when the subjects are nonhuman.

This project—and our path forward from here—is motivated by interrogating what is productive about reading these kinds of case studies together. What do we notice about the world when we bring these posthumanist, biopolitical, and political economic theories together with empirical cases of human and animal life and death—when we merge them, rather than read them side by side? The analysis derived from drawing these kinds of theoretical and empirical connections informs an enriched understanding of the way systems of power, privilege, and violence touch down on the ground and articulate with those embodied human and animal creatures living and dying in service to capital accumulation. Thus, this project is not just about drawing connections across species lines; it is also about laying bare the fundamental calculative technologies of *who* lives and dies—and *how*—and the economic logics that often drive these technologies of hierarchization. This project, then, is fundamentally about the violence of capitalism; it is about the cruelty of apathy and erasure; it is about what happens when economic interests eclipse ethics. But it is also about hope; it is about a radical disruption of the status quo; and it is about an enlarged ethic of care.

In reading these case studies together, as a set of testimonies to, and accounts of, the violence deemed 'necessary' to fuel capitalism, *Economies of Death* works to disrupt the ways in which ideas and ways of knowing are often siloed, separated by imagined and co-constructed disciplinary divides. The authors of these chapters are housed in departments as widely different as Art and Anthropology, English Literature and Geography, bringing with them the language and styles of their disciplines. And yet, there is an ease with which these chapters can be read together—they share many of the same questions and trace many of the same theoretical traditions, positioned as they are from within their own empirical and disciplinary frames. Taken individually, they hold within them their own critiques of particular processes and moments; taken together, they represent the possibilities for moving across disciplinary boundaries toward a broader ethical framework which begins to unwind the often closed systems of thinking.

This is not to suggest that disruptions, themselves, are discipline-bound. Critical epistemologies have opened up the ground for a proliferation of counter-discourses that seek to un- and re-narrate the past and present, recognizing what Chimamanda Ngozi Adichie (2009) calls "the danger of a single story." Indeed, postcolonial, anarchist, posthumanist, critical animal, feminist, and Marxist studies, among others, have seeped across disciplinary boundaries and beyond, seeking to disrupt taken-for-granted discourses of economic logics, species hierarchies, and circuits of power. These and others like them have served both to find new ways of speaking about and healing from the horrors wrought through global traumas such as the Holocaust, slavery, genocide, and colonialism as well as to build trans- and inter-disciplinary frames through which to engage across theoretical and ethical legacies (Braidotti 2013). What we are putting forward with 'economies of death' is an ethical framework that draws on these and other theories, reading them alongside one another and with empirical case studies to ground the theoretical strands. *Economies of Death* is a project of de-hierarchization; it is about fundamentally dismantling hegemonic power relations and value systems through an earnest re-evaluation of our own implicatedness in the presumed necessity of precarity and premature death in the continued primacy of capitalism and all that is incumbent in maintaining its dominance as a global force of relation.

It is through these disruptions of the status quo that an ethical framework emerges that we hope to carry forward into future work on calculative hierarchies of living and dying, violence and killing. This is a dual project of making political and ethical social relations that are mediated through economic relations. Ethics are often (and perhaps we might argue, *should always be*) at the foreground of empirical and theoretical studies, and yet, institutionally, ethics as a starting frame are often sidelined. In this project, we seek to (re-)center the ethical. Each of the chapters in this book is both ethically relevant and ethically charged. They seek to question the very ground on which the 'single stories' are built, sifting through the traces, memories, and hauntings (rubble) that are produced and left in the wake of history in order to draw us into a more ethically nuanced reading of these moments.

But what is it to speak of "ethics" or an ethical framework? There are so many different legacies of ethics—moral philosophies that range both historically and epistemologically—that to speak blithely of ethics is to reproduce moral ambiguities that flatten our individual and collective responsibilities to others. We take as our starting point care ethics, or the normative ontological frame that asserts the absolute centrality of physical and emotional care to life (Slote 2007; Lawson 2009). At the heart of an ethic of care is the recognition of the importance of attending to relationships—of listening *and* responding—and living in integrity with others (Tronto 1999; Gilligan 2014). It is about resistance against dominant systems of oppression as much as it is about resisting the urge to find universalisms against which to posit ethics as sets of rules and rights (Held 2004; Carmalt 2011). And as much as an ethic of care resists universalisms, it is also attentive to the slippages toward mere tolerance through notions of cultural relativism (Banks et al. 2008). Care ethics scholarship has focused on health care (Gordon et al. 1996; Mol 2008), domestic care (Bubeck 1995; Kittay 1999), gendered global divisions of labor (Raghuram 2008; Razavi 2011), and more recently, social policy and human security (Robinson 2011; Mahon and Robinson 2011). Many feminists and theorists of care ethics have asserted that at the root of a lack of a caring ethic is the feminization of care labor and the devaluation of the kinds of care necessary to maintain and reproduce life, more generally (Claassen 2002; Mitchell et al. 2004; Koggel and Orme 2013).

It is in praxis—not just in research, teaching, and public engagement, but also in our everyday living—that an ethic of care emerges. But it is in stretching it to encompass a posthuman ethic that 'economies of death' begins to take form. A posthuman ethic pushes the social ontology of relationality that is the foundation and bedrock of care ethics beyond just the human to embrace and recognize all that is *living*—human, nonhuman animal, and environment. We posit that it is no longer enough to reify the primacy of the 'human' in our ethical considerations, but rather, that we must acknowledge the importance of life and living for the sake of all living bodies. To be clear, we are not arguing that we should care because our lives are in danger, but rather, we are arguing for recognizing the absolute centrality of precarity and premature death in the continuation of capitalism as we know it. In this Anthropocenic age, we are attentive to, and critical of, the destruction wrought by *homo sapiens* and their social and economic systems of hierarchy, production, and consumption. As we, and the authors in this book, have argued, what is at stake is not merely *our* lives, but the lives of Others. And it is not the impact that the deaths of Others will have on our own liveliness that is our concern, so much as the absolute disinterest in the liveliness of Others—human, nonhuman animal, and environment.

In marrying an ethic of care to a posthuman ethic, we are asserting the importance of the recognition of the worth of all living beings (not just of recognizable lives, but of the very act of living itself) as the ground against which we consider our own ethical frame. Relationality, we are arguing, does not stop at the knowable (the recognizable other of the neighbor, the compatriot, or the ally) but rather, encompasses also the less-knowable (the less-recognizable Other of the stranger), *and* the un-knowable Other whose existence is relegated to a taxonomic definition of legibility. Relationality begins with the air we breathe, the ground on which we walk, and the trees and animals we encounter with ambivalence in our daily lives. It requires a relaxing of the hierarchical grid of intelligibility that we employ in our search for a definitional primacy that can be coded within a template of recognizability.

But more than mere recognizability, we seek to disentangle capitalism's tendency to construct relations through alienation, exploitation, and extraction, and by extension, the pervasive ideologies of the "autonomous, self-made man" (Tronto 1999). 'Economies of death' is about uncovering the often mundane ways in which we, individually and collectively, are implicated in the ongoing calculations that determine the worth of lives and the grievability of deaths through the circulation of capital and commodities, *and then challenging them.* Surely this is no easy task, particularly as we confront a closed system that materially produces the organization and practices that then sustain them (Gibson-Graham 2006; c.f. Foucault 2008). However, challenging these dominant orders and the 'making mundane' of this hierarchy of killability and grievability creates fissures in the hegemony of the system. It is through an ethic of care that these cracks form, and it is in them that an enlarged ethic of care can take root, spring up, and flourish. We are engaged in this shared project of caring and ethical commitments as a path forward for informing, and drawing connections between, our current and future politics and praxis.

As we conclude this volume, we suggest some future directions for taking economies of death forward in our research, teaching, and our lives in general. How does a theory of economies of death impact our research in relation to the topics we choose, the methodological concerns we have, and our fundamental motivations for doing the kind of work we do? How does 'economies of death' inform our teaching and how do we introduce a new kind of ethic into our pedagogical practice, even those courses that are not explicitly focused on death, killing, or the violence of capitalism? And finally, how do we incorporate the ethical commitments derived from the 'economies of death' framework into our daily lives? Moving forward, then, we hope to inspire further ethical consideration in how we do, teach, and live our scholarship, with a special attention to ways of resisting the economic logics that are often entangled with these facets of our lives and work.

Many of us do the research we do because we care deeply about our subjects. Often it is a deeply held ethic of care that propels us to choose to study certain aspects of injustice, domination and the creation and maintenance of uneven hierarchies of power and privilege. Thus, for many concerned with these inequalities, an ethic of care is always already embedded in the crafting and execution of our research activities. And yet, this ethic of care is often siloed, focused only on our particular topics. 'Economies of death' asks us to think about the ethical consequences of this kind of partitioning and the ways in which our interrogation of power and inequality might extend beyond our particular field site or topic of inquiry to link up with other projects of justice, politics, and ethics. From this starting point—of being open to drawing these connections with other ethically motivated research agendas—we advocate thinking critically and carefully about our research design and methodologies.

Even as we are often motivated by, and intentional about, our ethical commitments to our research subjects, there are also obvious and less obvious ways in which studying sites of injustice and suffering is fraught with ethically problematic imbalances of power. One theme threaded through *Economies of Death*, for instance, has been the ethics of using images of suffering and death. Several of our authors have chosen to use images of violence, pain, and death as central dimensions in their arguments about the nature of killing and violence. And indeed, the act of looking—of witnessing—can be a radical act of acknowledgment, memorialization, and remembering. The 'power of the visual' is, indeed, profound as it can often incite outrage, mourning, and empathy, and ultimately spur individual and collective action against injustice (Jenni 2005). And yet, as several of our authors have acknowledged here, there are also ethically problematic dimensions to this act of looking—a certain voyeuristic quality that can flirt with objectification in the act of viewing suffering, whether that suffering is witnessed firsthand or through secondary means (i.e., photographs, film, audio, etc.). This ethical tension—between the voyeurism of looking and the political act of witnessing—is a critical concern for research related to economies of death.

Methodologically, those of us who do research with living subjects are required to obtain approval from human and animal subjects ethics review boards. These are designed, in large part, to monitor and ensure that researchers engage in ethical research practice and are not causing harm to their subjects. However, ethics review boards do not operate outside of economic systems, as they are also concerned with avoiding liability issues and ultimately lawsuits, and, particularly in the biomedical field, large grants that fund university research are contingent on ethics review approval. Thus, the ethics review process is politically charged and ambivalent in nature (Martin 2007; Valentine 2005). Importantly, ethics is not a "kind of rational, distanced, objective reflection"; rather, "ethical reflection is a relational and situated process, less about being distanced and objective, and more about recognizing how our ethical decisions are shaped by our social and material environment" (Greenhough 2007, 1140). Research that involves nonhuman animal subjects is also further complicated by the fact that ethics review approval for animal subjects, monitored through Institutional Animal Care and Use Committees (IACUCs), is designed with biomedical research in mind (involving experimentation on animal subjects). Indeed, the use of animals in biomedical research is an economy of death all on its own—an appropriation of animal bodies in service to human supremacy and medical innovation, driven by economic and anthropocentric interests and only cursorily considering—in formalized, 'objectively' measured ways—the animals living and dying in service to this scientific inquiry. Thus, as we craft the methodological architecture of our research projects, we must take into consideration the ways in which we can and should go above and beyond base requirements for ethical practice instituted by ethics review boards. We should engender a kind of research practice that teases apart the economic interests that obscure an ethic of care from our considerations of the intimate, lived experiences of those we study.

Moving forward with a framework of 'economies of death,' then, requires consistent reflection on our research practices—how we design projects, how we execute our fieldwork, who is harmed and who benefits, and how we can strive to separate our ethical commitments from the impacts of underlying economic logics. Even as researchers, we are driven in part by economic logics—by our acquisition of degrees and accolades as a result of our research, by our need to publish and present on our research, and obtain funding, in order to advance our careers and so on. In part, we trade our research—the stories it tells, the political and intellectual implications of the conclusions we make—as currency in our professional advancement. Because we are academics making our living from the research and teaching we do, this is, to a certain extent, unavoidable. But it does not mean this moral ambiguity should go unnoticed and unremarked upon. Critical reflection about the ways in which we benefit directly and indirectly from the suffering of those we study—the way their suffering is a kind of dark currency—should always be in the back of our minds, motivating the (re)formulations of our ethical and political praxis.

In addition to how we research, 'economies of death' also suggests paths forward for how we teach. Through our respective teaching experiences, we have both found that students tend to be fiercely protective of capitalism and all that it affords them. This drive to defend capitalist tenets of innovation, consumption, and wealth is written into their personal politics and ways of being in the world. Involving a consideration of economies of death in teaching, then, offers a way to begin to dismantle the hegemony of capitalism in students' understandings of the world. Specifically, introducing 'economies of death' as a pedagogical framing helps students to understand in grounded, intimate terms the violence wrought by capitalism. Returning to the visual for a moment, students often respond in radical ways to the act of looking at suffering associated with poverty, inequality, and the appropriation of marginalized human and animal bodies for labor and commodity production. Thus, confronting with students, in respectful, self-reflexive ways, various hierarchies of death, killing, and subjugation can be an effective way to forge cracks in their unwavering faith in capitalist socio-economic systems. Asking students to think carefully about the various ways in which they are privileged is also a key feature of this project. Teaching, at its best, motivates students to see the world anew—to recognize their intuitions and then to challenge them, to question the comfort and privilege in which they live and learn, and to radically re-envision other ways of being in the world.

To illustrate what this might look like in practice, we offer two brief examples from our teaching. One of us (Lopez) often teaches courses that attract students who have visions of working in the global south in a non-profit capacity, often related to health. There is an enthusiasm for 'saving' those living in poverty in the global south that elides the complexities of historical legacies of dispossession (c.f. Roy 2010). Students, today, have been raised in the age of (RED) campaigns and on-the-fly philanthropy made possible through texting and donating their five cent refund at the grocery checkout. They are bombarded by the earnest, if uncritical, heroics of celebrity philanthrocapitalists who range from the The Giving Pledge billionaires to hands-on aid mercenaries like Sean Penn and adopters like Angelina Jolie and Madonna. It is often popular discourse that informs many young people's desires to 'do good' in the world. And thus, each course (regardless of its level) begins with an introduction to capitalism, neoliberalism, and the production of inequality. It is not enough to want to 'fix' the problem, but rather, requires students to better understand precisely how inequality arises and impacts the lived experiences of others. Students are invited to peel back the layers of discourse and materiality that celebrity (and their own everyday) philanthropy offers, to unmask the taken-for-granted and too-simply-articulated 'good' in order to develop a more robust ethical ground against which to mobilize attentive, responsible, competent, and responsive care in their chosen fields.[1]

One of us (Gillespie) teaches primarily on human–animal relations under capitalism. Designing courses around the mundane, everyday uses of animals (in food, fashion, etc.) proves to be a powerful entry into understanding the way animals' lives, deaths, and suffering are made invisible in service to capital accumulation. The role of animals in the food system, for example, offers a lens into an economy of death so thoroughly imbricated in our society as to be taken for granted. Students come into these classes believing that animals are here for our use, that breeding, raising, killing, and eating animals is necessary and natural, and they are often energetically defensive about confronting the violence inherent in raising animals for food. As an access point to a broader critique of capitalist economies of death, students begin to connect with the experience of animals raised for food—through readings, film, discussion, and through meeting and witnessing actual, living animals in the food system.

Throughout the term, they begin to question their protectiveness of a system built on such insidious violence and killing.

While it is important—in fact, essential—to ask students to challenge hegemonic discourses about capitalism and human and nonhuman others, it is also critical to offer some hope and alternative visions. Thus, while pedagogical enactments of 'economies of death' are about challenging dominant norms, uncovering mundane violence, and questioning the deeply hierarchized nature of the world we live in, we also advocate teaching about hope and possibility. What does a transformative politics of life look like and how does this challenge economies of death? One potential exercise for prompting this kind of generative conversation is to ask students to bring 'hopeful items' to each class. Beginning each class with 5–10 minutes of sharing individual or collective acts of resistance, transformation, and political action shifts the conversation away from solely one of critique and deconstruction to one of possibility and alternative praxis. As a teaching frame, then, 'economies of death' operates with these dual aims in mind—to tear down and to build up, to face somberly the stark realities of the world and to engage in joyfully imagining a different reality where ethical commitments eclipse economic logics.

Pedagogical considerations of economies of death, though, also must include an awareness and critique of the underlying economic logics of educational institutions. The corporatization of the university, the project of producing marketable, employable workers at the end of baccalaureate, graduate, and professional programs are all central concerns of ours (Bok 2003; Giroux and Giroux 2004; Nelson 2011). We ask, going forward, that these dimensions of education and the neoliberalization of educational institutions be a subject of critique and resistance. For instance, the university is driven by logics of maximizing efficiency and cutting labor costs. This is reflected in the radical increase of adjunct and temporary faculty, graduate student instruction, the declining number of permanent faculty positions, and the precarious positions of supporting staff (e.g., custodial staff, groundskeeping labor, etc.) (Porfilio et al. 2013; Washburn 2005). At the same time, class sizes increase, tuition jumps exponentially, and courses move online to maximize efficiency in the classroom and cut costs associated with providing educational services (Hill and Kumar 2009; Brown 2011).

Further, the university as an institution is implicated in reproducing economies of death. Every year, between 20 and 25 million animals are subjected to laboratory experimentation in the U.S. alone[2]—despite international pressure to move toward *in vitro* and computational modeling in toxicology sciences (Hartung and Leist 2008; Stephens 2010; Basketter et al. 2012). Laboratory animals, who have frequently been 'purpose bred' for research, live their artificially shortened lives in cages and are routinely subjected to painful and often debilitating procedures, and yet it is well documented that many studies consist of unnecessary duplication (Hooijmans and Ritskes-Hoitinga 2013). Further, human volunteers for drug development trials in the U.S. are overwhelming poor and often highly marginalized (mostly) men whose prime motivations are financial incentives, raising questions about the actual (versus the perceived) ethics of clinical trials (Shah 2006; Abadie 2010; Stunkel and Grady 2011). Beyond the laboratory, high schools, universities, and colleges are also often sites for military and intelligence recruiting, with the promise of a paid tuition and stipend—for many students the neoliberalization of the academy is offset by the militarization of their education (Allison and Solnit 2011; Armato et al. 2013). Students, mostly young people of color and from poor and marginalized communities, are targeted as early as middle school by military recruiters, marking them out as potential participators in the war economy—their entry into higher education and adulthood enabled by their enrollment in military life (Cowen and Siciliano 2011; Hagopian and Barker 2011). Admittedly, Federal Law stipulates that college campuses must allow recruiting in order to continue to receive federal funds; however, universities have long been centers of social and radical change. Indeed, some universities such as Yale, Stanford, and UC Santa Cruz have banned Reserve Officers' Training Corps (ROTC) programs without penalty from the Department of Defense (Galaviz et al. 2011).

Our research and teaching are central features of the work that we do as scholars, and they are primary mechanisms through which to theorize and understand economies of death. 'Economies of death' as a frame, though, should also inform the mundane ways in which we live our daily lives. As an ethically charged framework, it asks us to reflect on the ways that we are implicated in the suffering, killing, and premature deaths of unseen and unheard others. In keeping with the project of thinking across boundaries—of developing an enlarged and posthuman ethic of care—this consideration of our implicatedness in violent socio-economic relations should span across species boundaries. Even if our work is focused on the human realm of suffering and dying, we should also live our lives in accordance with commitments to nonviolence in our encounters with animals and ecosystems. Similarly, for those of us concerned with violence against animals, we should also be aware of, and responsive to, the ways in which these concerns can often sideline racialized, gendered, or classed social relations.

As we are all, to some extent, at least partially economic bodies living in a complex economic world, we should be consistently self-reflexive about the impacts we have. Often, this gets translated into conversations about whether and what we buy, how we consume, what waste we create. While these are important conversations to have—and are often the most direct and straightforward way to respond to our ethical concerns—we believe firmly that we cannot merely buy our way to more ethical living. In Ursula Le Guin's words, "You cannot buy the Revolution. You cannot make the Revolution. You can only be the Revolution. It is in your spirit or it is nowhere" (1974, 240). Living ethically is not just a matter of everyday lifestyle choices, such as consuming, voting, or donating along a preferred ethical line (although, admittedly, these are important choices). Rather, ethics and ethical living extend into every facet of the everyday: into our interpersonal interactions, our daily enactments of care and compassion for others, and the minute details of how we move through the world.

In the end, of course, we all die. We all, at some point—gradually or quite suddenly—reach our deaths and encounter the finitude of life. For our project here, it is not so much that we all die that we are concerned with. It is how we get to that death that is important, and why we reach the point of death when we do. It is about who is killed ('let die' or 'made to die') and who does the killing and under what political economic conditions. This book has been about these questions, with a focus on the characteristics of killings and deaths driven by economic logics. But 'economies of death,' as a theoretical perspective, is not just about death. It is also, importantly, about the inverse— life. It is about how we live, what choices we make, and how we respond to political economic conditions, inequality, hierarchy, privilege, and power. It is about what ethical commitments we make and carry through in our lives and work. It is about the moment of response and resistance, about driving cracks into the dominant order of violence and killing and imagining new ways of being, relationally, in the world. It is about grief and the act of making grievable those bodies who suffer and are killed, but it is also about a transformative politics of care and hope.

References

Abadie, Roberto. 2010. *The professional guinea pig: Big Pharma and the risky world of human subjects*. Durham, NC: Duke University Press.

Adichie, Chimamanda Ngozi. 2009. *TEDTalks Chimamanda Adichie— the danger of a single story*. New York, NY: Films Media Group.

Allison, Aimee and David Solnit. 2007. *Army of none: strategies to counter military recruitment, end war, and build a better world*. New York: Seven Stories Press.

Armato, Michael, Laurie Fuller, Nancy A. Matthews, and Erica R. Meiners. 2013. "Pedagogical Engagements: Feminist Resistance to the Militarization of Education." *Review of Education, Pedagogy & Cultural Studies*. 35 (2): 103–126.

Banks, Sarah, Richard Hugman, Lynne Healy, Vivienne Bozalek, and Joan Orme. 2008. "Global Ethics for Social Work: Problems and Possibilities-Papers from the Ethics & Social Welfare Symposium, Durban, July 2008." *Ethics and Social Welfare*. 2 (3): 276–290.

Basketter D.A., H. Clewell, I. Kimber, A. Rossi, B. Blaauboer, R. Burrier, M. Daneshian, et al. 2012. "A roadmap for the development of alternative (non-animal) methods for systemic toxicity testing - t4 report." *ALTEX*. 29 (1): 3–91.

Bok, Derek Curtis. 2003. *Universities in the marketplace: the commercialization of higher education*. Princeton, NJ: Princeton University Press.

Braidotti, Rosi. 2013. *The posthuman*. Cambridge, UK: Polity Press.

Brown, Wendy. 2011. "Neoliberalized knowledge." *History of the Present*. 1 (1): 113–129.

Bubeck, Diemut Elisabet. 1995. *Care, gender, and justice*. Oxford: Clarendon Press.

Carmalt, Jean Connolly. 2011. "Human rights, care ethics and situated universal norms." *Antipode*. 43 (2): 296–325.

Claassen, Rutger. 2012. "The commodification of care." *Hypatia*. 26 (1): 43–64.

Cowen, Deborah and Amy Siciliano. 2011. "Surplus Masculinities and Security." *Antipode.* 43 (5): 1516–1541.

Foucault, Michel. 1980. *Power/knowledge: selected interviews and other writings, 1972–1977*, Colin Gordon (ed.), Collin Gordon, Leo Marshall, John Mepham, and Kate Soper (trans.). New York: Pantheon Books.

——2008. "Interview: body/power." In Colin Gordon (ed.), *Power/Knowledge: nterviews and Other Writings, 1972–1977, Michel Foucault.* New York: Pantheon Books.

Galaviz, Brian, Jesus Palafox, Erica R. Meiners, and Therese Quinn. 2011. "The militarization and the privatization of public schools." *Berkeley Review of Education.* 2 (1): 27–45.

Gibson-Graham, J. K. 2006. *A postcapitalist politics.* Minneapolis: University of Minnesota Press.

Gilligan, Carol. 2014. "Moral injury and the ethic of care: reframing the conversation about differences." *Journal of Social Philosophy.* 45 (1): 89–106.

Giroux, Henry A. and Susan Searls Giroux. 2004. *Take back higher education: race, youth, and the crisis of democracy in the post-Civil Rights Era.* New York: Palgrave Macmillan.

Gordon, Suzanne, Patricia E. Benner, and Nel Noddings. 1996. *Caregiving: readings in knowledge, practice, ethics, and politics.* Philadelphia: University of Pennsylvania Press.

Greenhough, Beth. 2007. "Situated knowledges and the spaces of consent." *Geoforum.* 38 (6): 1140–1151.

Hagopian, A. and K. Barker. 2011. "Should we end military recruiting in high schools as a matter of child protection and public health?" *American Journal of Public Health.* 101 (1): 19–23.

Hartung, Thomas and M. Leist. 2008. "Food for thought … on the evolution of toxicology and the phasing out of animal testing." *ALTEX.* 25 (2): 91–102.

Held, Virginia. 2004. "Care and justice in the global context." *Ratio Juris.* 17 (2): 141–155.

Hill, Dave and Ravi Kumar. 2009. *Global neoliberalism and education and its consequences.* New York: Routledge.

Hooijmans, C. R. and M. Ritskes-Hoitinga. 2013. "Progress in using systematic reviews of animal studies to improve translational research." *PLoS Medicine.* 10 (7): e1–4.

Jenni, Kathie. 2005. "The power of the visual." *Animal Liberation Philosophy and Policy Journal.* 3 (1): 1–21.

Kittay, Eva Feder. 1999. *Love's labor: essays on women, equality, and dependency.* New York: Routledge.

Koggel, Christine M. and Joan Orme. 2013. *Care ethics: new theories and applications.* London: Routledge.

Lawson, Victoria. 2009. "Instead of radical geography, how about caring geography?" *Antipode.* 41 (1): 210–213.

Le Guin, Ursula. 1974. *The Dispossessed.* New York: Harper & Row.

Mahon, Rianne and Fiona Robinson. 2011. *Feminist ethics and social policy: towards a new global political economy of care.* Vancouver: UBC Press.

Martin, D. 2007. "Bureaucratising ethics: institutional review boards and participatory research." *ACME: An International E-Journal for Critical Geographies.* 6 (3): 319–328.

Mitchell, Katharyne, Sallie A. Marston, and Cindi Katz. 2004. *Life's work: geographies of social reproduction.* Malden, Mass: Blackwell.

Mol, Annemarie. 2008. *The logic of care: health and the problem of patient choice.* London: Routledge.

Nelson, Cary. 2011. "Higher education's industrial model." In *The global industrial complex: systems of domination*, Steven Best, Richard Kahn, Anthony J. Nocella II, and Peter McLaren (eds.). Lanham, Md: Lexington Books: 155–168.

Porfilio, Bradley J., Julie A. Gorlewski, and Shelley Pineo-Jensen. 2013. "The New Academic Labor Market and Graduate Students." Special issue, *Workplace: A Journal for Academic Labor.* 22.

Raghuram, Parvati. 2008. "Migrant women in male-dominated sectors of the labour market: a research agenda." *Population, Space and Place.* 14 (1): 43–57.

Raja, Ira. 2013. "Contractarianism and the ethic of care in Indian fiction." *South Asia: Journal of South Asian Studies.* 36 (1): 79–91.

Razavi, Shahra. 2011. "Rethinking care in a development context: an introduction." *Development and Change.* 42 (4): 873–903.

Robinson, Fiona. 2011. *The ethics of care a feminist approach to human security.* Philadelphia: Temple University Press.

Roy, Ananya. 2010. *Poverty capital: microfinance and the making of development.* New York: Routledge.

Shah, Sonia. 2006. *The body hunters: testing new drugs on the world's poorest patients.* New York: New Press.

Slote, Michael A. 2007. *The ethics of care and empathy.* London: Routledge.

Stephens, Martin. 2010. "An animal protection perspective on 21st century toxicology." *Journal of Toxicology and Environmental Health, Part B.* 13 (2–4): 2–4.

Stunkel, L. and C. Grady. 2011. "More than the money: a review of the literature examining healthy volunteer motivations." *Contemporary Clinical Trials.* 32 (3): 342–352.

Tronto, Joan C. 1999. "Care ethics: moving forward." *Hypatia.* 14 (1): 112–119.

Valentine, G. 2005. "Geography and ethics: moral geographies? Ethical commitment in research and teaching." *Progress in Human Geography.* 29 (4): 483–487.

Washburn, Jennifer. 2005. *University, Inc.: the corporate corruption of American higher education.* New York: Basic Books.

Notes

1 Attentiveness, responsibility, competence, and responsiveness are Joan Tronto's (1999) four ethical elements of care.
2 While these numbers represent *all* laboratory animals used in testing, it is difficult to tease out the number of strictly university test animals, particularly as many university laboratories are funded in part by corporations or are connected to other non-university entities such as local hospitals.

Index

For Product Safety Concerns and Information please contact our EU
representative GPSR@taylorandfrancis.com Taylor & Francis Verlag GmbH,
Kaufingerstraße 24, 80331 München, Germany

Printed and bound by CPI Group (UK) Ltd, Croydon, CR0 4YY

01/05/2025

01858452-0001